Property of Kenneth J. Collis

pd w/ ck #142

6 Sep 75 $11.90

D0423345

everyone's
book of hand
and small
power tools

everyone's book of hand and small power tools

George R. Drake

Reston Publishing Company, Inc., Reston, Virginia 22090

A Prentice-Hall Company

Library of Congress Cataloging in Publication Data

Drake, George R   1938–
    Everyone's book of hand and small power tools.

    1. Tools. I. Title.
TJ1195.D64   621.9   74–10554
ISBN 0–87909–260–2

© 1974 by
Reston Publishing Company, Inc.
A Prentice-Hall Company
Box 547
Reston, Virginia 22090

10 9 8 7 6 5 4 3

Printed in the United States of America.

to my mother
whose guidance and emphasis
on an education
has resulted in my writing career

and

to my dad
who taught me the skills
in the use of tools, woodworking,
and home repair

ACKNOWLEDGMENTS

The author would like to acknowledge and thank the following companies and persons who generously donated the many photographs in this handbook:

	Figure No.
Adel Tool Co., Chicago, Ill. 60656—Mrs. Donna Barone, Office Manager	10–6
Armstrong Bros. Tool Co., Chicago, Ill. 60646—Mr. Louis Ebersold, Advertising Manager	1–5, 4–1, 17–1, 17–3, 17–9
Bernzomatic Corp., Rochester, N.Y. 14613—Mr. Howard R. Debs, Manager Advertising/Sales Promotion	10–8
The Black & Decker Manufacturing Company, Towson, Md. 21204—Mr. Carl W. Starner, Public Relations Manager	13–1, 13–6, 13–9, 13–24, 13–31, 13–32
Brookstone Company, Peterborough, N.H. 03458—Mr. Steve Millard, Marketing Manager, and Judith Montaner, Assistant	4–1, 7–3, 10–3, 10–7, 10–11, 10–13
Dremel Manufacturing Co., Racine, Wis. 53401—Mr. E. A. Erdman, Vice President—Sales; Mr. B. R. Springhorn, Sales Promotion Manager; and Ms. Joyce Radwill, Secretary	13–1, 13–11, 13–12, 13–13, 13–14, 13–16, 13–17, 13–18, 13–19
The Foredom Electric Co., Bethel, Conn. 06801—Mr. Willard P. Nelson, Sales Manager, and Mr. Douglas E. Kellogg, President	13–1, 13–15
Heller Tool Company, Newcomerstown, Ohio 43832—Mr. C. E. McElhaney, Advertising Coordinator	6–1, 6–4
Klein & Sons, Inc., Mathias, Chicago, Ill. 60645—Mr. Howard R. Arnold, Advertising Manager	2–1, 2–3, 3–1, 9–1, 10–4, 10–15, 10–19, 12–1, 16–1, 17–1

CONTENTS

PREFACE

This handbook is directed to *you*—to the men, women, and young adults who enjoy creating, designing, and building furniture, lawn ornaments, wall projects, kit construction or personal gifts; to the hobbyist using small handtools, knives, and miniature power tools; to the home repairman; to the beginning craftsman, apartment renter, and technician; to the home automobile mechanic; and to the student taking shop courses in high school, vocational school, industrial arts school, or adult education programs. It is a reference text for the craftsman. It's a handbook completely covering the description, application, and care of each of the hand tools and hand power tools that these persons use—abrasive papers to wood gouges, carvers' knives to miniature power tools, coping saws to power hand circular saws.

This book presents *you* with the most important knowledge for accomplishing any repair or do-it-yourself job—*the selection of the proper tool for the job—the proper use of the tool—and the proper care of the tool.* The book starts you at the beginning and gives you the foundation upon which to build as you begin projects and perform home repairs. By doing your own repairs you save $ $ $, and you get tremendous personal satisfaction by building things for yourself, your home, and your friends.

Chapter 1—YOU AND TOOLS—is a reading must for each person. In fact, he should read it several times because it specifically recommends basic tools for each reader's particular use. It recommends in which chronological order to buy tools. It recommends quality tools for some applications and cheap tools for others. Finally, Chapter 1 suggests tool storage, work areas, and workbenches for use by various readers.

The primary section of each subsequent chapter (2 to 17) is also must reading because the primary section presents the basic tool description, applications, and care of the particular type tool described in that chapter. The reader then refers to the specific tool (listed alphabetically) within that chapter which he is interested in reading about for its specific description, application, and special care. Safety precautions are interspersed where required. Ample photographs and line drawings clearly convey the author's narrative on each tool.

Chapter 10 is a miscellaneous chapter containing the one-of-a-kind tools which do not readily fall into one of the other tool categories. Chapter 13 describes the application of hand power tools including the circular saw, electric drill, grinder, modeler's power tool, plane, reciprocating saw, router, saber saw, sanders, and soldering irons.

Appendixes, a glossary of terms, and a cross-referenced index conclude the handbook text. The appendixes include self study chapter review questions, suggestions for the instructor on how this handbook may be used in shop courses, practical benchwork problems, metric conversion tables, inch-millimeter equivalents, lumber conversion chart, nail and screw reference charts, decimal equivalents of number and letter size drills, and hardening and tempering procedures. The glossary lists definitions of terms used in the text which may not be familiar to the reader. Finally, a comprehensive cross-referenced index enables you to readily locate information on the description, use, and care of any tool described in this handbook.

George R. Drake
Baltimore, Maryland

you and tools
(your needs, beginning tool sets, storage, and work areas)

Figure 1–1 The home workshop.

If you have a need to use a tool, this handbook is for you. Toys broken? Electric light switch malfunctioning? Can't get your automobile oil filter off? Assembling an electronic, metal or wooden craft kit? Bathroom faucet leaking? Carving? Are you a mechanical, electrical, or electronic technician? Do you want to save money by doing your own repairs?

If the answer to any of the above questions is yes, or if similar situations arise in your household, apartment, automobile, hobby room, or occupation, this handbook can help *you*. It describes the proper use of hand tools and hand power tools in these and similar applications. This handbook provides you with basic training in the skills needed for doing the job yourself.

The keys to accurate and rapid completion of any task that involves the use of tools are

1. *Knowledge of the proper tool for the job.*

2. *Knowledge of how to use the tool correctly and skillfully.*

3. *Knowledge of how to care for the tool.*

This handbook provides you with this knowledge. You'll be your own boss and you can make repairs, build home improvements, and construct projects of professional quality. You can do this because you'll have complete knowledge of the use of tools and you'll have more time than the professional; he has to hurry to make money.

You can take your time and have the personal satisfaction that *you* did it. You'll save many dollars on home repairs and you can satisfactorily make emergency repairs. Why is it that all household emergencies happen on weekends or holidays?

1–1.   HOW TO USE THIS BOOK

To use this handbook properly, you should first read this chapter, which describes your tool needs; tool cost versus use; suggestions as to whether to buy, borrow, or rent a tool; recommended beginning tool sets; arranging your tools for convenience in toolboxes, tote boxes, workbenches, and storage areas; workshops; general tool care; and safety. This chapter tells you what tools you need, where you can store them, and how to set up a work area. You should understand this chapter thoroughly before reading on.

For your convenience, subsequent chapters have been arranged alphabetically by major tool groups: *boring tools; chisels and gouges; clamps and vises; fasteners; files; glues, adhesives, and cements; hammers; measuring and marking tools; miscellaneous hand tools; planes; pliers; powered hand tools; punches; saws; screwdrivers; and wrenches.*

Each of the tools described within a chapter is shown on the first page of the chapter. The introductory section of the chapter provides a general description, applications, and general care of the tool group described in that chapter. Subsequent sections describe each of the types of tools within the chapter category. For example, the beginning pages of Chapter 16, on screwdrivers, describe a general screwdriver and tell you how to use and care for it. Subsequent sections describe specific applications and care of various types of screwdrivers: conventional; jeweler's; offset; offset ratchet; Phillips head; Reed and Prince; screw-holding; spark-detecting; and spiral ratchet.

For effective use of this book, then, you should study the advice in Chapter 1 as you select your tools, locate your workshop, and set up your bench. You should then study the beginning sections of subsequent chapters so that you will have a general understanding of each tool, its applications, and its care. Finally, you should study the specific characteristics and applications of the tools that you own or contemplate owning.

Appendix A provides review questions to aid you in determining your comprehension of the material presented in each chapter. If you are using the book as a text, your instructor may assign selected questions from Appendix A and practical problems from Appendix C. Other appendixes provide you with conversion tables that are useful in everyday shop applications.

A glossary of terms near the end of the book will enable you to define terms with which you are unfamiliar. A comprehensive index enables you to locate readily all tool descriptions, applications, and methods of care discussed.

1–2.   WHAT ARE YOUR TOOL NEEDS?

Your tool *needs* are dependent upon your intended applications. These applications may result from your occupation, your avocation, as a result of a training or apprenticeship course in which you are enrolled, or because you are a do-it-yourself repairman, builder, handyman, or hobbyist.

Your tool *purchases*, on the other hand, are dependent upon application, necessity, probable frequency of use, cost, and budget. Sections 1–3 through 1–5 provide you with sufficient information so that you can determine which tools you need.

1–3.   TOOL COST VERSUS USE

In purchasing tools, consider their use. Are they used daily? Weekly? Only occasionally? Is accuracy required? Will they be subjected to abuse? Do you plan to use them for their intended purpose? Will the tool become part of your permanent workshop?

If your plans are to use the tools regularly and to keep them as part of your workshop, buy quality tools from a reputable manufacturer (some are listed as contributors of photographs to this book; refer to the Preface). Watch your newspaper—there are often sales that will lower your total costs—but be aware that inexpensive tools are often low in quality. Choose inexpensive tools for abnormal or infrequent use. For example, you might purchase an inexpensive medium-sized conventional screwdriver, a locking plier wrench, and an adjustable open-end wrench to carry in your automobile glove compartment to aid you in making emergency road repairs. Another inexpensive conventional screwdriver may be used to open paint cans, remove paint from painted screwheads, or as a pry bar.

Adopt the following rule, which is that of the professionals: *use quality tools only for their intended purposes.* This will ensure that the screwdriver tips, saw blades, chisel tips, plane cutters, and so on, are in proper condition at all times and are ready for you to use to perform their intended function in the most efficient and accurate manner.

It is advisable to buy certain tools in sets because the price of the set is often considerably less than the prices of the individual pieces. For example, screwdrivers often come in sets of four or five sizes that cover the normal range of screw sizes. Since you'll eventually need all the sizes (remember, you're going to use tools only for their intended purposes—which means the screwdriver tip of the proper size for the screw in use), why not (especially when you see a brand-name set on sale) buy a set initially?

But—let's consider that you're fairly well equipped with tools needed around the home. You'd like to do more automobile repairs and you suddenly see an advertisement for a complete mechanic's tool set at a tremendous saving. The savings look fantastic until you examine the 92 tools and discover that you already own the screwdrivers, center punch, combination wrenches, hacksaw, and 10 blades! You already own 25 of the tools! And the complement of the tools remaining in the set consists of 14 setscrew wrenches (total of $2 worth), 5 open-end wrenches (which you've covered in your toolbox with combination wrenches), and socket wrench drivers, sockets, and extensions. You have discovered that what you really need is the socket wrench set—and of course that's not on sale separately.

Also be aware of the sales on special tools. Many times these tools are on sale because no one else is buying them—no one else needs them. How about you? Is the tool an odd size? Is it only for special uses? Do you have another tool that can do the same job?

1–4.   BUY IT, BORROW IT, OR RENT IT?

The question often arises: shall I buy the tool or shall I borrow or rent it? The answer depends upon immediate need, anticipation of the frequency of use, cost of the tool, and your relationship with a friend or neighbor who owns the same tool. Obviously, if you need a ⅜-inch ratcheting socket wrench on a Sunday afternoon, you'll probably have to try to borrow it. In borrowing tools, though, keep three things in mind: use the tool only in its proper application; clean it after use; and return it as soon as you're finished. These acts will keep you at peace with the neighbors—and remember, that's how you'd like your neighbor to treat your tools.

Obviously, you need a basic set of tools for the type of work that you anticipate doing: apartment or home repairs, toy repairs, do-it-yourself projects, construction projects, hobbies, automobile or boat repairs, or whatever your particular use. For these principal uses, you need to buy the best tools you can afford. Buy the tools that you need the most first. Buy the others as your budget permits. Don't reject the idea of buying used tools. Many a good buy has been made from someone who has lost interest in a hobby and wants to sell the tools. Watch for sales in the classified section of your newspaper.

You can often rent individual hand tools. Perhaps you need a set of metric automobile mechanic's tools, sawhorses, a mallet, or large clamps. Refer to your telephone Yellow Pages under TOOLS—RENTING. Call the firm and discuss prices. You may decide that it would be cheaper in the long run to buy the tool. But you may be working on a project that requires some fancy wood engraving—then you should consider renting a router. Or perhaps you'd like to saw some paneling for a new wall—consider renting a circular saw, and you'll finish the job in a couple of hours.

The answer to the question of whether to buy, borrow, or rent depends, then, upon your needs, present and future. It also depends on your budget.

1–5.   RECOMMENDED BEGINNING TOOL SETS

Tables 1–1 through 1–7 list recommended beginning tool sets for the apartment dweller, home repairman, beginning craftsman (student), kit builder, hobbyist, home automobile repairman, and technician. Study the table that is applicable to your needs. Determine approximate prices from the current tool catalogs of reputable tool manu-

*TABLE 1-1. RECOMMENDED BEGINNING TOOL SET FOR THE
APARTMENT DWELLER*

Tools	Section Reference
Primary	
Conventional screwdrivers (set)	16-4
Locking plier wrench	17-8
Claw (curved) hammer	8-5
Folding or push–pull rule	9-11
Awl	10-3
Adjustable open-end wrench	17-4
Combination pliers (slip joint)	12-6
Putty knife	10-11
Needle-nose pliers (with cutting edges in the jaws)	12-12
Secondary	
Cross-cut saw	15-8
Forming tool	6-6
Coping saw	15-7
Electric drill and set of drills (1/16 to 1/4 in.)	13-5

facturers. If your budget does not allow you initially to buy all the tools in the set, consider buying the primary tools first, then the secondary tools, as your budget permits.

The home repairman should make his purchases with the goal in mind of obtaining the necessary tools with which he can perform most home repairs. The young apartment dweller should buy the tools that meet his immediate needs; his long-range plan should be to obtain the tools that he will need when he eventually buys a home.

The beginning craftsman may be a student in high school, vocational school, industrial art school, or adult educational shop program. Through courses conducted by an instructor, using this book as a text, the beginning craftsman learns the proper use and care of tools as he builds several shop projects. He has an advantage in that he can try different styles of the same tool that are available in the school shop and thereby select the tool that is the most useful to him.

The kit builder and the hobbyist fall into about the same group of tool users. Quite often, the basic tools needed to complete a kit are included in the kit. The hobbyist selects the specific tools that he needs to complete his projects.

The home automobile repairman purchases the tools he needs to perform the preventive and corrective maintenance tasks that he

TABLE 1–2. RECOMMENDED BEGINNING TOOL SET FOR THE HOME REPAIRMAN

Tools	*Section Reference*
Primary	
Conventional screwdrivers (set)	16–4
Locking plier wrench	17–8
Claw (curved) hammer	8–5
Folding or push–pull rule	9–11
Awl	10–3
Adjustable open-end wrench	17–4
Combination pliers (slip joint)	12–6
Putty knife	10–11
Needle-nose pliers (with cutting edges in jaws)	12–12
Combination square	9–8
Paint scraper	10–15
Miter box	15–12
Ripsaw	15–13
Secondary	
Phillips head screwdrivers	16–8
Combination wrenches (set)	17–7
Level	9–12
File (mill and saw)	6–8
Block plane	11–4
Nail set	10–7
Hacksaw	15–10
Center punch	14–4
Tin snips (straight or curved cut)	10–17
Pipe wrench	17–12
Circular saw	13–4
Soldering iron	13–13
Saber saw	13–11

TABLE 1–3. RECOMMENDED BEGINNING TOOL SET FOR THE BEGINNING CRAFTSMAN (STUDENT)

Tools	*Section Reference*
Primary	
Combination square	9–8
Folding rule	9–11
Cross-cut saw	15–8
Coping saw	15–7
Hand drill	2–7
Conventional screwdrivers (set)	16–4
Block plane	11–4
Rasp	6–9
Forming tool	6–6
Modeler's knife	10–5
Wood chisel	3–7
Claw hammer	8–5
Awl	10–3
Locking plier wrench	17–8
Adjustable open-end wrench	17–4
Combination pliers (slip joint)	12–6
Center punch	14–4
Needle-nose pliers (with cutting edges in the jaws)	12–12
Secondary	
Wood-marking gauge	9–21
Nail set	10–7
Level	9–12
Putty knife	10–11
Hacksaw	15–10
Combination wrenches (set)	17–7
Phillips head screwdriverss (set)	16–8
Tin snips (straight or curved cut)	10–17

is capable of performing. Perhaps he only changes the oil and checks the battery and radiator. Perhaps he replaces plugs, points, condenser, and performs a tuneup. Perhaps he is capable of replacing brakes and rebuilding carburetors and engines. The tools discussed in this handbook are for the minor preventive and corrective maintenance tasks; special automobile tools are not included.

The technician who would have need for the tools described in this book is usually trained in the electric, electronic, or mechanical field. He works with engineers and shop personnel in the con-

TABLE 1–4. RECOMMENDED BEGINNING TOOL SET FOR THE KIT BUILDER

	Section Reference	Electronic Kits	Wood Kits	Metal Kits
C clamp or hand screws	4–7, 4–10		×	
File (mill and saw)	6–8			×
Claw hammer	8–5		×	
Soft-faced hammer	8–8			×
Pocket rule (or 1-foot rule)	9–15	×	×	×
Scriber	9–16			×
Modeler's knife	10–5		×	×
Wire stripper	10–18	×		
Combination pliers (slip joint)	12–6	×	×	×
Needle-nose pliers	12–12	×		
Diagonal pliers	12–7	×		
Soldering iron	13–13	×		
Center punch	14–4			×
Conventional screwdrivers (set)	16–4	×	×	×
Phillips head screwdrivers (set)	16–8	×		×
Combination wrenches	17–7			×
Nut-driver wrench	17–9	×		
Terminal crimper	10–16	×		

TABLE 1–5. RECOMMENDED BEGINNING TOOL SET FOR THE HOBBYIST

	Section Reference	Model Building	Carving
Hand drill	2–7	×	×
Wood chisels	3–7		×
Rasp	6–9		×
Claw hammer	8–5	×	
Tack hammer	8–9	×	

	Section Reference	Model Building	Carving
Folding rule	9–11	×	
Pocket rule	9–15	×	×
Knives (modeler's, carver's)	10–5	×	×
Putty knife	10–11	×	
Sanding blocks	10–14		×
Wire stripper	10–18	×	
Modelmaker's plane	11–7	×	×
Spoke shave	11–6		×
Chain-nose pliers	12–4	×	
Electric drill	13–5	×	×
Modeler's power tool	13–7		×
Soldering iron	13–13	×	
Coping saw	15–7	×	×
Keyhole saw	15–11	×	
Conventional screwdrivers (set)	16–4	×	

TABLE 1–6. RECOMMENDED BEGINNING TOOL SET FOR THE HOME AUTOMOBILE REPAIRMAN

Tools	*Section Reference*
Primary	
Conventional screwdrivers (set)	16–4
Locking plier wrench	17–8
Phillips head screwdrivers (set)	16–8
Adjustable open-end wrench	17–4
Combination pliers (slip joint)	12–6
Oil-filter wrench	17–10
Combination wrenches (set)	17–7
Feeler gauges	9–10
Ball peen hammer	8–4
Mallet	8–6
Soldering iron	13–13
Secondary	
Socket wrenches (set)	17–14
Offset screwdriver	16–6
Box wrenches (set)	17–5
Open-end wrenches (set)	17–11

TABLE 1–7. RECOMMENDED BEGINNING TOOL SET FOR THE TECHNICIAN

	Section Reference	Electrical/ Electronic Technician	Mechanical Technician
Conventional screwdrivers (set)	16–4	×	×
Phillips head screwdrivers (set)	16–8	×	×
Open-end wrenches (set)	17–11		×
Adjustable open-end wrench	17–4	×	×
Setscrew wrenches (set)	17–13	×	×
Ball peen hammer (4 or 8 oz.)	8–4		×
Soft-faced hammer	8–8		×
Prick punch	14–7		×
Center punch	14–4		×
Pin punch (optional)	14–6		×
Combination pliers (slip joint)	12–6	×	×
Needle-nose pliers	12–12	×	×
Chain-nose pliers	12–4	×	×
Locking plier wrench	17–8	×	×
Cold chisel	3–5		×
Files	6–1		×
Mill file	6–8		×
File card	6–1		×
File handle	6–1		×
Hacksaw (and several blades)	15–10	×	×
Ball-joint vise	4–4	×	
Pocket rule	9–15	×	×
Scriber	9–16		×
Terminal crimper	10–16	×	
Wire stripper	10–18	×	
Nut-driver wrenches (set)	17–9	×	

struction, checkout, alignment, calibration, and repair of a product. He frequently works with hand tools to perform these tasks.

Figures 1–2 through 1–4 illustrate some beginning tool sets, which include the most common tools used for the application specified.

(A)

(B)

(C)

(D)

(E)

(F)

Figure 1–2 Beginning tool sets: (A and B) apartment owner's; (C) a beginning homeowner's kit—also a perfect starter kit for the young craftsman; (D) a larger set of tools for the handyman and craftsman; (E) a basic automobile kit; (F) a school tool cart with beginning tools.

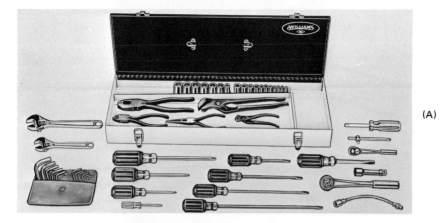

(A)

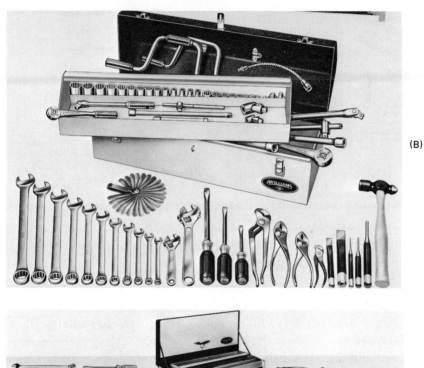

(B)

(C)

Figure 1–3 Specialized tool sets: (A) electrician's service
set; (B) general service set for the mechanical
technician; (C) industrial mechanic's basic service kit.

15

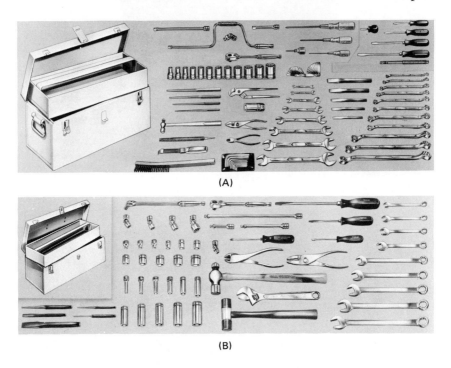

(A)

(B)

Figure 1–4 Other specialized tool sets: (A) mechanic's popular set; (B) apprentice tool set.

1–6.   ARRANGING YOUR TOOLS FOR CONVENIENCE

Once you begin to purchase tools, you'll want a place to store them.
The place depends upon the quantity, type, size, and intended use
of the tools.

A toolbox makes a convenient storage area if you have to trans-
port the tools often from place to place. It is also convenient in the
small apartment and for tools stored in the automobile.

A tote box is handy to use to carry tools within your home from
the normal storage space to the area where a repair is to be made.
The tote box is usually open, light, and small. Selected tools, parts,
and fasteners needed for the particular repair are placed into it.

The workbench is the ideal storage area for the home repairman
and the hobbyist. Drawers and hangers can be arranged to accom-

modate your tools in a neat and orderly fashion. You can hang tools by hooks on pegboard, nails, spring clips, magnetic strips, strips of leather or inner tubing, wooden pegs, or holes or notches in a piece of wood.

No matter how the storage area is arranged, you should allow for the arrangement, convenient selection, and protection of each tool. Common tools should be grouped together; for example, different lengths of conventional screwdrivers may be placed in one drawer compartment and Phillips head screwdrivers in another. Tools should also be located for convenient selection; place the tools that you use most often in the most convenient locations. Tools that are used less often should be placed in the backs of drawers, in the lower drawers, or in storage cabinets away from the normal working area.

Many tools need to be protected from each other and therefore should be specially located. For example, files should not come into contact with one other. Similarly, some tools require their own holders and may require application of a preservative or rust inhibitor.

Make a habit of always returning the tool to its own storage space—in essence, *provide a home for each tool.* By doing this, you will usually know exactly where your tools are when you need them (this is often a difficult task if there are some young craftsmen in your family).

1–7.   TOOLBOXES AND TOTE BOXES

If you have only a few tools or if you have some special tools you'd like to protect from dust or misuse, you may choose to keep them in a toolbox. As Figure 1–5 illustrates, many types and sizes of toolboxes are available. In selecting a toolbox, don't consider only your present needs; consider your future needs as well. Select a sufficiently large box of sturdy construction. Tote trays are handy for carrying smaller tools, fasteners, and parts. Compartments allow you to segregate your tools by size, type, or function. Larger boxes should have two lever-type clasps to keep them closed; padlock hasps are available on some models and are recommended if you have to take your tools away from home (or if you'd like to keep the children out). A handle is convenient for carrying.

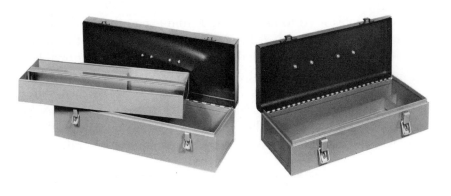

Figure 1–5 Various types and sizes of tool boxes.

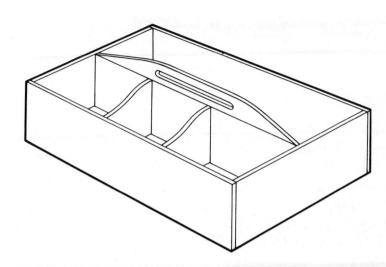

Figure 1–6 Tote boxes are used to carry tools, small parts, and fasteners, and are easy beginning construction projects.

Tote boxes are made of metal or wood (a good beginning construction job) and are used to carry tools, fasteners, and parts to the work area. Since the tote box is not covered, it does not protect your tools. Figure 1–6 illustrates a tote box that has compartments for tools, small parts, and fasteners.

1–8.   WORKBENCHES AND STORAGE AREAS

Workbenches and storage areas are the places where you'll do your work and store your tools, supplies, parts, and partially completed projects. The size, shape, and quantity of workbenches and storage areas depend upon your needs.

Figures 1–7 to 1–9 suggest some ideas for workbenches and storage areas. You can buy a complete workbench or make one to your own design specifications. A workbench is a good construction project to begin with because no finishing is required. If you don't like the idea of building drawers, consider buying two unfinished chests of drawers. Then screw two or three 2- by 12-inch boards across the top. You may also consider placing an old door on top of

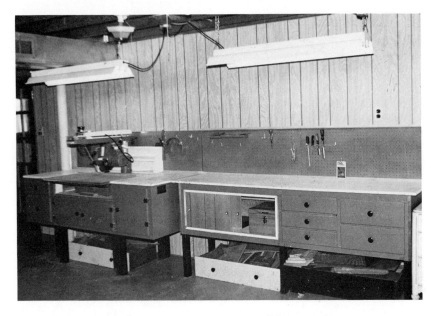

Figure 1–7 This workbench provides a large work area and
storage. Note that lumber is stored underneath.

the chests (Fig. 1–9). The bench work surface should be waist high.
If you want to put a fairly durable and tough top on the bench, nail
or glue a piece of tempered Masonite to the top. Paint the chests
with a good enamel paint, but don't paint the workbench top.

Unfinished kitchen cabinets make excellent storage cabinets,
or perhaps you know someone who is remodeling his kitchen and
discarding old cabinets. Also consider buying second-hand cabinets.
Give the cabinets a coat of paint.

Pegboard and assorted hooks make excellent hangers for many
hand tools. Place a piece behind your bench for easy access to the
tools that you use most often. Place other pieces next to the bench
or around the workshop at convenient places. Paint the pegboard
with glossy white paint to protect it and to reflect light. Magnetic
bars may be used to hang iron-alloy tools.

Wood (or metal) storage areas can be made by dropping U-
shaped frames from the rafters or by placing 2- by 3-inch supports
from the rafters to the floor. Place cross braces as required (Fig. 1–
10). Store your wood by type and size in the spaces created by the
dividers.

Figure 1–8 Different sized cabinets and drawers have been built for storage. Old kitchen cabinets make ideal storage areas.

Figure 1–9 A sturdy workbench can be constructed from two unfinished chests of drawers and a door.

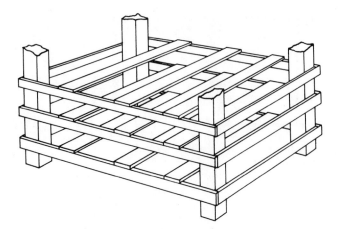

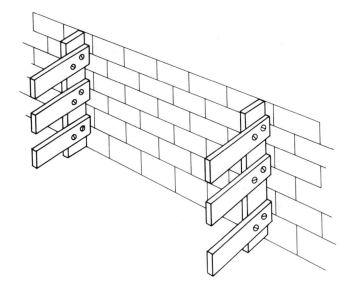

Figure 1–10 Wood storage areas.

1–9.   WORKSHOPS—BASEMENT, ATTIC, OR GARAGE?

The location of your workshop depends upon the size of your home, the availability of a spare room, basement, attic, or garage, and upon the type of workshop and space needed. For example, the model or kit builder can often work in a spare room or part of a room because he doesn't need much space and he doesn't create much noise or dirt. On the other hand, the craftsman needs room for a large workbench, tool storage, lumber storage, and an assembly-and-painting area. Other considerations include adequate ventilation, temperature control, dampness control, and lighting.

The basement probably provides the most adequate area for a workshop. It is isolated from most of the rest of the home, so noise disturbances to other parts of the home are held to a minimum. Dirt from sawdust, and the smell of glue and paint, are also partially isolated from the rest of the home. As the basement is normally below ground level, the surrounding earth tends to aid in keeping the basement warmer in the winter and cooler in the summer. Registers are easily placed in the heat and air-conditioning ducts as required. Basements are often damp in the summer and can cause tools to rust, but dampness can be limited by use of a dehumidifier.

Attics provide another area for consideration of a workshop. Attics usually provide sufficient area and some isolation from the rest of the home. Dust, however, has a tendency to settle to the lower floors and to work its way into stored items. The attic is also usually too hot in the summer and too cool in the winter for comfortable working conditions, although additional heating or air-conditioning ducts or portable units can be used.

Garages provide an adequate area and isolation from the rest of the house; dirt and noise are not problems. Competition for space from the automobile(s), lawn and garden tools, and bicycles and toys often significantly limit shop space in garages. Winter cold, summer heat, and dampness are problems that are difficult to contend with.

1–10.   WORKSHOP FLOOR PLANS

Floor plans for your workshop are dependent upon your needs, both present and future. How large an area do you need? What are your storage requirements? Can you place cabinets on the walls? Do you need a lumber or metal storage area? Will you eventually expand your workshop to include bench power tools?

Figures 1–11 and 1–12 present some ideas for floor plans of different shops. Use the ideas to construct a plan for your workshop. You might want to make a scale model of your work area. Use a piece of ¼-inch grid-line paper and let one square equal 1 square foot. Mark out the overall space you have available. Use another piece of grid-line paper and glue it to a piece of thin cardboard. Draw scaled outlines of the probable size of the workbench, storage cabinets, wood storage areas, power tools, and other items that you will have. Label the areas and units on the outlines and cut them out. Place the scaled unit cutouts on the first drawing and arrange them until you have a satisfactory and convenient layout.

Next consider lighting (Section 1–11) and electricity. Have wiring installed, considering present and future installation of power

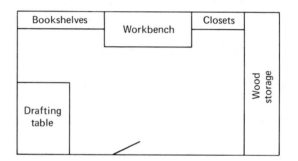

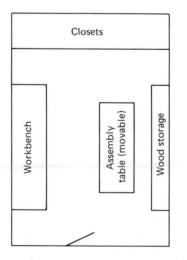

Figure 1–11 Workshop floor plans.

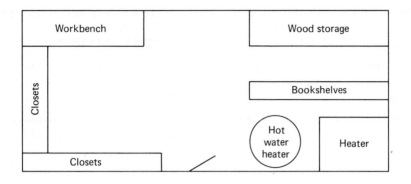

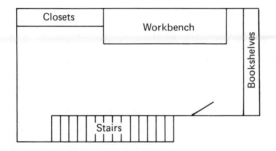

Figure 1-12 Workshop floor plans.

tools. It's a good idea for safety to put all your power tools on a
separate circuit breaker that is out of the reach of children and can
be locked in the OFF position. The walls and ceiling should be
painted white or a light color to reflect light around the workshop.
Floors may be painted so that lost parts may be more rapidly found
and dust and dirt may be more readily removed; but be sure that
the floor is not slippery. In some shops, a piece of linoleum is placed
on the floor. If your shop is an electronic shop, be sure to place a
rubber runner on the floor just in front of the workbench. This acts
as an insulator between the electricity in your equipment and the
floor, which is damp in many basements.

1-11.   LIGHTING THE WORK AREA

Once you have established your workshop, you are ready to locate
the workbench. Since most of your work will be done at the bench,

consider locating it near a window, which will aid in lighting the work area during the daylight hours. You might like to have a curtain or shade that can be drawn to block direct sunlight.

Artificial light can be provided by incandescent lights, fluorescent lights, high-intensity lights (also incandescent), and flexible-arm lamps. Incandescent lights of 100 to 150 watts can be placed into reflector sockets. The complete unit can be hung by a half-knot in the line cord to a pulley. The pulley can be attached to a cable (as AWG No. 8 or No. 10 aluminum television-antenna guy wire) so that it can be drawn across the work area. This enables you to place the light where you need it (Fig. 1–13). If you'd like to vary the intensity of the light, install a dimmer switch or light-dimmer control box.

Fluorescent lights are available as wall or overhead fixtures. Models with from one to four tubes are available. A fluorescent fixture may also be hung with pulleys from cables (as AWG No. 8 or No. 10 aluminum television antenna guy wire) as shown in Fig. 1–14. The pulleys are attached to the fixture with eye bolts. Turnbuckles attached to one end of each cable enable the cables to be drawn tight. This method of suspending the fixture allows the light to be moved to a convenient location over the work area or to any other work area along the length of the cables. Fluorescent light fixtures with light diffusers installed provide light that is nearly free of shadow.

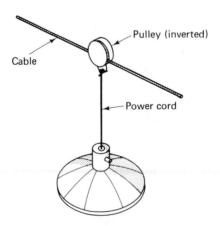

Figure 1–13 Incandescent lights installed in reflector sockets can be hung by a pulley on a length of cable.

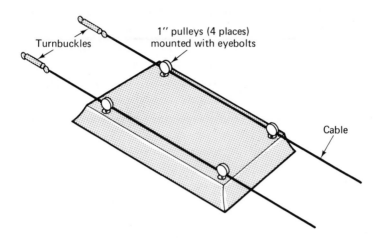

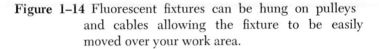

Figure 1–14 Fluorescent fixtures can be hung on pulleys and cables allowing the fixture to be easily moved over your work area.

High-intensity lamps can be mounted on the work surface or mounted on a wall behind the workbench. These lamps are recommended where high-intensity light is needed over a small work area. They are perhaps best used for hobby workbenches.

Flexible-arm lamps are fluorescent lights that may be bench- or wall-mounted. These lamps provide more overall surface light than the high-intensity light. They are most useful for hobby benches and drawing tables.

1–12.   GENERAL TOOL CARE

The simplest and best way to care for hand tools and hand power tools is to *use them in the proper way and only for their intended purposes.* For example, the proper size of conventional screwdriver should be used to apply torque to a slotted screw; the screwdriver should *not* be used to open paint cans, bang holes in a lid, pry out bent nails, or to chip rock! Proper use ensures that the tool is always in the best condition to enable its use in completing a job accurately, rapidly, and precisely. It also ensures longevity of the tool.

Tools should be kept clean and sharp at all times. Burrs and dirt or other foreign matter should be removed immediately. Tools should be stored either by hanging or by placing them in drawers. If tools with cutting edges, such as chisels, files, punches, knives, or saws, are kept in drawers or a toolbox, they should be kept from touching each other. Keep metallic tools thinly coated with light oil. If tools are to be stored for a long period of time (more than one month), apply a rust preventative, such as a light grease, to all metal parts.

If one of your tools becomes worn or dull, the most practical solution is usually to buy a new one. Keep the old tool to use for a task for which you'd rather not employ a good tool. Some tools, such as screwdrivers, punches, chisels, and plier cutters, can be reground. Specific procedures are discussed in the applicable "care" section of each chapter.

When tools such as screwdrivers, punches, chisels, or plier cutters are ground to resharpen or reshape them, the tool should be dipped frequently in cold water to keep it cool. Too much heat from grinding can cause loss of temper of the metal; this condition is usually indicated by the appearance of a blue color on the metal. Tempering is discussed in Appendix O.

1–13.   GENERAL SAFETY

Always concern yourself and others with safety. Hand and power tools can be very harmful and can maim a person permanently. Read the following lists of DOs and DON'Ts and reread it frequently. Use the safety checklist of Table 1–8 now and recheck it on occasion—in fact, schedule periodic safety checks for your work area. A "yes" in every column indicates a safe work area.

DO take your time in working with all tools.

DO plan ahead.

DO wear rubber-soled shoes when working on electrical work, cutting metal, and chiseling.

DO take work breaks to reduce fatigue.

DO follow the manufacturer's recommendations.

DO store your tools properly.

DO keep your tools sharp. Sharp tools are the easiest to use and the safest.

But remember:

DON'T wear neckties, long-sleeved shirts, or shorts while working in the shop.

DON'T work when you're tired.

DON'T allow your children to use sharp tools or power tools unless you are supervising them closely.

1–14. SUMMARY

This chapter has provided you with much to consider. You should have an idea of the tools you need for your uses and whether you should buy expensive or inexpensive tools or rent the tools you need. You should also have some ideas on the location of your work area, have a floor plan in mind, and have a scheme for lighting your work area. You should know some general procedures to be used in caring for your tools, and you should know some safe rules and procedures to use to guard against injury.

TABLE 1–8. SAFETY CHECKLIST

	Yes	No
Tools are properly stored.		
Tools are sharp.		
Wood and metal are properly stored. Nails have been removed from used lumber.		
Power tools, cords, and plugs are in good condition.		
Power can be shut off by a central circuit breaker.		
Safety glasses, goggles, or a face shield is available.		
A rubber mat is located on the floor in front of the area where electrical work is done.		

boring tools

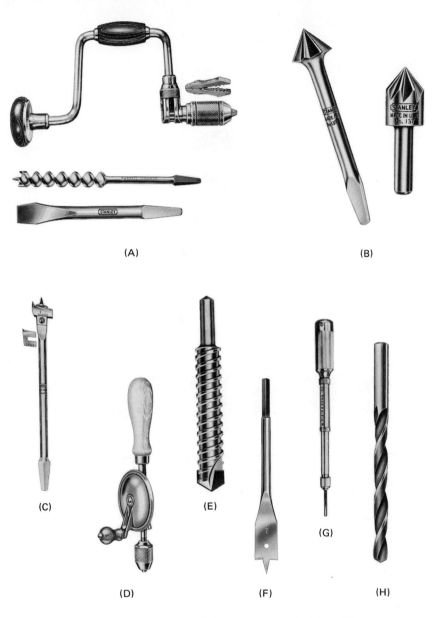

(A)

(B)

(C)

(D)

(E)

(F)

(G)

(H)

Figure 2–1 Boring tools: (A) bit brace and bits; (B) countersinks; (C) expansive bit; (D) hand drill; (E) masonry drill; (F) power wood boring bit; (G) push drill; (H) twist drill.

2-1. GENERAL DESCRIPTION

Boring tools are used to bore a round hole into a piece of wood, metal, plastic, masonry, or other material. The hole may be used for a fastener, such as a screw, bolt, rivet, pin, or dowel. The hole may also be for another assembly, such as a lock or as an opening to pass an object, such as an electric wire, through.

The boring may be performed with hand tools or electric (or air)-powered tools. The actual cutting process is done with a tool known as a **bit**, **drill**, or **point**. This chapter describes both hand and power-driven bits. Hand bit drivers are discussed in this chapter, but electrical power drills (the machine, not the bits) are discussed in Section 13–5.

Bits, drills, and points are driven by *braces, hand drills, push drills*, and *electric drills*. *Reamers* are used to enlarge a small-diameter hole into a larger one. *Countersinks* are used to drill a tapered hole below the surface so that a screwhead can be driven flat with the surface; a *counterbore* drills a hole such that the head can be sunk below the surface.

2-2. APPLICATION OF BORING TOOLS

The application of boring tools can be divided into three parts: boring into wood, boring into metal, and boring into other materials, including plastics and masonry. Predetermined drill depths are bored into these materials by placing a piece of tape around the drill at the predetermined depth measurement. Drill into the material until the tape meets the workpiece surface. Variable-depth gauges can be purchased commercially and assembled onto auger bits or twist drills.

Boring into Wood

To bore a hole into wood, first carefully measure and mark the center point of the hole to be drilled. Determine the size of the hole and select your boring tool. Use an awl to make a small prick point into the wood. The point should be of sufficient diameter and depth to accept the point of the boring tool.

To bore a small-diameter hole into wood with a hand-driven tool, select either a hand drill (for a hole up to $\frac{1}{4}$ inch in diameter) or a push drill (for a hole up to $\frac{11}{64}$ inch in diameter). Insert the tool point into the prick point made by the awl. Make several easy movements with the driving tool until the boring tool is through the surface of the wood and is aligned properly. To check that the boring tool is straight, check it visually by using a try square or a block of wood (Fig. 2–2). Continue boring. Reduce the pressure when you think the boring tool is nearly through the wood. When the boring-tool point comes through the other side of the material, pull or turn the tool out. Place the boring-tool point on the opposite side of the wood, where the point came through, and bore gently from the back until the hole is complete. This process will prevent the tool from splitting the wood where the tool comes through.

To drill a hole larger than $\frac{1}{4}$ inch in wood with a hand-driven tool, use a brace and bit (Section 2–4). Mark the hole location and use the awl in the way described previously. If the material is hardwood, drill a small hole, called a *pilot hole*, described previously in connection with small holes. This pilot hole (about $\frac{1}{16}$ inch) leads the boring-bit lead point through the wood. When the lead point projects through the other side, reverse the boring bit to the opposite side and complete the hole (Fig. 2–2). The expansive bit (Section 2–6) can be used with the brace to make a variety of large-sized holes.

The first power tool that should be purchased is the **electric drill** (Section 13–5). It can be used to drive twist drills, power-wood-boring bits, and masonry drills into various materials to produce fast,

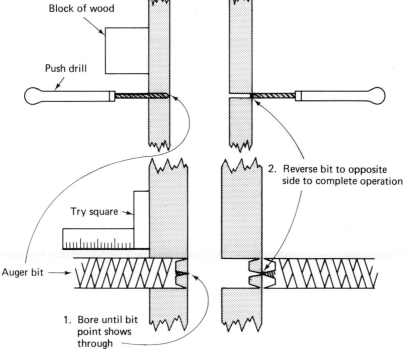

Block of wood

Push drill

2. Reverse bit to opposite side to complete operation

Try square →

Auger bit →

1. Bore until bit point shows through

Figure 2–2 Sighting a push drill and an auger bit for correct alignment and drilling from both sides to prevent splitting.

accurate holes (Sections 2–12, 2–9, and 2–8, respectively). In using the electric drill, make a starting hole with an awl. For drilling, say, a $\frac{1}{4}$-inch-diameter hole in hardwood or metal, you should drill a $\frac{1}{16}$-inch-pilot hole first.

In using the electric drill as a bit driver, be careful not to let the drill (bit) get too hot. In wood that is difficult to drill, pull the drill partially out occasionally to remove the dust. Light oil, wax, or soap can be used as a lubricant to aid in drilling. However, lubricants may prevent you later from using the wood finish you desire (such as penetrating oil stain), so use lubricants on wood with discretion. Use a try square or block as previously discussed to aid you in drilling straight holes.

Power-wood-boring bits are driven by the electric drill. Take care not to overheat them. In boring deep holes, partially remove the boring bits occasionally to remove dust and shavings.

If a variable-speed electric drill is used, start the hole at a slow speed. Then increase the speed to maximum. When the bit or twist drill is about to come through the opposite side of the workpiece, reverse the boring tool to the opposite side and finish the hole. Another method of preventing the back side of the wood from splitting as the drill point breaks through is to clamp a piece of scrap wood to the back.

Use as much pressure as is required to keep the tool cutting. Use little pressure at the start and at the end when the boring tool is about to come through the workpiece. Use only light pressure on very thin drills to prevent their bending and breaking.

Boring into Metal

Twist drills are used to bore holes into metal. These may be hand driven by a brace, a push drill, or a hand drill. Twist drills used to bore metal are more effectively driven by an electric-powered drill.

After the proposed center point of the hole has been carefully located, use a center punch to make an indenture in the metal. Place the center-punch point against the marked point and hold the punch perpendicular to the workpiece. Strike the anvil end of the punch with a hammer to make the indenture. The angle of the conical indenture made by the point matches the angle of the tip of a twist drill.

If a small-diameter hole is to be drilled, place the tip into the indenture and begin drilling at a slow feed and pressure. The drill speed should also be slow. Increase pressure and feed as the drill enters the metal. For deep holes, lubricate the drill point and hole with light oil. Occasionally raise the drill point; this causes the metal chips (or ribbons) to break off. As the drill point is about to break through the metal, decrease the feed and pressure. This will help prevent burring of the metal. Don't let the drill get too hot.

Boring into Other Materials

Two other materials that are frequently bored are plastics and masonry. Plastics are bored with the same tools as those used for wood. Drill at low speeds to minimize heat, and back the workpiece boring area with a piece of wood.

Masonry, including brick, slate, concrete, and cinder block, is bored at medium speed with a special carbide-tipped drill (refer to Section 2–8).

2–3.   CARE OF BORING TOOLS

Boring tools have cutting or screw lead points, cutting edges, and, in some cases, cutting flutes. To prevent damage to these tools, store them so that they cannot bang into each other or into other tools. Use a soft wire brush to remove clogged wood, metal, or other particles from boring tool flutes after each use. Wipe them occasionally with a rag dampened with light oil; this will discourage rust. Remove burrs from the shanks of drills with a metal file.

2–4.   BIT BRACE AND BITS (AUGER, COUNTERSINK, AND SCREWDRIVER)

A **bit brace** is a hand tool that holds bits of various size and, through pressure and rotation of the brace, causes a bit to bore, countersink, or drive screws. The bit brace and bits are useful to the person who only occasionally drills a few holes. But its most important use is in outdoor areas where no electricity is available. The major parts of the brace are illustrated in Fig. 2–3.

Brace jaws are of two types. One type accepts only tapered square tang bits; a universal jaw accepts square and round shanks (drills) as well. The sweep of the handle and bow determines the amount of torque that can be applied; the greater the sweep, the greater the torque. Sweeps are generally 8, 10, and 12 inches. Ratchets are optional but are definitely recommended. The ratchet allows the bow direction to be reversed without the jaw and bit turning. This is a valuable asset that allows boring or fastener tightening in close quarters, such as at the corners of a room.

To use the brace, place the bit shank into the jaws. Rotate the shell until the jaws tighten securely on the bit shank. Ensure that the bit is in straight. Place the bit to the workpiece. Press the head with one hand or with your body while rotating the bow in a clockwise direction for boring or driving fasteners. If you are working in

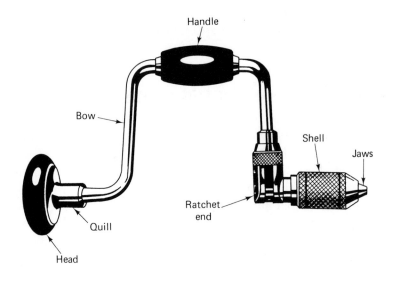

Figure 2–3 Major parts of a brace.

a confined area, engage the ratchet and reverse the bow direction as required.

Occasionally place a drop of light oil at the handle collars, the quill–bow interface, the ratchet, and the chuck shaft and shell. Damaged chucks, jaws, shells, ratchet pawls, heads, and quills can be replaced easily by following the manufacturer's instructions.

Bits are the movable boring, drilling, or turning part of a tool. Bits used in the bit brace are of three types: auger, countersink, and screwdriver. The bit is secured into the brace, which is used as the driving mechanism.

An **auger bit** is a corkscrew-shaped bit with a lead screw on the tip and a tapered square tang on the other end of the shank for insertion into the jaws of the bit brace. To use the auger bit, make a starting hole with an awl at the point where the hole is to be drilled. Place the bit lead screw into the starting hole and rotate the brace handle. The lead screw draws the bit into the wood. Use care as the cutters make contact with the wood. The corkscrew body removes wood from within the hole.

Two types of auger bits are available: the *Jennings*, or *double-twist*, type and the *solid-center* bit. The double-twist bit produces a smoother hole, whereas the solid-center bit is stiffer and better suited to boring deep holes or holes in wavy-grained wood. Diameters from ¼ to 1 inch in lengths of 7 to 10 inches are available. Deeper holes may be bored by using a bit extension. Larger holes are drilled with an expansive bit.

Auger bits can be sharpened (Fig. 2–4) with an auger bit file. Do not remove any more metal than is necessary. The cutters are beveled on the surface toward the bit shank. Also, file the rounded spurs at the perimeter of the bit tip, filing only from the inside. Do not sharpen the lead screw; remove accumulated wood from the lead screw. Remove burrs from the tang.

Countersinks are used in wood or soft metal when it is desired to place the head of a fastener such as a flatheaded screw or a bolt flush with the surface. The fastener hole is drilled first. The countersink tip is then placed into the fastener hole and the brace is revolved. Periodically remove the countersink and hold the fastener head to the hole to gauge the proper depth. Use a try square or wood block to check proper alignment of the countersink with the workpiece. Figure 2–5(A) shows a screw inserted into a countersunk hole.

Screwdriver bits of various sizes with conventional or Phillips-head tips are available with square tapered tangs for use in a hand brace. The brace allows the bits to rapidly drive screws into predrilled holes. The brace also provides leverage to aid in tightening the screws.

Choose a tip that is the proper size for the fastener being used.

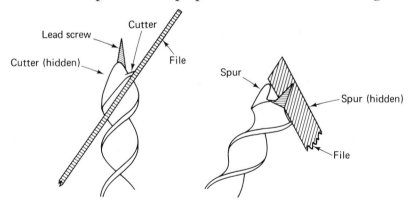

Figure 2–4 Sharpening an auger bit.

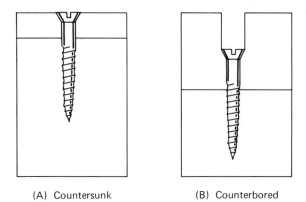

(A) Countersunk   (B) Counterbored

Figure 2–5 Illustration of a screw inserted in (A) a countersunk hole and (B) a counterbored hole.

This will prevent damage to the fastener head (refer to Section 16–2). Place soap on the screw threads to ease the driving power required. Reverse the turning direction of the brace to remove fasteners.

2–5.   COUNTERSINKS/COUNTERBORES (SCREW BITS)

Countersinks/counterbores for electric drills are sold in combination-size sets for use with screws. The combination countersink/counterbore drills the proper screw thread and shank size, countersinks, and counterbores for plug or filler filling in one operation. The shanks of the countersink/counterbores are ¼ inch in length. The depth of countersinking/counterboring is adjustable. (*Countersinking* is the boring of a conical-shaped hole such that the conical head of a flat-headed screw will recess flat with the surface. *Counterboring* is boring below the surface of the wood such that a screw will go below the surface. The hole may then be plugged with dowel or dowel buttons or filled. Refer to Fig. 2–5).

In using the countersink/counterbore, no predrilling of a pilot hole is required, but a pilot hole is recommended for accurate drilling in hardwoods. Use an awl to start a point for the countersink/counterbore. Do not let the point become excessively hot during use.

2–6.   EXPANSIVE BIT

The **expansive bit** is used to bore holes of various sizes (up to 35 standard holes) in wood. The shank, which has a tapered square tang usable only in hand bit braces, contains a tapered lead screw and a gearlike driven adjustable cutter that expands the hole diameter in $\frac{1}{16}$-inch increments from $\frac{7}{8}$ to 3 inches. It is a useful tool in that you don't have to stock a large variety of fixed-size auger bits (Section 2–4).

Prior to using the expansive bit, drill a $\frac{3}{16}$-inch pilot hole to accept the bit lead screw. Set the adjustable cutter (Fig. 2–6) to the desired diameter by rotating the adjusting screw with a screwdriver. Insert the bit tang into the bit brace and ensure proper alignment; tighten the bit-brace jaws. Place the tip of the bit into the pilot hole and rotate the bit brace, drawing the expansive bit into the wood. Ensure that the bit is straight as it enters the wood; the first *scratched circle* of the cutter into the wood indicates that you are aligned properly.

For drilling holes larger than $\frac{1}{4}$ inch with an electric drill, refer to Section 2–9. Sharpen the expansive bit in the same way as sug-

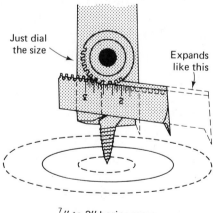

Just dial the size

Expands like this

$\frac{7}{8}''$ to 3'' boring range

Figure 2–6 Expansive bit.

gested for the auger bit (Section 2–4). File only the original bevel surfaces. Cutters, clamping screws, adjustment screws, and beveled washers may be purchased separately if replacement is necessary.

2–7.   HAND DRILL

The **hand drill** is operated by the rotation of a gear against one or two pinions, which in turn drive the drill chuck. The chuck jaws accept any drill or countersink with shanks from $\frac{1}{16}$ to $\frac{1}{4}$ inch, which makes the hand drill useful for drilling pilot holes for larger bits or drills and for drilling holes in wood, plastic, or metal for small screws or nails. Some models store drills in a hollow handle.

Loosen the chuck jaw shell and insert the drill point. Close the jaws until they lightly grip the drill; check that the drill is properly aligned in the chuck. Then hand-tighten the jaws against the drill. For accurately drilled holes, start a pilot hole with an awl. Place the drill point into the pilot hole and hold the hand-drill handle (or the side-grip handle, if available) with one hand and the gear-drive handle with the other hand. Rotate the gear-drive handle. Additional force may be applied to the drill point by pressing your body against the drill handle—but let the drill do the work.

Occasionally apply a few drops of oil to the gear and pinions of the hand drill. It is possible to replace chuck assemblies, jaws, gears, cranks, knobs, handles, and drill points with new parts as required without the need of special tools or procedures.

2–8.   MASONRY DRILL

Masonry drills are carbide-tipped drills used to drill holes into concrete, slate, brick, or other masonry materials. A wide spiral fluted shank provides fast, easy drilling and quick dust removal. Drill sizes range from $\frac{3}{16}$ to 1 inch, with shank chuck sizes of $\frac{1}{4}$ inch for the smaller drills and $\frac{1}{2}$ inch for the larger drills.

To start the drill at the desired spot, use a nail to make a pilot punch point for the drill tip. During drilling, alternately push the drill in and pull it out; this removes the dust. Use a medium drill speed. Protect the eyes with goggles.

A **star drill** is a hand drill used to make holes in masonry. It is a bar of steel with a star-shaped point. The drill is held in one gloved hand or may be held with a locking plier wrench; the other end of the drill is hit with a hammer. After each hammer blow, rotate the drill slightly. Remove the drill occasionally and blow out the dust. Wear goggles when using this tool.

2–9.   POWER-WOOD-BORING BITS

Because many electric drills accept drills with shanks only up to ¼ inch, wood drills with ¼-inch shanks (for ¼-inch or larger chucks), with the capability of drilling from ¼- to 1½-inch holes, are available. Various sizes are often available in sets of 4, 6, or 8. Hollow-ground points start the hole and guide the drill. Machine-sharpened cutters bore the large-diameter holes.

To use **power-wood-boring bits,** insert the shank into the drill chuck of an electric drill. Align the drill shank flats against the chuck flats and hand-tighten the chuck. Check proper seating of the drill by trying to rotate it in the chuck as you continue to snug the chuck flats against the shank flats. When properly aligned, tighten the drill chuck with the chuck wrench.

To accurately drill a hole, predrill a ³⁄₁₆-inch pilot hole into the wood, then place the hollow-ground point into the pilot hole and begin to drill. Carefully hold the bit perpendicular to the surface in which the hole is being placed. For rough hole drilling, as through a rafter for placement of cables, no pilot hole is required. The hollow-ground point will lead the drill through the hole. Hold the drill tight and in alignment. This prevents chattering of the drill within the wood. Reduce pressure on the drill when the drill is nearly through the wood. Do not let the boring bit become excessively hot while drilling. Excessive heat can damage the hardened cutting edge.

To sharpen a boring bit by hand, clamp the bit in a vise and stroke it with a flat 8-inch mill file at an angle of 15°. Power-sharpen on a fine-grained round corner wheel. Use an oilstone to remove burrs.

2–10.   PUSH DRILL

The **push drill** is a small one-hand-operated spring-action return drill. It is a convenient tool for making holes in models, for drilling pilot holes for larger boring bits or drills, and for making holes for small screws or nails. The push drill comes complete with drill points that range from $\frac{1}{16}$ to $\frac{11}{64}$ inch. The points are held in a magazine in the handle. Separate sets of points or individual points may be purchased. The overall push-drill length is about 11 inches.

To insert a drill point, loosen the shell surrounding the jaws. Insert the drill point and rotate the point until the notch in the point seats in the chuck jaws. Rotate the shell until the jaws are tight on the drill point.

To accurately drill a hole, start a tiny pilot hole at your mark with an awl. Then place the drill point into the pilot hole, grasp the push-drill handle, and push toward the workpiece. At the end of the push, release the pushing force and let the push-drill internal mechanism return the handle to the starting position. Use a try square or a square block against the workpiece as a sighting device so that your drilled hole is perpendicular to the workpiece.

Push drill parts including chucks, cylinders, pistons, magazines, spindles, and springs may be replaced without the need for special tools or procedures.

2–11.   REAMERS

Reamers (Fig. 2–7) are used to remove burrs from pipe and conduit and to enlarge holes in steel or wood. The reamer flutes do the hole cutting by a shaving action (this is opposed to a twist drill, where the flutes do not cut—only the tip cuts). Reamers are often classed as deburring reamers and taper reamers. The *deburring reamer* removes burrs from the inside of a cut pipe. After a pipe has been cut and before the pipe is removed from the vise, use the reamer. Medium pressure should be applied through the brace and reamer into the pipe. Continue to rotate, ensuring that the reamer is being applied straight into the pipe, until the burr is completely removed.

The *taper reamer* is used in a similar manner. To eliminate

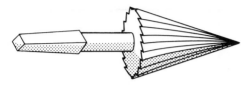

(A) Deburring

(B) Taper

Figure 2–7 Reamers: (A) deburring; (B) taper.

some of the taper in the hole, use the taper reamer from both sides
(Fig. 2–8). Taper reamers are about 5 inches long and taper from
about ¼ to 1 inch. It is necessary, therefore, to have a minimum
hole size of ¼ inch before the reamer can be used.

2–12.   TWIST DRILLS

Twist drills are among the most popular bits because they can be
used to bore holes in both wood and metal. The point is the only
cutting area; the flutes (two spiral grooves) remove cut material
from the boring and allow lubricant to flow to the cutting point.
Twist drills are made of either carbon or of high-speed steel.

Twist drills vary in diameter; their length is proportional to
the diameter. Twist drills are sold singularly or in sets of 13, 15, 21,
or 29 sizes. The bits in these sets are incremented in size by ¹⁄₆₄ inch
and provide a convenient storage medium. Twist drills normally
have shanks the same diameter as the tip and flute area, up to the
¼-inch-diameter shank size. Shank size may then remain at ¼ inch

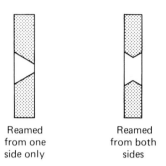

Reamed
from one
side only

Reamed
from both
sides

Figure 2–8 Effect of the use of a taper reamer on a piece of
metal (cross sections shown).

while the tip and flute diameter increase. One-half inch is another
standard shank size.

In using twist drills, start the drill in a hole started with an awl
(in wood) or in a center-punched indentation (in metal) to ensure
starting at the proper point. Use high speeds for wood and slow
speeds for metal. Keep the drill from overheating. Use soap as a
lubricant in hardwoods, light oil for steel and wrought iron, and
kerosene or turpentine for aluminum. No lubricants are required
for drilling cast iron, brass, or bronze. Let the drill bit do the cutting; don't force it. When drilling small wood or metal workpieces,
tightly clamp the workpiece. Twist-drill accessories, such as right-
angle drives, flexible drive couplings, depth gauges, and extensions,
are available for special uses.

Twist drills may be sharpened on the grinding wheel using a
drill-point gauge and holders, available commercially. The correct
angle at the cutting edge of the drill-point lip is 59°. After the cutting edge is ground, the lip heel is ground at 12°. Unless you use
drills extremely often and wear them out often, it is more practical
to purchase replacement twist drills than to regrind the points.

3

chisels
and
gouges

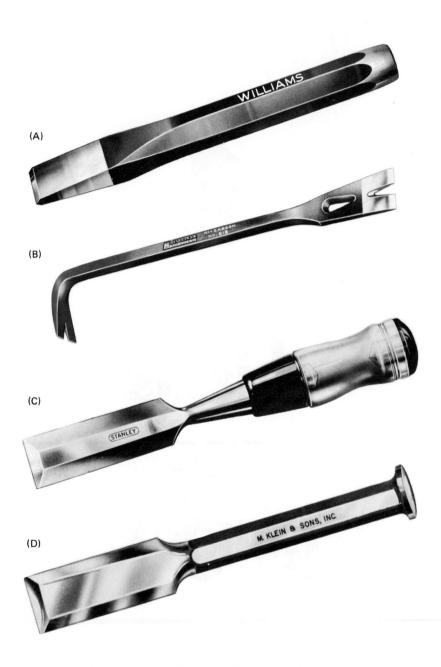

Figure 3–1 Chisels: (A) cold; (B) ripping; (C) wood chisel with molded handle; (D) all steel wood chisel.

3-1. GENERAL DESCRIPTION

Chisels are cutting tools. There are two categories: metal- and wood-cutting chisels. *Metal-cutting chisels* are used to remove metal from a workpiece; to cut rod, rivets, or wire; and to cut sheet or metal plate. Metal-cutting chisels are used only when there is no other means available (such as machinery, saws, etc.) to perform the cutting.

Wood-cutting chisels are finishing tools. The cutting edges are razor-sharp and are used where other tools, such as saws, planes, or drills, cannot remove the necessary wood.

Chisels must always be kept sharp for fast, accurate, and safe cutting. The heads (called *anvils*) must be kept from *mushrooming*, spreading out. When mushrooming occurs, immediately file or grind the material away. Buy only top-grade chisels because tempered high-grade alloy steel produces cutting edges that remain sharp longer, and the anvils resist mushrooming.

3-2. APPLICATION OF CHISELS

Chisels are hand-held and, in the case of wood chisels, are usually driven by hand. Under some conditions, such as cutting hardwoods or across grain, wood chisels are tapped with a wooden mallet or a plastic-tipped hammer. Metal chisels are tapped with a ball peen hammer; a metal chisel-holding device is described in Section 14–8.

Because chisels are very sharp, special caution must be taken to protect yourself from being cut. Do not lay chisels unprotected on the bench. When using metal chisels, you must protect against flying chips. Always wear safety glasses, goggles, or a face shield to protect yourself. Place a curtain or screen around your area to protect others.

3–3.   CARE OF METAL-CUTTING CHISELS

To work effectively, metal-cutting chisels must be kept sharp. Grinding is necessary when the cutting edge has been badly nicked or the bevel has been rounded. The included angle formed by the two bevels should be about 65°. Set the grinder tool rest for the angle and hold the chisel against the grinding wheel as shown in Fig. 3–2(A). Move the chisel back and forth across the wheel with moderate pressure. Grind the cutting edge slightly convex, as shown in Fig. 3–2(B). Dip the chisel often in cold water to prevent loss of tool temper from overheating. Grind both bevels, taking equal amounts of material from each side. If a chisel head mushrooms, file or grind off the excess metal.

3–4.   CARE OF WOOD-CUTTING CHISELS

Do not abuse your chisels. Sharpening will seldom be required. A properly ground chisel can be honed many times with an oilstone before it needs regrinding. Separate chisels from each other during storage. When necessary, hone the chisel on a combination oilstone that has been lubricated with light oil. Place the beveled edge of the chisel flat against the coarse-grit side of the oilstone. Hold the chisel at about 45° from the length of the oilstone and stroke the chisel back and forth with even strokes; do not vary the angle of contact with the surface. Now repeat on the fine-grit side of the oilstone. Next, turn the chisel over and very carefully place the chisel flat against the stone. Move the chisel a few light strokes in a sideways direction to remove the burrs and wire edges left from the

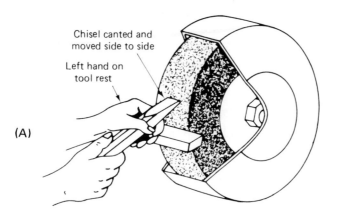

(A)

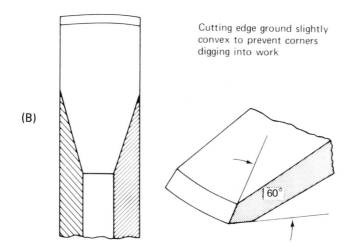

(B)

Figure 3-2 (A) Grinding a cold chisel; (B) the cutting edge
of the cold chisel is ground slightly convex to
prevent corners from digging into the workpiece.

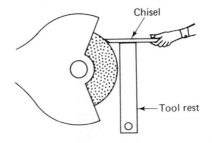

Figure 3–3 Set the tool rest so that an angle of 25 to 30° will be ground on the chisel.

beveled edge honing. Finally, strop the finished edge on a piece of heavy leather or rub across the end grain of a piece of hardwood. Stropping gives a fine razorlike sharpness to the chisel.

To grind a new edge, first check the cutting edge for squareness and nicks. Place a try square against the edge and sight through it to determine squareness. If the edge is unsquare or nicked, hold the chisel edge against the edge of a grinding wheel and slide the chisel back and forth.

Determine the angle of the chisel bevel and properly set the grinding-wheel tool rest (Fig. 3–3) for the determined angle. The angle is between 25 and 30°. Prior to applying power to the grinding wheel, practice holding the chisel on the tool rest against the wheel. This will help you to grind the correct angle once power is applied. Use a medium and then a fine grit grinding wheel.

While grinding, keep the chisel from becoming hot by using only light pressure against the wheel and by frequently dipping the chisel in cold water. Overheating the metal will cause the metal to lose its temper; it will no longer be able to hold a sharp edge. After grinding, hone the edge.

The handles of some wood chisels can be replaced. Place the chisel into a vise and tap the old handle off with a light hammer. Place the new handle into position. Tap the new handle into position with a plastic hammer or rubber mallet.

3–5.   COLD CHISELS

The **cold chisel**, also called a *flat chisel*, is used to cut metals and other materials and to shear old bolt heads, nuts, and rivets. The

cold chisel is identified by its flat cutting edge, which ranges from
3/16 to 1 inch. Lengths vary from 5 to 12 inches.

Cold chisels are used for four types of metal-cutting operations:
chipping, a term applied to the removal of metal with a cold chisel
and a hammer; cutting wire or round stock; cutting sheet or metal
plate that is too thick for tin snips and too wide for a hacksaw; and
cutting rivet heads. Chipping is done where machining is difficult
or inconvenient. The cold chisel may also be used to make an opening in cinder block.

To chip metal away from a workpiece, first fasten the workpiece into a vise in a manner such that the chipping will be done
toward the stationary vise jaw (Fig. 3-4). Copper covers over the
vise jaws will prevent the workpiece from becoming marred. Place
a canvas barrier a few feet beyond the vise to prevent accidents
from flying chips.

Grasp the cold chisel with one hand and hold the cutting edge
of the chisel to the workpiece at an angle of about 35° from the horizontal. All four fingers should encircle the chisel; the third and
fourth fingers grasp tightly and the little finger is used to guide the
chisel. The thumb remains on top to absorb a blow if you miss with
the hammer! In this position it can give a little. Strike the chisel
anvil with a ball peen hammer that is large enough to do the job.
Use the bevel of the cutting edge as a guide. Reset the chisel after

Figure 3-4 Chipping a workpiece with a cold chisel.

each blow. Cuts of from $\frac{1}{32}$ to $\frac{1}{16}$ inch deep should be made. The depth of cut is determined by the angle of the chisel; raise or lower the chisel to obtain the proper depth of cut. Don't use the chisel to chip to the finished level desired; leave enough material so that it may be finished with a file. Work should progress from the outer edge of the workpiece toward the center.

When chipping wrought iron or steel, the edge of the chisel should be wiped with an oil-saturated cloth. This lubricates the contacting surfaces and protects the edge of the chisel. When chipping cast metal, begin at the ends and work toward the center; this prevents the breaking of edges and corners.

The cold chisel may also be used for cutting wire or round stock when a hacksaw is not available. Place the workpiece on an anvil or other working surface. Place the chisel cutting edge on the cutting mark. Lightly tap the chisel with a ball peen hammer; examine the chisel mark to be sure that it is in the correct place. Place the chisel on the mark and strike the chisel with successive hammer blows. The last few blows should be lighter. On thick round stock, cut halfway through in one direction. Then turn the piece over and finish the cut.

Sheet or plate metal is cut with a chisel when metal cutters or machines are not available. If the workpiece is small enough, secure it in a vise so that the guideline is even with the vise jaws (Fig. 3–5).

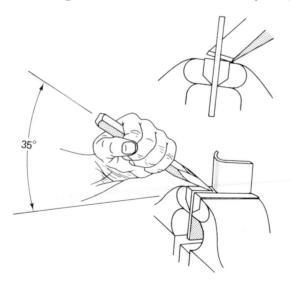

35°

Figure 3–5 Shearing a small workpiece with a cold chisel.

Figure 3–6 Using a cold chisel to make a cutout in a workpiece.

If the piece is large, place it on a suitable work surface. Sheets
should be backed up with a wood or metal plate to prevent bending.
Start at one edge of the workpiece and work across. Strike the end
of the chisel sharply, keeping the chisel cutting edge firmly against
the workpiece.

To make a cutout in a metal workpiece, scribe the hole, center
punch, and drill a series of overlapping holes within the cutout near
the scribed line. Use a cold chisel to clean up the edges (Fig. 3–6).
Finish with a file.

To cut off a bolt or rivet head, place the edge of a cold chisel
against the head and split it in two. Then place the edge against the
side of the head (as near the shaft as possible). Strike the chisel anvil
sharply with a ball peen hammer. (If you'll be doing a lot of rivet
busting, it is advisable to use a special chisel called a *rivet buster,*
specifically designed for the purpose.) To split a nut, place the cutting edge on top of one-half of the nut. Split that side. Then split the
opposite side, if required.

There are several other types of metal-cutting chisels, but they
are usually only used in machine shops. These types are the *cape
chisel,* used to chip narrow grooves; the *round-nose chisel,* for cutting groves and relocating incorrectly started drilled holes; and the
diamond-point chisel, for cutting V grooves and cleaning out corners.

3–6.   RIPPING CHISELS

The **ripping chisel** is similar to a ripping bar except that the chisel end is flatter and is ground to a sharper edge. Ripping chisels are about 18 inches long, with cutting edges from 1½ to 2 inches wide. The cutting edge is slotted for nail pulling. The ripping chisel illustrated in Fig. 3–1 is an offset pattern; the back of the offset cutting edge can be hammered to place the edge into position, and the offset enables the rest of the chisel length to increase ripping leverage. The offset end can also be hammered to drive the straight end in between boards. Other types of ripping chisels have no offset and have only one cutting edge; the other end is an anvil that may be hammered with a large ball peen hammer or a small sledgehammer.

To remove a nail, place the V notch in the offset end cutting edge around the nail. Pull on the arm using the offset bend as a pry. For a long nail, increase tool leverage by placing a piece of scrap wood under the offset bend.

To *rip* or *split* a board with the ripping chisel, place the cutting edge against the end of the board in line with the wood grain. Strike the chisel sharply with a heavy ball peen or light sledgehammer.

3–7.   WOOD CHISELS AND GOUGES

The **wood chisel** is a *finishing* tool; that is, it is used, preferably, after other tools, to make the finishing cuts on a piece of wood. To make final cuts accurately and easily, the wood-chisel edge must be very sharp and free of nicks. Therefore, only high-quality wood chisels that will maintain sharp edges and resist nicking should be purchased. You should use them properly, store them properly, and keep them sharp by frequent honing.

Wood chisels are named by size. The shortest is the *butt chisel*, which is from 7 to 9 inches long. It is used in tight corners. The *pocket chisel* is from 9 to 10½ inches long and is for general shop use. The *mill chisel* is about 16 inches long and is used for heavy work. Chisels are also named by use: *paring chisel* and *firmer chisel*. The paring chisel is a thin-bladed hand-driven chisel used to make precision shaving cuts. (To *pare* is to cut off the outer coating). The firmer chisel is thick-bladed for heavy driving.

Wood chisels have cutting edges from ⅛ to 2 inches wide; most homeowners need only ¼-, ½-, ¾-, and 1-inch chisels, which can often be purchased in sets. Some wood chisels have a one-piece blade and shank which meets a steel cap. With this type of construction, the end may be tapped with a light hammer, mallet, or soft-faced hammer. Other wood chisels have a one-piece blade and tang with a tough, impact-resistant molded handle. Molded handles should be tapped only with a mallet. All-steel wood chisels are also produced.

The wood-cutting chisel is used only when other tools cannot make the desired cut into your workpiece. If you can make the cut by another method, such as sawing, drilling, or planing, use the other method. For example, if you want to cut a mortice in a door for a lock, remove some of the wood first by using an auger bit. Overlap several holes and drill each hole to a depth *close to* the final depth. Then use the wood chisel for the final cuts.

To make cuts with the wood chisel along the grain of the wood, hold the chisel in one hand with the handle end firmly against the palm of your hand. Place the chisel on the workpiece in the direction of the wood grain. Place your other hand on the blade. This hand is used to guide the wood chisel blade. A number of shallow cuts are to be made rather than a few deep cuts. Angle the wood-chisel cutting edge slightly along the wood (Fig. 3–7) and into the grain (not with the grain). Push the chisel with one hand and guide the blade

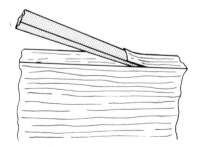

Figure 3–7 The chisel blade should travel into the grain. This causes the chips to break off and prevents the chisel from cutting and running with the grain too deeply.

with the other. If a better angle is required in cutting, as when deep cuts are made, turn the chisel over so that the bevel side is down. Cross-grain cuts are best made with the blade at an angle of about 45° to the grain. Work from each end toward the center; this prevents end splitting. The workpiece should always be securely supported or vise-held.

Mallets and rubber- or plastic-faced hammers are used with wood chisels when making rough cuts, when cutting across grain, or when cutting hardwoods. Tap the mallet with a series of light taps rather than with heavy blows. Do not use a metal hammer (unless a special steel-headed chisel is used) because it will damage the chisel anvil.

If possible, make cuts in scrap wood first, progressively working backward to the good area of the workpiece. Make a series of short, thin cuts rather than long, deep cuts. This method is more accurate and is safer. In cutting recesses, such as are used for door hinges, use the chisel first in a vertical position. Tap with a mallet. Then make long cuts along the grain up to the vertical cut. Increase the depth of the vertical cuts as required.

Gouges are hollow-blade chisels that are bevel ground inside or outside. Paring and firmer gouges are available. Gouges are used to match curved patterns such as molding and as carvers' tools. Woodcarving gouges are discussed in Section 10–5.

4

clamps and vises

(A) (B) (C) (D) (E)

(F) (G) (H)

(I) (J)

(K) (L) (M)

Figure 4–1 Clamps and vises: (A) ball joint vise; (B) bar clamp; (C) bench stop; (D) C clamp; (E) corner and miter box clamps; (F) drill press vise; (G) hand screws; (H) machinist's vise; (I) parallel clamp; (J) saw horse brackets; (K) spring clamp; (L) strap clamp; (M) wood vise.

60

4–1.   GENERAL DESCRIPTION

Clamps and **vises** are tools used for holding workpieces together with pressure during gluing, soldering, or welding or to hold a workpiece while another operation, such as drilling, planing, sanding, or fastening to another workpiece, is performed. As defined by a dictionary, a clamp is a device designed to bind or constrict or to press two or more parts together so as to hold them firmly. A vise is defined as any of various tools with two jaws for holding work; the vise usually closes by a screw, a lever, or a cam. The clamp is considered a portable tool, whereas a vise is normally mounted to a bench or table. Many types of clamps and all vises work on the principle of the screw.

In this chapter you are introduced to *bar clamps, C clamps, corner and miter-box clamps, hand screws, improvised clamps, parallel clamps, spring clamps*, and *strap clamps*. You are also introduced to the *ball-joint vise, drill-press vise, machinist's vise*, and *wood vise*. Two related tools are included also: the *bench stop* and the *sawhorse*.

Clamps are handy items to have around the shop (and the home). You'll find endless uses for them. Right now I have a recreation-room chair temporarily clamped together with a C clamp waiting until I get a chance to repair it. You'll find the C clamp, bar clamp, and the hand screw the most used clamps around the home and in the workshop. Buy at least one hand screw; two bar clamps with several lengths of pipe; and a couple of C clamps in 1-, 6-, and 12-inch sizes (openings).

Vises are handy in the shop, too. I'd suggest a machinist's vise with at least 3-inch jaws and a wood vise with 6-inch jaws.

There are many times when you'll need to improvise ways to hold workpieces. Refer to Section 4–11 for numerous ways to improvise clamps.

4–2.   APPLICATION OF CLAMPS AND VISES

The most important concern that you should have when using clamps and vises is that the workpiece is protected from being marred by the jaws of the clamp or vise. Protection can be as simple as cardboard for lighter-pressure clamps, scrap wood for heavier clamps and vises, and soft metals such as copper or aluminum when a metal workpiece is held in the jaws of a vise.

In addition to ensuring that the jaws are covered to protect the workpiece, be sure that the jaws are firmly and evenly placed against the workpiece; the jaw pressure must be evenly distributed. When clamps are used during gluing, don't apply too much pressure because too much glue will be squeezed out. You can also warp, bend, buckle, or crack the workpiece if too much pressure is applied.

Wood vises are mounted under one of the workbench top corners. The top of the jaws are flush with the top of the workbench. The machinist's vise is mounted on one of the front corners and on the *top* of the workbench.

4–3.   CARE OF CLAMPS AND VISES

Clamp and vise jaws should be cleaned occasionally and wire-brushed, as required, to remove clogged dirt or metal chips. Occasionally rub metallic surfaces with an oily rag to aid in rust prevention. Many quality wood, machinists, and drill-press vises have parts that can easily be replaced. These replaceable parts include jaws, slides, swivels, bases, and angle plates.

4–4.   BALL-JOINT VISE

The **ball-joint vise** is a small versatile vise used by model makers, electronic technicians, instrument makers, and jewelers to position a workpiece in any direction (in a full circle) horizontal to vertical. The jaws can be positioned to any compound angle and are locked at that angle by tightening one clamp knob. The ball-joint vise is die-cast and can be bolted down by its base to a bench or a drill press. A portable vacuum-base version is also available; the base is secured to any flat smooth surface by simply turning a handle.

The ball-joint vise is $6\frac{1}{2}$ inches high with jaw widths of $2\frac{1}{2}$ inches. The jaw capacity is about $2\frac{1}{2}$ inches. Horizontally grooved or flat nylon jaws and flat steel jaws are available.

4–5.   BAR CLAMP (CLAMP FIXTURE)

The **bar clamp**, known also as a *clamp fixture*, is a versatile clamp adjustable over an almost unlimited length. It is used in clamping wide glued-up wood strips, for clamping furniture, and for holding parts during assembly.

Several types of bar clamps are manufactured: one that uses black pipe (Fig. 4–1), one that uses wood, one that is of *I-beam* construction (lengths of 2 to 7 feet), and one that uses a notched bar. Of the four types, I recommend the bar clamp that uses black pipe because you can buy several sets of different lengths of pipe. This enables you to have a number of different-sized clamps, and you need only buy a set of *frame* and *slide* assemblies.

The frame assembly screws onto a threaded end of pipe. The screw adjusts a flat jaw over a length of 2 inches. The slide assembly fits over the pipe, slides along into the desired position, and then locks and remains locked in position by a cam with milled teeth.

In clamping a large workpiece made up of a series of strips of wood, you should use three bar clamps, one on each end on top and one in the center on the bottom of the workpiece. Place the pipe flat against the workpiece. This method will prevent the workpiece from buckling. To further ensure against warping, clamp the pipes against the workpiece with hand screws.

Make *one* bar clamp as follows: buy a set of bar clamps. The set consists of one frame and one slide (the set will be for either ¾-inch pipe or for ½-inch pipe, not both). Determine the pipe length(s) you'd like; I use 24- and 40-inch pipes. Select extra-heavy black iron pipe for ordinary clamping, double extra heavy when greater pressure is required. Buy different lengths of pipe, have them cut, and have 1 inch of *one end* of each piece threaded. If it didn't come with your bar-clamp set, buy a threaded cap to place on the threads of each piece of pipe except for the one on which the bar-clamp set will be assembled; the caps protect the threads from damage. Now, press the cam on the slide, place it over the pipe, and slide it along the pipe (Fig. 4–1). Slide the jaw of the frame over the pipe; screw the threaded section of the frame onto the pipe thread.

To use the bar clamp, retract the frame jaw by turning the screw handle. Press the cam of the slide and position the slide so that the opening between the jaws is about ¼ inch longer than the workpiece. Release the cam. Place the bar clamp over the workpiece with the pipe against the workpiece. Rotate the frame screw and tighten the jaws against the workpiece. If you're gluing, don't tighten so tightly that all the glue is squeezed out.

4–6.   BENCH STOP

The **bench stop** is a handy accessory for your workbench. It is used in conjunction with a wood vise (Section 4–17) to clamp a workpiece to the surface of your workbench for performing such work as planing or sanding. The bench stop is placed into a ⅝-inch hole; the stiff spring on the 3-inch bench stop holds it in place at the desired height.

For example, let's assume that you'd like to plane the surface of a 12-inch board. You insert the bench stop in the applicable ⅝-inch hole in your bench. You raise the retractable *dog* (Section 4–17) on your wood vise and open the movable jaw until the distance between the dog and the bench stop is greater than 12 inches. Insert the board and tighten the vise jaw. If you don't have a dog on your wood vise, remove the wood plate on the movable jaw of your wood vise and insert a plate that is about 2 inches higher than the top of

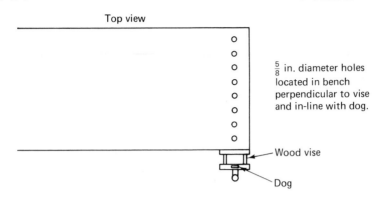

Figure 4–2 Locating holes for a bench stop.

your workbench. Use this plate with the bench stop as you would use a dog.

Figure 4–2 illustrates the placement of ⅝-inch holes in your workbench for use with a wood vise in clamping a workpiece. Remove the bench stop from the workbench when the stop is not in use.

4–7.   C CLAMP

The **C clamp** is named after its physical shape. It is a very useful clamp for woodworkers, hobbyists, and model makers; it is used extensively in aircraft construction, pattern making, and allied trades. The C-shaped malleable frame has one fixed flat jaw and one movable jaw. The movable jaw has an anvil that is flat and sits on a ball-joint swivel, making the clamp useful for clamping surfaces that are parallel or are nearly parallel. An acme thread screw with a sliding pin handle adjusts the opening of the clamp.

In purchasing a C clamp, two dimensions are important: the *opening of the jaws*, which varies from 1 to 18 inches, and the *depth* of the clamp, which varies from 1 to 4 inches. The depth is referred to as the *throat* and is from the center of the screw to the frame; *deep-throated* C clamps have throats that vary up to 16 inches. The depth dimension is important because it determines how far away from the edge the workpiece can be clamped.

In use, open the C-clamp jaws slightly larger than the material to be clamped. Sandwich thin blocks of wood over the workpiece to protect it. Using the pin handle, tighten the clamp. Don't use a

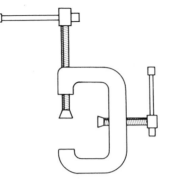

Figure 4–3 A special C clamp used for edge gluing.

wrench or pliers on the pin handle because it may bend the handle and may also possibly bend the clamp frame.

A special type of C clamp (Fig. 4–3) is used for edge gluing. Close the C-clamp jaws first; then tighten the side clamp. Don't clamp so tightly that the glue is all squeezed out.

4–8.   CORNER AND MITER-BOX CLAMPS

Corner and miter-box clamps are used to clamp a rectangular frame together for gluing, nailing, or stapling. The clamps are sold in a set of four, one miter-box clamp and three corner clamps. The **miter-box clamp** has guides for a backsaw that is used to cut 45°-angle cuts into workpieces for right-angle joining. The workpieces fit exactly with no gaps. This makes a strong joint. The **corner clamp** only holds two pieces together at right angles; it has no saw-blade guides. Corner and miter box clamps are made of cast aluminum alloy and clamp workpiece widths up to 3½ inches.

The miter-box clamp is fastened to the workbench with two wood screws. The frame is marked for proper length, is clamped into the miter-box clamp, and is cut at an angle of 45°. Glue is applied to the two frame sides with their ends cut at angles of 45° and the sides are then clamped into a corner clamp, assuring that the mitered frame ends are tight together. Ensure that you do not tighten the clamps so tight that you mar the frame pieces. The mitered joint can then be nailed or stapled for additional strength.

If you have a miter box and backsaw already, you may prefer

to buy a complete *frame clamp* instead. With a frame clamp, all four corners are clamped at one time. Four long screws (capacity of 2 to 14 inches) are screwed through four aluminum-alloy right-angle corner blocks. Ensure that you don't tighten the screws so tight that you buckle the frame. Any number of extension screws may be added to extend the capacity of the frame.

4–9.   DRILL-PRESS VISE (ANGLE VISE)

The **drill-press vise**, also known as an *angle vise*, is used most often for clamping small workpieces while drilling, tapping, and grinding operations are performed on the workpiece. It can also be used as a small bench vise for hand operations on workpieces. The cast-iron drill-press vise can be placed on end or on either side for making quick setups without clamps or wedges. Vises that are mounted to a tilting-type base (Fig. 4–1) or a combination swivel/tilting base are even more versatile because the jaws can be set at an angle of from 0 to 90° in a 360° circle.

The jaw faces of drill-press vises are flat, but additional accessory pieces for holding irregularly and round workpieces are available and in fact are included with some drill-press vises. Jaw widths are about 2½ inches with depths of 1½ inches; the jaws may be opened about 3 inches. Jaw faces are easily replaced by removing two screws. Mounting lugs are provided on the bases for mounting to the drill-press table or to the workbench.

Move the jaws of the drill-press vise by rotating the screw with the pin handle. Set the angle of the vise with respect to the base by loosening the winged thumbscrew on the base. An indicator on the side of the vise indicates the angle in degrees from the horizontal. Ensure that the vise angle is set at 0 (zero) when you are not intentionally using the vise at an angle.

4–10.   HAND SCREWS

Hand screws are used in the woodshop primarily to clamp pieces of wood together while gluing; they may also hold wood while a hobbyist carves or drills. The jaws of the hand screws are made of seasoned hardwood, usually maple. Some manufacturers make jaws of cast-magnesium-alloy steel. Jaw lengths and openings vary from 4 to 18 inches and from 2 to 14 inches, respectively. I prefer the wood jaws because of their inherent advantage—that no pads of scrap wood are needed to prevent marring of the workpiece.

The jaws of the hand screws can be set to any angle by means of the two cold-rolled-steel acme-threaded screw spindles. One half of each spindle is right-hand-threaded; the other half is left-hand-threaded. The handles are made of fluted hardwood to provide a good grip. The middle spindle provides compression of the jaws against the workpieces; the end screw causes the jaws to pivot about the middle spindle.

Revolving the spindle advances or retracts both jaws simultaneously. To revolve both spindles at the same rate to open or close the jaws, grip both handles and revolve the handles as you would pedal a bicycle; one direction opens the jaws and the other closes the jaws. In use, open the jaws to a point close to the correct size and place the jaws over the workpiece so that the middle screw is as close to the workpiece as possible. Lightly tighten both spindles, ensuring that even pressure is being applied along the entire length of the clamp. Then tighten each spindle with equal pressure.

Keep wooden-hand-screw jaws coated with wax to prevent glue from sticking to them. Occasionally place a light coat of oil on each spindle. Do not store the hand screws with the jaws tightly closed.

4–11.   IMPROVISED CLAMPS

There will be many times when you will need to improvise a clamp for a special purpose. The following ideas may be used or expanded upon to suit your needs.

1. Use alligator clips to hold tiny parts together. You can use a vise to hold the handle of the clip or you can fasten the clip to a block of wood. Alligator clips are excellent as a third hand when soldering.

2. Use spring-loaded clothespins to hold small objects. You can screw or nail one handle of the clothespin into a block of wood or into your workbench.

3. Rubber bands are useful to clamp small wooden or plastic pieces together while glue is drying. For longer

rubber-band lengths, tie several together; for shorter lengths, loop the rubber bands over and over or tie knots in them. Rubber bands resist slipping, won't scratch or mar, and conform to odd shapes. They are ideal for regluing antiques. Large rubber bands can be made from old inner tubes. Giant rubber bands are available up to 56 inches in circumference by ½ or ¾ inch wide.

4.   You can use tape as a clamp. However, tape stretches and therefore is used only with quick-setting glue.

5.   You can pile weights on top of workpieces being glued. Protect the workpiece with a flat piece of scrap wood; then place a brick, hammer, sledgehammer, or similar weight on top. Ensure that the weight is evenly distributed across the workpiece.

6.   Broken chair rungs should first have glue worked into the break. Next, wrap waxed paper over the break. Finally, wrap the rung with heavy cord and tie the ends.

7.   Loose chair rungs or similar repairs can be made by gluing and then applying a rope *tourniquet*. Protect the workpiece with cardboard under the rope, which is looped between the chair legs and is tied together. Place a heavy stick between the loop and twist it to tighten the joint (Fig. 4–4).

8.   To drill a round bar of metal or wood when you don't have a drill-press vise, make a holding device by bolting two round pieces of pipe or dowel together (Fig. 4–5). Place the round workpiece in the curved opening created by the joined pipes or dowels.

9.   To hold workpieces for planing, you can nail two pieces of scrap wood (the thickness must be less than the workpiece thickness) into your workbench. Place the workpiece in position and use wooden wedges (Fig. 4–6) to hold the workpiece. Don't wedge with too much force or you'll mar the workpiece.

10.   To clamp a mitered joint, make a 2-inch L-shaped jig from a piece of ¾-inch scrap wood; the sides must be perpendicular to each other. Place the mitered pieces along the sides of the L jig. Use C clamps to clamp the workpieces to the L jig. Use a piece of smooth scrap wood against the workpiece to protect it from being marred by the C clamp (Fig. 4–7).

Figure 4–4 Apply a rope or string tourniquet as an improvised glue clamp.

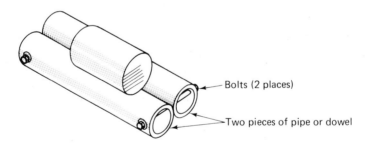

Figure 4–5 Jig for holding round objects.

4–12.   MACHINIST'S VISE

The **machinist's vise** is used at home, machine shops, and garages for metal work. It consists of a base, a fixed jaw with a small flat anvil surface, an adjustable jaw (the front jaw), a screw, and a pin-type handle. Bases are fixed, swivel (Fig. 4–1), clamp-on (Fig. 4–1), or vacuum. The swivel-base vise has a great advantage over the fixed-base vise because the vise can be swiveled around at least 165° (most home models) and up to 365° (on industrial models). A positive lock fixes the vise at any desired angle. Tighten the base by hand with the pin; don't hit it with a hammer or you'll bend the pin. Fixed and swivel-base models are bolted to the workbench top, whereas the clamp-on is a semipermanent installation. The vacuum base must be placed on a flat smooth surface.

The jaws are replaced on some models by driving out pins and

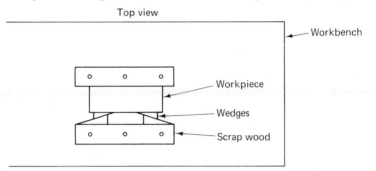

Figure 4–6 Using wedges to hold a workpiece in place.

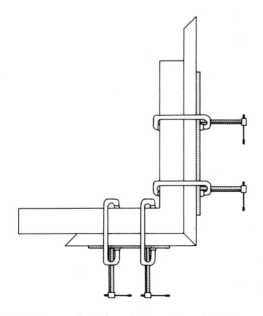

Figure 4–7 L shaped jig for gluing mitered joints.

on others by removing flatheaded bolts; both smooth jaw faces and gripping faces are available. Pipe grips are located below the front and rear jaws on many vises. If you plan to do any plumbing, I suggest that you obtain a vise with this added feature. On industrial models, the rear jaw can pivot when a stop pin is removed. This feature is handy when working with workpieces that are tapered or are irregularly shaped. Machinist's vises come in a range of sizes:

Jaw Width	Jaw Opening	Throat Depth	Weight
2½ to 8 in.	2½ to 12 in.	3 to 6 in.	25 to 180 lb

Light-duty machinist's vises (Fig. 4–1) are usually fixed, swivel, or clamp-on bases. The jaws are 2½ inches wide and open 2½ inches. They can be mounted to surfaces up to 2 inches thick.

Bench-mounted machinist's vises are bolted to the top front corner of a workbench. Mark and drill holes through the top of the bench and fasten with three bolts, lock washers, and nuts.

Place workpieces between the open jaws of the vise. Protect the workpiece from being marred by placing brass or aluminum *caps* or *soft faces* over the jaws. You can purchase soft jaws or make them yourself by bending pieces of brass or aluminum.

There are two types of jaw-face mounts: pins or flatheaded bolts. To replace jaw faces held on by pins, use a solid punch and ball peen hammer to start driving out the pins. Follow the solid punch with the proper size of pin punch to drive the pins completely out. Replace the jaw faces and reinsert the pins. If the jaw or faces are bolted in, simply remove the flat screwheaded bolts, install the new faces, and reinstall the bolts.

4–13.   PARALLEL CLAMP

Parallel clamps are similar to hand screws (Section 4–10) but, by comparison, are miniature. The steel parallel clamps have 1- to 2½-inch capacities and have smooth jaws to prevent marring. The screw caps have holes through them so that a pin can be placed through the hole to increase the torquing ability of the screw. A spring clamp holds the loose jaw in constant alignment when the jaws are opening or closing.

The parallel clamp provides positive clamping to hold work-pieces together in drilling, tapping, engraving, and grinding operations. It is used by hobbyists, machinists, toolmakers, and mechanics.

Place the clamp over the workpiece until the workpiece edge nearly meets the center screw. Finger-tighten both screws. If additional torquing is required, place a pin through each of the screw-cap pin holes. Simultaneously hand-tighten each screw. Do not use pliers on the screw caps. Wipe the complete clamp occasionally with an oily rag.

4–14.   SAWHORSE BRACKETS

Sawhorse brackets are not really tools, but when combined with some 2- by 4-inch wood, the combination becomes a sawhorse, which is very useful in the shop for holding large workpieces. The brackets are steel and have predrilled holes in them for attaching the brackets to wood.

Figure 4–8 illustrates how to make sawhorses. You need two sawhorses, which means that you should buy two sets of brackets (a total of four brackets). The bill of materials of Fig. 4–8 suggests lengths for the various pieces of wood, but you can alter the length dimensions to your own requirements. The base of each leg should be cut at an angle of 15° (75° complementary angle) so that the legs fit flush to the ground. After all the pieces of wood are cut, nail or screw the legs into the brackets. Then place the cross member into the brackets and nail or screw it into place (use 7d common nails or 1½-inch No. 5 roundheaded screws throughout).

The top supports are optional additions to the sawhorses. I find them very useful because you can place a sheet of wood on top of the sawhorses and rip it with a circular saw (Section 13–4). The saw-horses support both sides of the cut and the separation between the top supports allow the blade to pass through. Glue and nail on the top supports. Use 4d finishing nails and countersink the nails ½ inch below the surface so that there is little possibility that your saw blade can cut into them. Instead of gluing on the top supports, you could also cut away a piece of the cross member.

For large sheets of wood such as 4 by 8 feet, you can give the sheet additional support by laying 2-inch by 4-inch by 8-feet lengths

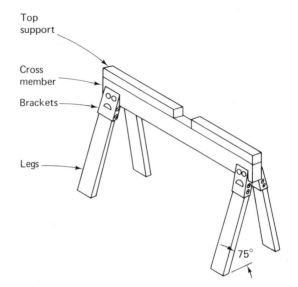

Figure 4–8 Plans for building sawhorses.

of wood between two sawhorses. Place the sheet of wood on top of the supports, keeping two supports on either side of the saw kerf.

4–15.   SPRING CLAMP

Need a third hand for clamping flat or round workpieces? The **spring clamp** may be your answer. It's a heavy-gauge steel clamp with vinyl tips to prevent marring. It can be applied and removed instantly, which makes it ideal for fast-drying glue jobs, where a number of clamps need to be placed on the workpiece quickly.

Spring clamps are available in lengths of 4, 6, and 9 inches, with maximum openings of 1, 2, and 3 inches, respectively. Clamp pressures range from 27 to 80 pounds/square inch.

If you suspect that there may be too much pressure from the clamps on your workpiece, add scrap wood under the clamp jaws to distribute the pressure over a larger area. For light-duty clamping jobs, you can use a clothespin.

4–16.   STRAP (BAND, WEB) CLAMP

The **strap clamp**, also called a *band clamp* or a *web clamp*, consists of 12 to 15 feet of nylon webbing and a *ratchet and pawl* buckle mechanism. The strap clamp holds all sizes and irregular shapes under positive even pressure. It is very useful for clamping when chair parts or large-diameter workpieces are being glued.

In use, the strap is placed around the workpiece. The strap is pulled tight at the buckle mechanism. A wrench or large screwdriver is used on the ratchet nut to tighten the clamp (one manufacturer's strap clamp uses a handle crank). The pawl continually prevents the ratchet from rotating backward; that is, the pawl locks the ratchet and strap tight.

To release the strap clamp, use a wrench or large screwdriver on the ratchet nut. Rotate the ratchet nut in the *same direction as for tightening* the clamp until the ratchet tooth is off the pawl. Press the spring-loaded pawl and let the clamp loosen.

4–17.   WOOD VISE

The **wood vise** is used in all shops where woodworking is done. It has replaceable wood-faced jaws from 3 by 6 inches to 4 by 7 inches that open from 7 to 12 inches and hold workpieces for sanding, planing, carving, drilling, gluing, or other operations. The wood vise is normally permanently fixed to a front corner of the workbench, but portable clamp-on vises are available. The wood vise in Fig. 4–1 is well suited for home use. More expensive models have rapid-action screw mechanisms: counterclockwise operation disengages threads and permits fast jaw movement, clockwise operation engages the threads and produces continuous jaw movement and nonslip holding power. A retractable dog is available on some vises and is used with a bench stop (Section 4–6) or an improvised stop to hold larger workpieces.

The wood vise is mounted on a front corner of the workbench such that the jaws are flush with the workbench top; the underneath part of the vise is screwed into the underneath surface of the top of the workbench, and the fixed jaw is screwed into the front of the workbench top. Hold the vise into place and carefully mark the underneath hole locations. Drill pilot holes under the workbench and install lag screws (lag screwheads are tightened with a wrench) from the bottom (you may need to build up the underneath surface of the workbench top so that the jaws are flush). Install a wooden jaw face made from a piece of ¾-inch hardwood the size of the fixed jaw against the fixed jaw. After drilling pilot holes in the wooden face and workbench, drill countersinks (Section 2–5) in the jaw face. Then screw flatheaded screws through the wooden jaw face and vise into the workbench. Install another piece of ¾-inch hardwood against the movable jaw; use short stove bolts and countersink the flatheads. When the wooden jaw faces become damaged, you can remove them, plane them smooth, and return them to the vise; or you can replace them.

5

fasteners

5-1. GENERAL

It is true that **fasteners** are not tools, but this handbook describes all the tools used to cut workpiece materials and all the tools necessary to drive fasteners. It is only fitting, then, that a chapter should be included to describe the common fasteners utilized by the craftsman, the hobbyist, and the professional to join workpieces together.

This chapter describes some easy-to-use fasteners, some difficult ones, some temporary ones, and some permanent ones. It provides you with sufficient information so that you can select the applicable fastener for your job. Some tabular data that are useful in the shop are contained in Appendixes L and M.

The fasteners discussed in this chapter include *anchoring devices; bolts, washers,* and *nuts: corrugated fasteners; nails; rivets; screws; setscrews;* and *turnbuckles.*

Purchase fasteners in large quantities (by the box or by the pound) as you need them for a particular job. Then store the leftovers. You might also buy some assortments of fasteners, but watch out because merchandisers have a habit of throwing together as an assortment what they can't sell. At any rate, if you buy an assortment, sort the pieces and store the same types and sizes together. You can store fasteners in plastic or cardboard storage bins, jelly jars, baby-food jars, or similar types of containers. Store the fasteners in a dry place and don't mix different kinds of metals together.

For the most satisfactory results from fasteners, use the proper fastener for the particular job. Use the proper type and size of tool to drive the fasteners.

5–2.   ANCHORING DEVICES

Anchoring devices are special fasteners for use in attaching items to hollow, plaster, concrete, brick, and stone walls. Three types are available (Fig. 5–1): spring toggle bolts, molly bolts, and expansion shields.

The **spring toggle bolt** is used in hollow walls. Drill a hole large enough for the toggle to pass through when the toggle wings are folded back against the bolt. Before installing the device, remove the bolt from the toggle. Insert the workpiece onto the bolt and reattach the toggle to the bolt. Fold the toggle against the bolt and push the toggle through the drilled hole. Use a screwdriver to tighten the bolt.

The **molly bolt** is also used in hollow walls. Drill a hole of the diameter recommended by the manufacturer for the size of molly

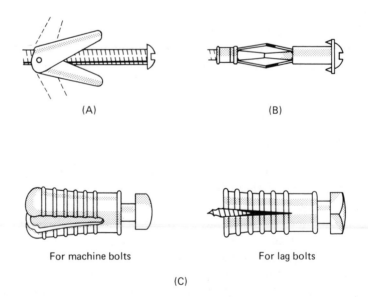

(A)   (B)

For machine bolts   For lag bolts

(C)

Figure 5–1 Anchoring devices: (A) spring toggle bolt; (B) molly bolt; (C) expansion shields.

to be installed (molly bolts are sold on cards with installation directions on the back of the card). Push the molly bolt through the hole. Tap the assembly lightly with a hammer until the points (under the bolt head) are inserted into the wall. Using a screwdriver, tighten the bolt; this draws the molly sleeve tightly up against the wall. Remove the bolt, install the workpiece on the bolt, and reinstall the bolt into the anchor.

Expansion shields are used in concrete, brick, and stone. Use a masonry drill (Section 2–8) to drill a hole the diameter of the (unexpanded) expansion shield into the masonry. Tap the expansion shield into the masonry until it is flush with the masonry. Install the workpiece on the bolt and screw the bolt into the expansion shield. As the bolt goes into the shield, the shield expands against the masonry material and makes a secure fastening.

5–3.   BOLTS, WASHERS, AND NUTS

When a bolt, a washer, and a nut are combined as a fastener to join two workpieces together, a very strong joint is accomplished. This section describes the types, characteristics, and uses of the various kinds of bolts, washers, and nuts used to join metal, wood, plastic, combinations of the aforementioned materials, and other materials together.

Bolts

A **bolt**, used to fasten objects together, consists of a metal rod or pin with a head at one end and a screw thread at the other end; the rod is secured by a nut. The diameter of a bolt is the same over the length of the rod. Bolts are used with washers and nuts to fasten metal workpieces together; bolts are also used to fasten metal to wood, wood to wood, and for other fastening applications.

Bolts come with a variety of heads and different-threaded rods, as shown in Fig. 5–2. Bolt materials include steel, brass, and plated steel. Various lengths (from ⅜ to 30 inches) are available in each style. First determine your application—what type of head is needed? What length is needed? (Lengths of bolts are measured from the part of the head that is *flush with the surface of the workpiece* to the rod

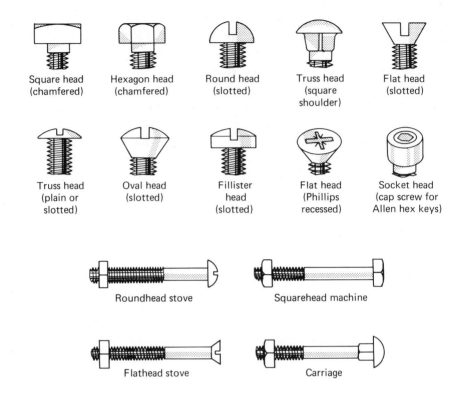

Figure 5–2 Bolt head styles and typical bolts.

end.) Is a lock washer or a flat washer needed? What type of nut is needed? Once these decisions have been reached, you can obtain the bolt/washer/nut combination that is required for your particular application.

When installing bolts, push the bolt through predrilled holes in the workpieces to be joined. The predrilled hole diameters should be slightly greater than the bolt diameter. Install a lock washer. Install a nut. Hold the bolt head with the proper type and size of screwdriver or wrench (depending on the type of head) and, using the proper tool on the nut, tighten the nut.

Washers

Washers are thin flat rings or perforated plates used in joints or assemblies to ensure tightness, prevent leakage, act as spacers, prevent friction, and to act as locking devices on bolt-and-nut assemblies.

Washers may be leather, fiber, rubber, or metal. Metal washers are most commonly used with fasteners and so will be discussed further. Rubber and fiber washers are used in plumbing.

Washers are shown in Fig. 5–3. The plain flat washer is used to protect, prevent friction, and act as a spacer. Flat washers are available in different thicknesses and diameters. Larger-diameter washers are used where it is desired to spread the fastening load over a larger area. Thinner washers are used to prevent marring. Flat washers are available through the complete range of screw sizes up to 3-inch diameters. The size of a washer is the size that will pass a particular threaded fastener through its bore. For example, a No. 5 washer allows a No. 5 threaded fastener to pass through it.

Lock washers prevent fastener hardware from loosening and eventually falling away from assemblies where either a rotational or a vibrational motion is encountered. They are either of the spring- or toothed-lock design. The spring-lock washer has a spring action that closes to a flattened condition when it is tightened between a nut and workpiece. In the compressed condition, the washer split ends spring out and dig into the nut, keeping the nut from unscrewing. Spring-lock washers are available in sizes from No. 2 through a $1\frac{1}{4}$-inch screw size.

The toothed-lock washer works on the principle that the teeth dig into the surface of the nut and the workpiece, locking the assembly together. Toothed-lock washers are available in screw sizes from No. 2 through a $1\frac{1}{4}$-inch size.

Nuts

A **nut** is a perforated block, usually made of metal, that has an internal screw thread and is used on a bolt or screw for tightening or holding workpieces. Nuts are shaped as shown in Fig. 5–4. The hexagon and square nuts are commonly used. The wing, hex cap, and

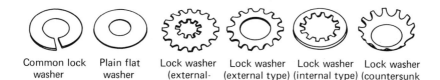

Common lock   Plain flat   Lock washer   Lock washer   Lock washer   Lock washer
washer   washer   (external-   (external type) (internal type) (countersunk
                           internal type)   type)

Figure 5–3 Washer styles.

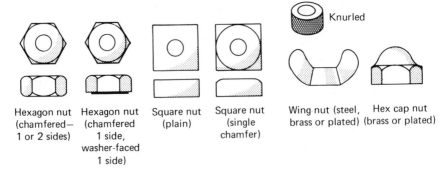

Figure 5–4 Nut styles.

knurled nuts are special-purpose nuts. Nuts are made of steel, plated steel, and brass.

The square nut is inexpensive and is generally used in the construction field; it is not normally used in machine building. Square nuts are available in machine-screw sizes from No. 0 to No. 12 and in fractional sizes from ¼ to 1½ inches. Hex nuts are generally used in the machine field because the hex (six-sided) shape allows for tightening in cramped areas; the six sides also provide additional edges for gripping with a wrench for tightening and loosening. Sizes range in machine-screw sizes from No. 0 through No. 12 and in fractional sizes from ¼ to 4 inches.

The wing nut and knurled nut are used in special applications where only a hand-tight fit is necessary and where frequent removing and reinstalling is expected. The hex cap nut is used to protect the ends of screw or bolt threads or to protect objects from catching on the protruding screw or thread; they are also used for decorative purposes.

The most important fact to remember in installing nuts is to use a wrench of the proper size for the nut. Use 12- or 6-point wrenches on hex nuts and 8- or 4-point wrenches on square nuts. Refer to Chapter 17 for a complete discussion of the use of wrenches.

5–4. CORRUGATED FASTENERS

Corrugated fasteners (Fig. 5–5) are used to fasten mitered or butted wood joints together. They are usually used for rough construction and in concealed construction. Typical uses for corrugated fasteners are in the joining of the mitered corners of wood window screens and picture frames. Corrugated fasteners have one sharpened edge and come in a variety of sizes and with parallel or tapered corrugations. The tapered corrugated fastener is the most effective because it draws the pieces together as the fastener is installed. Once driven into place, it is difficult to remove these fasteners without ruining part of the workpieces.

To join two pieces of wood together with corrugated fasteners, mate the pieces flush with each other. Clamp the pieces in position if possible. Position the corrugated fastener so that it is divided equally over the two pieces; if possible, do not locate the fastener near the edges of the wood. Use a hammer to drive the fastener flush into the workpieces.

5–5.   NAILS

A **nail** is a slender pointed and headed metal fastener designed to be pounded into a workpiece. Nails are the most common fasteners used and are quick and easy to install. They are relatively strong. Nails are used in carpentry, building, house framing, roofing, trimming interiors, in box making, and in upholstering to fasten wood to wood, metal, asbestos, slate, plasterboard, and composition board. Nails are made of steel wire, iron, brass, copper, and galvanized steel. Nails range in size from tiny tacks or brads to railroad spikes. Nails are sized by "d" sizes. The letter d is derived from the English symbol for pence or penny. Originally it meant the number of nails that could be bought for a penny. Appendix L lists various nail sizes.

When a nail is driven into a workpiece, it bends, breaks, and

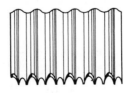

Figure 5–5 Corrugated fastener.

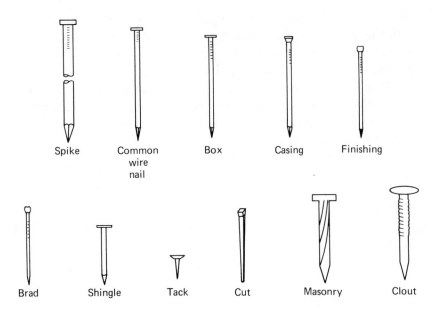

Figure 5–6 Nail styles.

splits wood fibers; it is the force of the fibers trying to return to their original position that holds the nail into the workpiece.

Brads and finishing nails have small heads with indentations. These nails are used primarily in furniture making and are driven below the wood surface with a nail set (refer to Section 10–7). Common nails are driven flush with the surface.

The following hints are provided to aid you in making secure fastenings with nails. Be sure to refer to Sections 8–5 and 10–7 for discussions on how to hammer nails properly, how to toe-nail, how to clinch-nail, and how to countersink finishing nail heads. Now for the hints:

1. In hardwood, near workpiece edges, or in narrow strips of wood, predrill nail holes with diameters slightly smaller than the nail diameters.

2. Locate nails a minimum of ¾ inch from any edge. If this is not possible, predrill the nail holes.

3. Apply a little glue to the nail or to the predrilled hole before driving a nail. This gives added strength to the joint.

4.   When nails are placed along the grain of the wood, splitting of the wood along the grain can be prevented by staggering the nails instead of placing them in a straight line.

5.   Don't drive nails near or through knots in the wood.

6.   The strongest nailed joint is made when workpieces are both glued and nailed together (refer to Chapter 7, Glues, Adhesives, and Cements).

5–6.   RIVETS

A **rivet** is a soft metal pin or bolt with a head, used to join pieces of metal, thin wood, fiber, leather, plastic, or similar materials by passing the shank through a hole in each piece. The plain end of the rivet is then beat or pressed down to make a second head. Rivets are used for permanent fastening, where removal is not anticipated. Rivets are of five types (Fig. 5–7): two-piece hollow, tubular, solid, split, and blind (the blind rivet is very useful for home use and is used with a special rivet tool; refer to Section 10–13).

Solid, tubular, and split rivets are used to fasten sheet metal, thin wood, and thick plastics. Tubular and split rivets are used to fasten canvas and leather, and two-piece hollow rivets are used on soft materials.

All riveting is begun by drilling a hole the size of the rivet diameter through the pieces to be fastened. Insert a rivet through all pieces to determine if a rivet of the proper length is being used, one that protrudes no more than one rivet diameter through the thickness of the materials to be joined. A flat washer can be used to increase material thickness. Now proceed to rivet per the instructions

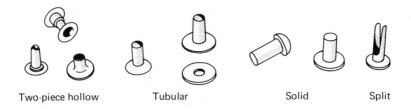

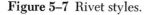
Two-piece hollow   Tubular   Solid   Split

Figure 5–7 Rivet styles.

given for that type of rivet. In each case, place one side of the rivet against a metal block, such as a vise anvil.

two-piece hollow rivets   Insert the tapered portion of the rivet. From the other side of the workpiece, place the hollow portion of the rivet over the tapered portion. Drive the two parts of the rivet together with a hammer.

tubular rivets   Place a center punch into the hollow rivet. Strike the punch with a hammer; this causes the rivet to start spreading. Now hit the rivet with the ball of a ball peen hammer to spread and flatten the rivet walls.

solid and hollow rivets   Use the ball of a ball peen hammer to spread and flatten the rivet.

split rivet   Drive the rivet through the materials onto a steel block. The legs of the rivet will spread and flatten out.

blind rivet   Insert a blind rivet with a riveter tool (refer to Section 10–13).

Procedures for removing a rivet are discussed in Section 3–5.

5–7.   SCREWS

A **screw** (Fig. 5–8) is a metal-pointed and headed cylindrical fastener that is helically or spirally threaded and designed for insertion into material by rotating, as with a screwdriver. It has greater holding power than a nail and taps its own thread on its way into a workpiece. Though harder to insert than a nail, it is easier than a nail to remove. Screws are also more expensive than nails; they are available in stainless steel, aluminum, soft steel, iron, galvanized steel, chrome-plated steel, nickel-plated steel, blued steel, brass, bronze, and in material with tinned finishes. Brass, brass- and nickel-plated steel, and galvanized steel screws are for use where there is water.

Screwhead shapes include flat, round, oval, square, Phillips, and Frearson (refer to the bolt-head illustration, Fig. 5–2). Screws are available in gauge sizes 0 to 24 and in lengths from $\frac{1}{4}$ to 5 inches

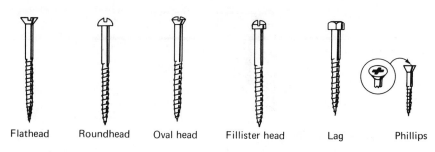

Flathead   Roundhead   Oval head   Fillister head   Lag   Phillips

Figure 5–8 Screw styles.

(Appendix M). (Gauge numbers are shank-size numbers.) Screws are purchased by specifying the gauge number and the screw length.

To install a wood screw, proceed as follows (refer to Fig. 5–9 to help you determine the size of the pilot hole, shank hole, and countersink hole):

1. Using an awl, make a small indentation at the point where the screw is to be installed.

2. Drill shank and pilot holes. Drill the shank hole in the top piece of wood; the shank hole is to be of the same diameter as the screw shank. In the bottom piece of wood, drill the pilot hole (the same diameter as the root thread —the screw thread minus the thread thickness) partway into the wood.

3. If the screw is to be countersunk or/and counterbored, drill a countersink/counterbore hole (of the same diameter as the screwhead) to the required depth.

4. Use the proper type and size of screwdriver (Chapter 16) to drive the screw into the wood. You can use soap or wax on the screw threads to reduce friction, thus making the driving process easier. You can also apply glue to the screws to make them hold better.

NOTE: The shank, pilot, and countersink holes can be drilled in one operation using a countersink/counterbore screw bit (Section 2–5).

Screws don't hold well in end grains of wood. To alleviate this problem, drill a hole perpendicular to the end grain and install a

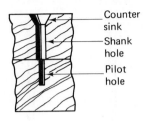

Figure 5–9 Drilling holes for screws.

dowel (glued in). Drill a pilot hole and drive the screw into the end grain and through the dowel.

Sheet-metal screws (Fig. 5–10) are used to join pieces of sheet metal. The screws do their own threading and thus require only that holes be predrilled. The hole diameters should be slightly less than the diameter of the screws. Round, oval, binding, and flatheaded styles are available in shank diameters from No. 2 to No. 14, with lengths from ⅛ to 2 inches.

Screw hooks, screw eyes, and cup hooks (Fig. 5–11) are special screws made of steel, brass, or galvanized steel. They are used to hang pictures, curtains, hammocks, clotheslines, etc. These special screws are available in many sizes. Predrill a hole with a diameter equal to the screw diameter minus the thread thickness. You may need a pair of pliers to screw these special screws into harder woods.

5–8.   SETSCREWS

A **setscrew** is a screw that is screwed through one part tightly upon or into a second part to prevent relative movement between the two parts. An example of this use is in the application of a setscrew in a

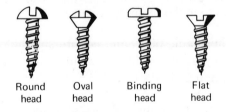

| Round head | Oval head | Binding head | Flat head |

Figure 5–10 Sheet metal screws

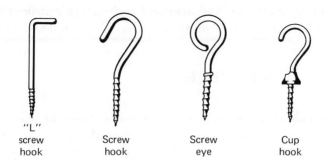

"L"
screw
hook   Screw   Screw   Cup
                    hook   eye   hook

Figure 5–11 Screw hooks, screw eyes, and cup hooks.

motor pulley that *sets* the pulley to the shaft of the motor, preventing movement between the pulley and the shaft. Setscrews are also used to regulate valve openings or spring tension.

Setscrews (Fig. 5–12) are available with square, socket (hex), slotted, and thumbscrew heads. The socket and slotted heads are used in applications where the setscrew is screwed completely inside a part; this prevents a protruding head that can catch on other parts. The thumbhead setscrew is used in applications where frequent removal and replacement or adjustment are expected. Setscrews come in screw sizes from No. 2–56 to No. $\frac{1}{2}$–13.

A setscrew that leaves no marks or burrs on the mating part has a nylon insert that protrudes from the bottom inside. When this setscrew is tightened into threads against another part, the nylon insert compresses into the thread, acting as a self-locking mechanism.

Another type of setscrew has a soft silver grip insert that flattens against the second part; it conforms to the surface of the second part, preventing marring, scratching, or deformation. This type of set-

Square head   Socket set-   Headless   Thumb screw
setscrew   screw (for   setscrew
                     Allen hex keys)   (slotted)

Figure 5–12 Setscrews.

screw can be used over and over and is therefore excellent in applications where a setscrew must be removed or loosened frequently.

5–9.   TURNBUCKLES

A **turnbuckle** (Fig. 5–13) is a device that consists of a link (sleeve) with screw threads at both ends or a screw thread at one end and a swivel at the other end. Eye bolts or hook bolts are threaded into each end of the link. The turnbuckle link is turned to bring the eye or hook bolts closer together and hence to tighten a rod or cable attached to the eye or hook bolts. Turnbuckles range in size from 4½ to 20 inches (open).

Turnbuckles are used in sailboat stays, antenna guys, and diagonal supports across doors meant to prevent sagging.

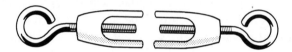

Figure 5–13 Turnbuckles.

6

files

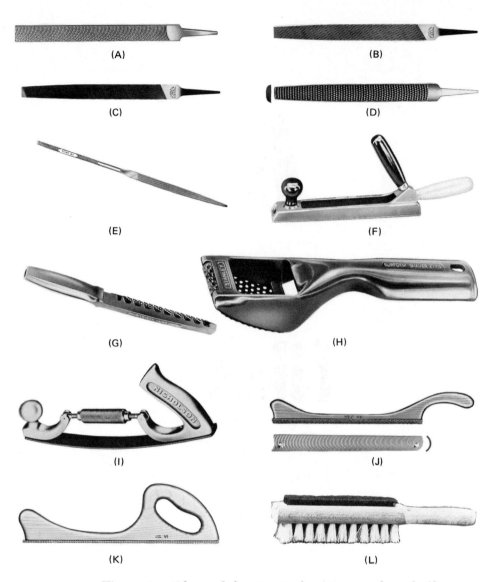

Figure 6–1 Files and forming tools: (A) curved tooth file (rigid); (B) machinist's file; (C) mill file; (D) rasp file; (E) Swiss pattern file; (F) forming tool; (G) mini file forming tool; (H) shaver forming tool; (I) adjustable holder for flexible curved blades; (J) holder for half oval curved file shell; (K) holder for flat flexible curved tooth file; (L) file card.

6–1. GENERAL DESCRIPTION

Files are used to cut, smooth, and remove small amounts of material from workpieces. Metal files are used with metal workpieces; wood rasps, files, and forming tools are used on wood, plastic, and soft metal workpieces. Often, the file is the finishing tool used to make machined parts fit accurately together in prototype or small-quantity production runs or to make wood workpieces fit together properly.

Figure 6–2 illustrates the various parts of a file (a half-round file is illustrated). The flat side is termed the *face* and the opposite side is termed the *back*. Edges that may be flat or rounded are said to be *safe* when there are no teeth cut into them. The length of the file is the distance from the point to the heel (length excludes the tang). Handles are readily removed and are not normally sold as part of the file.

Files are characterized by their cut, coarseness, length, and cross-sectional shape. The cut of a file is the arrangement of the

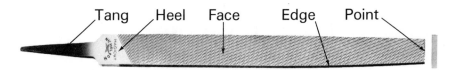

Tang   Heel   Face   Edge   Point

Figure 6–2 File nomenclature.

teeth that the manufacturer has cut into the face of the file. Four cuts are available (Fig. 6–3): single, double, rasp, and curved-tooth. The *single-cut file* has a single set of parallel rows of teeth at an angle of 60 to 80° to the length of the file, extending the length of the file. The single cut produces a smooth finish or a keen edge on a knife, shears, sawteeth, or other cutting tool. Light pressure is used on the tool against the workpiece. The *double-cut file* has a double set of parallel rows of teeth; the first parallel set is cut at about 45° and the second set is at 60 to 80°. The double-cut file is used to remove metal rapidly. Medium to heavy pressure is used on the tool. The *rasp cut* has many short separate teeth, each separately formed during manufacturing by a single-pointed tool or punch. The rasp is used primarily for fast removal of wood. It is also used to file leather, hoofs, and soft metals such as aluminum and lead. It is used with a pressure suited to the hardness of the material. The *curved-teeth cut* has rows of curved teeth along the length of the file. It is used for surface filing of aluminum and steel.

File-teeth row spacing determines the *coarseness* of the file; the larger the number of rows of teeth to the inch, the smoother the cut.

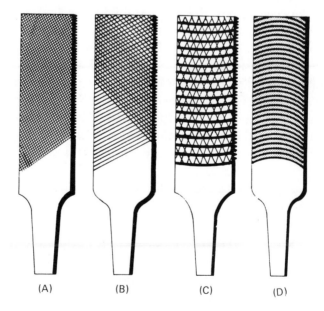

(A)   (B)   (C)   (D)

Figure 6–3 File cuts: (A) single; (B) double; (C) rasp; (D) curved tooth.

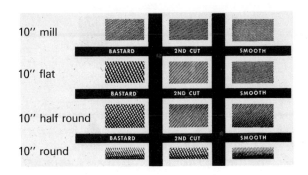

Figure 6–4 File coarseness.

The files are categorized into *coarse* (greatest distance between rows of teeth), *bastard* (medium coarse), *second cut*, and *smooth teeth* (Fig. 6–4). Two other grades, *rough* and *dead smooth*, are also available from some manufacturers. Spacing of the teeth changes with file *length*, increasing proportionately to the increased length of the file; the longer the file, the coarser the file (Fig. 6–5). However, the same relative difference always exists between the cuts for any file in any particular length.

The *shape* of the file is determined by its cross-sectional view (Fig. 6–6). Many shapes are available, but the file shapes used most often are the *round, flat, half-round, three square,* and *square*. The round file is usually tapered toward the point and is used to enlarge or smooth circular openings or concave surfaces. The flat file tapers toward the point in both width and thickness. It is used to file flat surfaces. The half-round file incorporates the features of both the round and flat files into one file that is useful to remove material from flat, convex, and concave surfaces. The half-round file shape is recommended as the first shape of a file to purchase for filing both wood and metal.

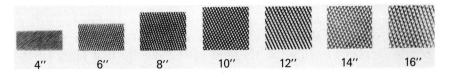

Figure 6–5 Coarseness range of a typical machinist's flat bastard file.

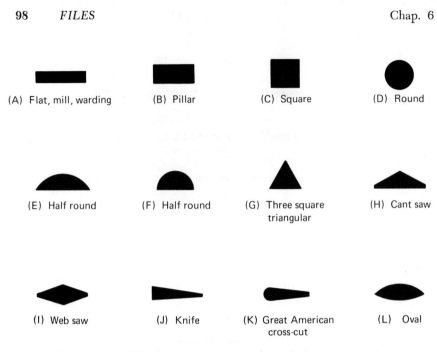

Figure 6–6 File shapes—cross sections of those most often used: (A) flat, mill, warding; (B) pillar; (C) square; (D) round; (E) half round; (F) half round; (G) three square-triangular; (H) cant saw; (I) web saw; (J) knife; (K) great American cross-cut; (L) oval.

The three square file is triangular. It is used to file internal angles that are more acute than a right angle. It is used to clean out square corners and to file taps, cutters, sawblade teeth, and serrated jaws. The square file is used to file square and rectangular slots, keyways, and splines. Some square files have three faces that are double cut and one face that is safe. The safe face can be placed against one inside edge of a workpiece while another edge can be filed.

Most files are tapered toward the point, both in width and thickness, and are made of high-carbon tool steel.

File handles are made of soft wood *without* a finish (such as varnish, etc.) so that the wood absorbs moisture from sweating hands. A metal ferrule (on the end of the handle that slips on the tang) protects the wood from splitting. Handles range in approximate sizes as follows: 4-inch handle for files of 3 to 6 inches; 4½-inch handle for files of 4 to 8 inches; 5-inch handle for files of 6 to 10 inches; 5½-inch handle for files of 8 to 12 inches; and 6-inch handle for files 12 to 18 inches.

The following files are recommended as the first files for your workshop. The selection provides you with an overall range of file sizes and types: 12-inch half-round bastard wood file; 10-inch half-round bastard file for rough work and concave surfaces; 6-inch mill file for smooth cutting on small workpieces; 6-inch three square file for sharpening sawblade teeth and for repairing serrated jaws; and several 4- to 6-inch small, slim needle files—round, flat single cut, and flat double cut for filing small precision parts. You'll also find numerous uses for a standard forming tool and a file brush is a necessity (if you have a wire brush and a fairly stiff bristle brush in the shop, you can substitute them for the file brush).

A *file brush* is a two-sided tool that has a stiff wire brush on one side and a soft hair brush on the other side. The wire brush is used for general cleaning of coarse file teeth; the hair brush is used for finer cut files. A *file card* has only one brush and that is a stiff wire brush for use on coarse file teeth.

Files are manufactured in numerous shapes and sizes. For discussion in this chapter, I have categorized the many types of files as follows: *bent rifflers, curved-tooth files, forming tools, machinist's files, mill files, rasps, special-purpose files, Swiss pattern files,* and *wood files.*

6–2.   APPLICATION OF FILES

Prior to filing, you must first consider the job. What material is to be filed? How tough is the material? Is there a lot of material to be removed or just a little? Is the surface flat? Is it rounded? Use the knowledge you have gained from the introduction to this discussion of files, the latter part of this chapter, and Table 6–1 to determine the answers to these questions. Then select the proper file for your application. Never file without placing the proper handle on the tang. A handle protects your hand.

It takes practice to be able to properly file a surface flat, but it is a skill that you should acquire. Practice slowly and carefully to meet this objective.

Clamp the workpiece to be filed into the protected jaws of a vise

TABLE 6-1. FILE CUT USE

General	
Small work	Short file
Medium work	8-inch file
Large work	Most convenient size
Metal workpieces	
Heavy, rough cutting	Large coarse, double cut
Finishing cuts	Second or smooth cut, single cut
Cast iron	Start with bastard; finish with second cut
Soft metal	Start with second cut; finish with smooth cut
Brass, bronze	Start with bastard cut; finish with a second or smooth cut
Aluminum, lead, babbitt	Bastard-cut curved tooth
Wood workpieces	
Heavy, rough cutting	Rasp, coarse curved tooth, or forming tool
Finishing cuts	Wood files

located approximately at elbow height (Fig. 6–7). The material should be parallel to the jaws and should protrude slightly above the jaws. Clamping of the workpiece prevents vibrations that sometimes damage file teeth. Hold the file in one hand, thumb on top, and hold the point of the file with the fingers of the other hand; again the thumb should be on the top. Keep the file strokes in a straight line. When filing wood, file in the direction of the grain.

New files should be used carefully. Do not apply too much pressure, because it may break off the teeth. If the file becomes clogged, clean it with a file card (Section 6–3). If the file continually clogs,

Figure 6–7 Proper filing procedure.

perhaps you can use a file with teeth that are farther apart. This will give you a rougher cut, however.

In using a file, apply even pressure with both hands on the forward (away from the body) stroke only. The return stroke does not cut; therefore, if you are filing a hard material, lift the file from the material for the return stroke. This prevents the file from becoming dull faster than it should. If you are filing soft metals, light pressure on the return stroke helps keep the file teeth clear of waste metal. Keep the file flat, preventing any rocking motion as the file is stroked across a flat workpiece. Use a rocking motion only when filing rounded edges. File slowly, lightly, and steadily at a rate of about one stroke per second. The proper speed and pressure come with experience. Do not force the file. Check the squareness of the work repeatedly with a steel square. When the file becomes clogged, clean it with a file brush or card.

Small files are used to remove small burrs or excess material in tight locations. Hold a small file in one hand with your index finger extended along the file face for added control (Fig. 6-8). Note from the illustration that even small workpieces should be held in a vise or other clamp. This clamping gives added control to the filing, which results in precisely constructed workpieces. As with the larger files, material is cut only on the forward (away from the body) stroke.

Another filing technique that produces a very smooth and true surface is known as *draw filing*. It is used on narrow surfaces and edges. A single cut file with a second cut or smooth teeth spacing is used; files with successively finer teeth should be used.

To draw-file, place the workpiece in a vise with protected jaws. Grasp the file with both hands (Fig. 6-9) close together (to prevent bending and breaking the file) and draw the file across (at right angle to) the workpiece. Work in both directions. Use moderate pressure on both the draw and back strokes. For an extra-smooth surface, wrap a piece of emery cloth around the file and stroke in the same manner.

The forming tool is easy to use (Fig. 6-10). Examine the blade first to determine the direction of the teeth. This will determine if the tool is to be pushed or pulled along the grain of the workpiece. Also, note the direction of the rows of teeth. Are the rows curved? Are the rows at an angle to the holder? If the rows are curved or are at an angle to the tool holder, then the tool is pushed or pulled di-

Figure 6–8 Filing with a small file.

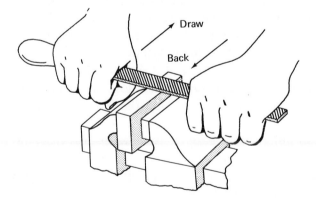

Figure 6–9 Draw filing.

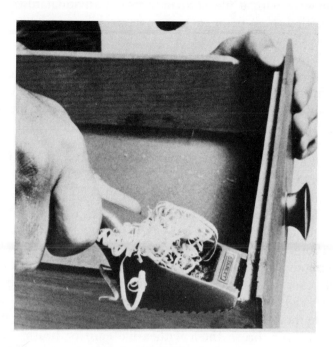

Figure 6–10 Use of a forming tool.

rectly in line with the workpiece. For rough cuts or grooves, stroking across the grain is permitted. However, for smoothing cuts, move the tool with the wood grain. Use the forming tool carefully on end grains to prevent splitting wood chips off of the sides.

6–3.   CARE OF FILES

Break in a new metal-cutting file by first using it on brass, bronze, or smooth iron. Do not use a new file to remove fins or scales from cast iron and do not use it on a narrow surface such as sheet metal, because the teeth will break off. Wood files do not require breaking in.

Chalk may be rubbed into the rows of teeth of a file to help prevent particles of metal from clogging the teeth. When the teeth do become clogged, the file slips, scratches, and is inefficient. Clean a file frequently with a file card or brush. Individual rows may be cleaned with a sharp point such as an ice pick or a nail when the file card or brush cannot get the chips out. Use the file card or brush by drawing it in a direction parallel to the rows of teeth.

Use files properly and only for the intended purpose. Always use a firmly attached handle (except for some Swiss pattern files in which the file and handle are one piece). Do not strike a file to clean chips from it; clean it properly and often with a file card or brush. Do not oil a file, as this causes the file to slip across the surface, preventing filing. Store files separately so that they do not rub against each other or other tools.

To install a handle on a file, insert the tang into the handle socket. Hold the handle in your hand and tap the handle on the workbench top until the file is seated. Do not hammer the handle onto the tang.

To remove a handle, hold the file with one hand and the handle with the other. Pull the handle from the file while striking the handle (at the ferrule) on the edge of the workbench.

Shake the shavings from the teeth of a forming tool. If the teeth become clogged, brush them with a file card or brush. Pitch and other foreign materials stuck to the blade may be wiped clean with a cloth dampened with kerosene.

Replace the blades of forming tools by removing the one or two screws that hold the blade to the holder.

6–4.   BENT RIFFLERS

Bent rifflers are files that are specially designed for wood carvers, metal workers, and stone workers for use in shaping and finishing the irregular shapes of their creations. Rifflers are made in different shapes such as half-round bastard, three square rasp, round rasp, three square bastard, flat bastard, and flat with safe sides. The rifflers are 8 inches in length including handles (which come with the riffler). About two-thirds of the length of the riffler is straight; the one-third toward the point is gradually curved to an angle of about 45°. The curvature allows the riffler to reach into difficult-to-reach areas on models, sculptures, and the like.

6–5.   CURVED-TOOTH FILES

A **curved-tooth file** has rows of teeth cut in a curved contour across the file. The curved-tooth file is widely used in the automobile manufacturing and repairing industries for work on aluminum and sheet steel. It is also used on soft metals, including brass, babbitt, and iron. The curved teeth of the file clears the chips away. It is available in pillar, square, half-round, and flat shapes from 8 to 14 inches in length.

The curved-tooth file is available as a rigid file with a tang [Fig. 6–1(A)] or as a flexible *plain file* (called a *shell* if it is curved rather than flat) that attaches to a holder [Fig. 6–1(I), (J), and (K)].

An adjustable tool holder has a turnbuckle-like arrangement that allows a flexible blade to be positioned concave for shaving convex surfaces or convex for shaving concave surfaces. Adjustable and nonadjustable holders have two screws or other means of clamping replaceable blades.

Both rigid and flexible blades are made. The flat blades are for flat and concave surfaces; the flexible blades are for adjustable and curved holders and are for shaving concave surfaces. Half-round blades are for compound curves. Rigid shell files [Fig. 6–1(J)] have curved teeth on the convex side for cutting concave surfaces and teeth on the concave side for cutting convex surfaces. Flexible blades often have teeth on both sides.

Blade lengths range from 8 to 14 inches. There are from 8 to 18 teeth per inch. As with a file, the more teeth per inch, the finer and smoother is the finish.

6–6.   FORMING TOOLS

A **forming tool** is a mixture of a rasp and a plane; it has characteristics of both. It may be included as part of either the file or the plane family of tools. It is sometimes known as a *rasp plane.*

The forming tool consists of a blade and a holder. The replaceable blade is made up of hundreds of curved teeth that are actually miniature milling cutters. Holes are provided in front of each cutter for chip clearance. The chips are actually shavings similar to those cut with a plane or on a power lathe. Close examination of a single hole and tooth reminds you of a tiny plane (Chapter 11); the only difference is that the depth of cut of the forming-tool "blades" is not adjustable.

The forming tool is used to shape wood, plastic, laminates, fiberglass, and soft metals, including aluminum, copper, and other metals up to the hardness of mild steel. Forming tools are often used as cutting tools for work on the lathe. The tool is used extensively by the woodworker, automobile body repairman, machinist, and patternmaker. It's an inexpensive tool and I recommend that you equip your shop with several models.

Forming-tool holders are made in several shapes, including straight, block type, and round. One model [Fig. 6–1(F)] has a folding handle that makes it similar to a plane (handle up) or a rasp file (handle down). Various forming tool shapes are shown in Fig. 6–1(G) and (H).

The shaver forming tool is a small one-hand-held tool that shaves, trims, scrapes, and smoothes with an easy pulling action. It is ideal for curves, turns, and tight inside corners.

The minifile is similar to other straight forming tools, but it is specifically mentioned because of its small size, ½ inch wide. It is held in one hand and is used to cut grooves and notches, to smooth joints, and to square corners.

6–7.   MACHINIST'S FILE

The **machinist's file** is used for the rapid removal of metal. It produces a rough finish in respect to the mill file (Section 6–8). It is used by machinists, automobile repairmen, and do-it-yourselfers. The machinist's file is double cut on both sides and is single cut on the edges. It is available in bastard, second cut, and smooth teeth. Machinist files range in length from 4 to 18 inches.

6–8.   MILL AND SAW FILES

The **mill file** is used in draw filing (Section 6–2) to produce a smooth finish on metal workpieces. The mill file is also used to sharpen mill and circular saws, knives, lawn mower blades, axes, and shears. The two faces of the mill file are parallel and the edges are flat or rounded. The faces and edges are usually single cut and are available in bastard, second cut, or smooth cut coarseness. A round-edged mill file is used where rounded gullets are preferred as compared to sharp corners or squared gullets. Mill files are available in widths from $\frac{7}{16}$ to $1\frac{1}{2}$ inches and lengths from 4 to 16 inches.

6–9.   RASPS

Rasps are used by wood craftsmen, plumbers, leather and aluminum workers, blacksmiths, and hobbyists. Rasps may be used on wood and other nonmetallic surfaces for fast removal of the material. A round surface is left remaining, but the rough surface may be smoothened with a wood file (Section 6–12) or with abrasive papers. Wood rasps range from 6 to 16 inches and are available in bastard and smooth cuts on the faces. Edges are flat or rounded and are single cut. Rasp shapes are flat, half-round, and round.

6–10.   SPECIAL-PURPOSE FILES

As was mentioned in the introduction to this chapter, there are numerous types and lengths of files. Some of the unique types, called **special-purpose files**, are worth mentioning here: *auger bit file; rotary mower blade file* (also sharpens edges of hoes, hatchets, and other garden tools); *farmers file* (ideal for sharpening scythes, mowers, and other tool edges); *all-purpose file; ignition file* for automechanics (cleans contact points on magnetos, switches, electric bells); and *voltage-regulator file* (used on automobile voltage regulators, circuit breakers, relays, and other electrical contact points).

6–11.   SWISS PATTERN FILES

Swiss pattern files are manufactured more accurately than other files. They are generally slender and narrow in both width and thickness; the tapered files have finer points. Swiss pattern files are delicate cutting tools used by precision craftsmen, jewelers, gunsmiths, watchmakers, and patternmakers to file delicate instruments and mechanisms for final fitting and for use in tool and die work. On the small files, the fine tang is shaped into a handle. Cuts are identified differently for the Swiss files; the cuts are made in seven grades, 00 (coarsest, 34 teeth/inch), 0, 1, 2, 3, 4, and 6 (finest, 184 teeth/inch). There are many shapes available in lengths from 3 to 12 inches.

Swiss files are used as finishing files for removing burrs, rounding out slots, and for cleaning out square corners. Swiss pattern files are also useful for enlarging small holes and for shaping and finishing very narrow grooves, notches, and keyways.

6–12.   WOOD FILES

The **wood file** is used by woodworkers on wood only. It is used after the rasp (Section 6–9) to finish smoothing a workpiece. Wood files are from 8 to 14 inches long and from ¾ to 1⅜ inches wide. The file teeth are coarse to prevent clogging.

7

glues, adhesives, and cements

7–1. GENERAL DESCRIPTION

The terms **glue, adhesive,** and **cement** are used interchangeably when applied to the viscous solution used to permanently join two workpieces together. Additional fasteners, such as nails and screws, are often used in addition to the solutions to give added strength. The solutions and the fasteners complement one another to produce very strong joinings.

The most common glues, adhesives, and cements have been included in this handbook. Likewise, they have been named by their most common name. Included in this chapter are: *animal glue, casein glue, contact cement, epoxy glue* and *(epoxy) paste, modeler's glue, plastic cement, plastic resin glue, rubber cement,* and *white glue*. A description of *tub sealers* and of the *hot glue gun* are included also because of their importance.

In the complete field of glues, there are two basic types of glues: natural and synthetic resin. The natural-origin glues are made from animals, vegetables, casein, and soybeans. The synthetic resin glues are urea-resin, phenol-resin, resorcinol-resin, melamine-resin, and polyvinyl emulsion. The synthetic glues are becoming increasingly popular.

7–2.   APPLICATION OF GLUES, ADHESIVES, AND CEMENTS

Six general procedural steps that apply to every gluing operation are: preparation, providing proper temperature and ventilation, spreading, clamping, removing excessive glue, and setting and curing. These general procedures are discussed in the following paragraphs; specific procedures are included with each glue discussed. It is also important that you follow the manufacturer's directions on the container.

Proper surface preparation is essential in establishing strongly glued joints and laminations. First, ensure that the workpieces to be joined fit together properly. Don't apply the glue and then place the pieces together only to find that the pieces do not join; ensure that the workpieces fit together first. Next, remove all sawdust, dirt, grease, wax, paint, old glue, and so on. Use a brush or vacuum cleaner for loose dust and dirt. Use denatured alcohol, lacquer thinner, lighter fluid, turpentine, or another agent to remove grease, wax, and fingerprints. Roughen hard, dense, smooth surfaces with sandpaper to ensure a stronger glue bond.

Do your preparations in a room that is at a temperature of 70° Fahrenheit or above. Workpieces, glues, and the room temperature should all be the same. You can't, for example, bring workpieces in from the outside cold and expect glue to adhere at room temperature; you must wait several hours until the workpieces are at room temperature. When you are ready to spread the glue, check the specific paragraph in this handbook and the manufacturer's directions regarding ventilation and danger of fume explosions. Adequate cross ventilation can be provided by opening windows and doors. An exhaust fan may also be installed and is, in fact, recommended for your shop. When using flammable glues, ensure that *all* sources of fire are removed; extinguish all fireplace flames, gas pilots (such as in gas driers, stoves, ovens, etc.), and other open flames. Prevent electrical sparks that can be caused by applying power through a switch or by static electricity.

Apply the glue in thin coats to both sides (unless the manufacturer or the specific glue description that follows directs otherwise).

Spread the glue carefully, but completely, with a brush, scrap of wood (Fig. 7-1), tube lid, or your finger. Keep the glue off of adjacent surfaces of the workpieces.

Press the workpieces together and fasten them with nails or screws or secure with clamps, a vise, or other improvised devices. I prefer to apply the glue, clamp the workpieces together, and then nail or screw the workpieces together. Screw your clamps only fingertight, until the glue oozes out slightly. Don't tighten so tightly that all the glue is squeezed out. Refer to Chapter 4, Clamps and Vises.

Remove excessive glue from the workpieces immediately. Failure to remove excessive glue can prevent a wood finish, such as oil stain, from penetrating; the workpiece can become stained by the glue; or the glue will harden and be difficult to remove. Allow sufficient drying time for the glue before removing the clamps. Different glues and different materials require different drying times; refer

Figure 7-1 Glue may be applied by brush, scrap of wood, tube lid, or your finger.

to the specific section in this chapter and to the manufacturer's recommendations. Heat decreases the setting and curing time of glues. You may use heat lamps, regular lights directed toward the glued area (remember, heat rises!), or place small workpieces near the furnace to hasten drying. Allow sufficient curing time before applying maximum stress to glued joints.

> *CAUTION:*   Keep all glues out of the reach of children. Many glues cause skin irritations, have harmful vapors, and have volatile flammable fumes. Provide adequate ventilation, eliminate sources of spark or flame, and avoid prolonged breathing of vapors and repeated contact with the skin. Flush the eyes and skin with water if they are irritated by glue.

7–3.   CARE OF GLUES, ADHESIVES, AND CEMENTS

Store glues in a dry place at room temperature away from open flames. When using glues, keep the lids on as much as practical and don't mix more glue than is required for a particular application.

7–4.   ANIMAL GLUE

Animal glue is made from various animals. It comes in caked, flaked, or granulated form and is soaked in water and then heated in a double-boiler glue pot; hence it is often referred to as *glue-pot glue*. It is applied with a brush.

When animal glue is hot and ready to apply, it should run freely and should not have lumps; however, it shouldn't be so thin that it breaks into drops. It congeals rapidly as it cools. It is important to remove excessive glue from clamped joints immediately because the hardened glue is difficult to remove.

Animal glue is not waterproof. It does not stain the wood when it is applied. Animal glues are not used today as they were in years past because of the new synthetic glues. Some new liquid animal glues are available.

7–5.   CASEIN GLUE

Casein glue is a white powder that is mixed with water (follow the manufacturer's directions carefully). It is a popular glue for inside work, especially for oily woods such as lemonwood and teak, and is okay for outside work if the glued joints are protected by paint or varnish. Casein glue resists moisture.

Casein glue may stain certain woods, including oak and mahogany. To prevent staining, immediately wash off any excess glue. Stains can be removed with crystals of oxalic acid dissolved in water. Use rubber gloves when applying the oxalic acid solution.

7–6.   CONTACT CEMENT

The most popular cement for laminating two surfaces, such as countertopping to a counter or plywood or hardboard panels to walls and studding, is **contact cement**. It is also used for bonding other porous or nonporous materials such as linoleum, masonry, metal, ceramics, plastics, hardboard, flakeboard, canvas, and leather to wood or metal. It is not for gluing joints together.

Contact cement dries very rapidly because of its chemical makeup. Its vapors are harmful and very flammable (some nonflammable contact cements are available), making it necessary to provide adequate cross ventilation by opening your windows and doors. Ensure that there are no sparks, open flames, pilot lights (such as on your gas water heater, stove, or drier), or cigarettes in the area. The cement and vapors are also irritants to the eyes and skin.

The contact nature of this cement is so important that it is necessary to discuss its use in detail. When the cement-coated pieces that are to be bonded to one another come together, the bond is *instant* upon *contact*. The pieces cannot be moved. Therefore, it is important that (1) the pieces are prefit before the cement is applied and (2) that the following directions are followed exactly (if the manufacturer's suggestions differ from the following, obey his directions).

The cementing should be done when the cement, workpieces, and room temperature are all 65° or above. Ensure that all pieces fit together properly and that you know in what direction and order the pieces must be assembled. Stir the cement thoroughly. Brush, roll, or use a spreader to apply a thin coat of the cement to *both* surfaces. Apply the cement in one direction only; do not apply in a back-and-forth motion. On porous materials, apply a second coat of cement after the first coat has dried. Dull spots on the glued surface indicate that a second coat is required; a gloss indicates proper coating. The drying time is usually between 15 to 30 minutes, depending upon the temperature and humidity. You can check that the cement is dry by touching it with a piece of kraft wrapping paper. When the paper does *not* stick, the cement is dry. When the cement on both workpieces is dry, align the pieces and place them together. Remember, once mated, the workpieces cannot be moved. In joining larger pieces, put wrapping paper between the surfaces and gradually slide the paper out as the surfaces are placed together. Use pressure on a small (less than 3 inches) rubber roller and roll from the center of the cemented workpieces toward the edges of the workpieces; this prevents trapped air. If you don't have a roller available, tap the surface with a rubber mallet or with a hammer against a soft wood block. No weights, clamps, or presses are needed.

Cemented workpieces should be joined within 2 hours. After 2 hours, reactivate the cement by applying another coat. Use lacquer thinner for cleaning cement from spilled areas and from brushes. Don't buy more than you can use; the shelf life of contact cement is 12 months.

7–7.   EPOXY GLUE AND PASTE

Epoxy makes a stronger bond between two workpieces (Fig. 7–2) than any other glue; it is also one of the most expensive glues. Epoxy bonds everything to anything except polyethleyne, bronze, nickel, or lead. It's even effective for mending masonry, glass, marble, water pipes, china, ceramic tile, and for installing bathroom fixtures such as soap dishes. **Epoxy putty** is for filling holes, dents, cracks in concrete, metals, and wood. Epoxy has strength and durability, is waterproof, and cures with a catalytic action. It expands and contracts with the joint.

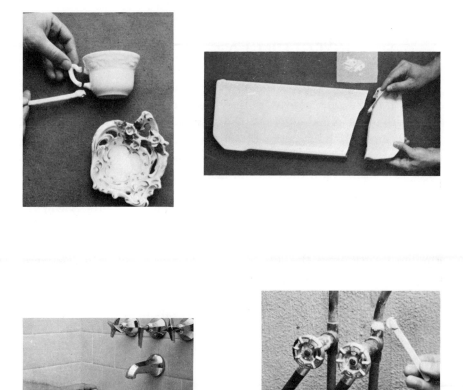

Figure 7–2 Epoxy glue bonds almost everything to anything.

Epoxy is a two-part glue consisting of a *hardener* and a *resin.* Equal amounts of each are thoroughly mixed together on a clean surface, but don't mix more than you can use. Apply the mixture to a clean and roughened surface. Follow the manufacturer's recommendation for drying time; it is usually 2 to 4 hours, although a 5-minute epoxy is available. Epoxy reaches its full strength in 24 hours.

Epoxy putty is also mixed in equal parts. Apply it and let it cure. Then file, sand, and paint the epoxy.

7–8. HOT GLUE GUN

The **hot glue gun** (Fig. 7–3) is used to apply a pinpoint of hot glue to wood, metal, tile, canvas, pottery, plastics, and leather when two items are to be joined together. A dry stick of glue is placed into the electric gun; at the squeeze of the trigger, the needed amount of glue is squeezed from the gun. The workpieces are strongly bonded in 60 seconds without the need for clamps. The bonds are permanent and are waterproof.

The hot glue gun operates from 115 volts ac house power. It heats up rapidly and is thermostatically controlled to remain at the proper temperature. An antidrip check valve keeps glue from continuing to exit from the gun after the trigger is released. The gun case is shockproof plastic.

Load a dry stick into the hot glue gun and plug the gun into an electrical outlet. After the glue is heated (about 3 minutes), touch the point to the workpiece and squeeze the gun trigger until sufficient glue is applied. Immediately join the second workpiece and hold the pieces together for about 60 seconds. Do not allow the workpieces to shift after they have been joined. Remove excessive glue with a knife.

> *CAUTION:* Molten glue sticks get hotter than 300°. Take care in using.

Figure 7–3 Hot glue gun.

Caulking sticks are also available for use in glue guns. Squeeze out the caulk and move the gun at the required rate to fill the gap.

7–9.   MODELER'S GLUES

By the term **modeler's glues**, I mean the fast-drying glues used to join pieces of wood or plastic models together. These glues are often referred to as airplane glue because of their use in the building of model airplanes.

Two types of modeler's glues are available, one for use with wood models and one for use with plastic models. Both types of glues provide fast drying, strong, transparent bonds. The wood glue bonds wood to wood and paper to wood. The plastic glue bonds polystyrene to polystyrene (polystyrene is a rigid transparent thermoplastic used in molded products, foams, and sheet materials). The plastic glue is available in regular or in nontoxic form for use by small children. Wood glue is available in regular or hot fuel-proof form for use in areas where model engine fuel is used.

In using the glues, apply the glue sparingly to one piece. Hold the parts together until the glue sets (about 30 seconds). Allow 2 hours' drying time for maximum strength. To hold and glue adjacent wooden model parts over a pattern, use straight pins to pin the parts through a piece of waxed paper and the pattern into a piece of heavy cardboard.

7–10.   PLASTIC CEMENT

Different plastics have different chemical properties, and there are cements made for the various plastics. Buy the type of **plastic cement** for the kind of plastic you are cementing. If you don't know the type of plastic, test an area of the plastic that will not be noticeable upon completion with a drop of cement. If the plastic and the cement are compatible, you may then use the cement with the plastic.

In using plastic cement, apply the cement to both workpieces. When the workpieces are tacky, join and clamp the pieces for 10 minutes. Let the joint dry for 12 hours.

Provide adequate ventilation when using this cement. Follow the specific manufacturer's instructions. (Refer to Section 7–9 for a discussion of modeler's glue for plastics.)

7–11.   PLASTIC RESIN GLUE

Plastic resin glue is used for all indoor wood gluing applications; to adhere plastic laminates (such as countertops) to wood, plywood, or hardboard; and to adhere leather to itself or to wood, hardboard, cloth, or cardboard. Plastic resin glue provides a very strong bond for all porous and semiporous materials. It is particularly good for joints. It provides a strong bond that is highly water resistant. Full strength and moisture resistance develop after a few days of curing.

Plastic resin glue may only be used when room, glue, and workpiece temperatures are above 70°. Mix the powdered glue with water, following the manufacturer's directions, until the mix has the consistency of heavy cream. When mixed, the glue is ready for use; only mix what is needed. The *pot time* of mixed glue is 4 to 5 hours. Once the glue is spread, the workpieces must be joined within 10 to 15 minutes. Clamping pressure is required for 8 to 12 hours.

Apply a thin coat of the glue with a brush. Clamp, nail, or screw the joint together with sufficient pressure to force some glue from the joint. Let the joint cure for 8 to 12 hours.

Clean applicator brushes with water immediately after use. The powder and glue may irritate the skin. Wash the affected skin area with plenty of water. Store the powder in a closed can in a dry place.

7–12.   RUBBER CEMENT

Rubber cement is the ideal cement for paper. It does not shrink, curl, stain, or wrinkle photographs, paper pasteups, scrapbooks, layouts, etc. It can also bond paper to wood or cardboard.

If you plan a temporary bond, as when making a layout, apply the cement to one piece of paper (or cardboard) only and place the piece down immediately. If you desire a permanent bond, apply cement to both pieces of paper and let the cement dry (2 to 3 minutes is ample drying time). Join the pieces firmly together, smoothing from one edge to the other edge or preferably from the center of the pieces out to the edges. When the cement is applied to both pieces, the cement acts like a contact cement; once contact is made, the pieces can't be relocated. Remove excessive dry cement by rubbing the cement with the fingertip or with an eraser.

7–13. TUB SEALER

Tub sealer is leakproof silicone rubber used to seal mating surfaces such as wall-to-tub and wall-to-wall to keep water out of the walls. Apply only to clean dry surfaces. Cut the spout of the tube and squeeze a *bead* out of the tube as you slowly move it along the joint. Wipe off excessive sealer.

7–14. WHITE GLUE

White glue is a polyvinyl emulsion glue that is used to bond paper, wood, cork, Styrofoam, fabric, leather, and other porous materials. It is easily recognizable by its white color; it is usually sold in plastic squeeze bottles. It is safe, has no harmful fumes, and can be wiped off with a water-dampened rag *before* the glue hardens. White glue is fast setting and is very nearly transparent when dry. Its only disadvantage is that it is affected by moisture and water. It is for interior use but can be used outdoors if the completed workpiece is properly sealed with several coats of exterior paint or varnish.

After proper surface preparation and when the workpieces are at a temperature above 60°, apply a thin spread of glue for paper or fabric. For softwoods, plywood, and composition board, apply glue to both of the surfaces to be joined. For wood end grains, apply a preliminary spread of glue to both surfaces to be joined; after 15 to 20 minutes, apply a final spread of glue to both surfaces. Join the surfaces and let the glue set for 3 to 4 minutes before joining and clamping the workpieces. For softwoods, maintain clamping pressures for 25 minutes; 30–45 minutes for hardwoods. Allow a minimum of 4 hours for curing, overnight if possible. Full strength is reached in 24 hours. Immediately wipe off excessive glue with a damp rag.

You can fill holes, nicks, and cracks in a workpiece and match the wood color quite well by mixing sawdust from the workpiece with white glue. Press the mix into the hole, nick, or crack and let it dry thoroughly. Smooth the filled surface with sandpaper.

8

hammers

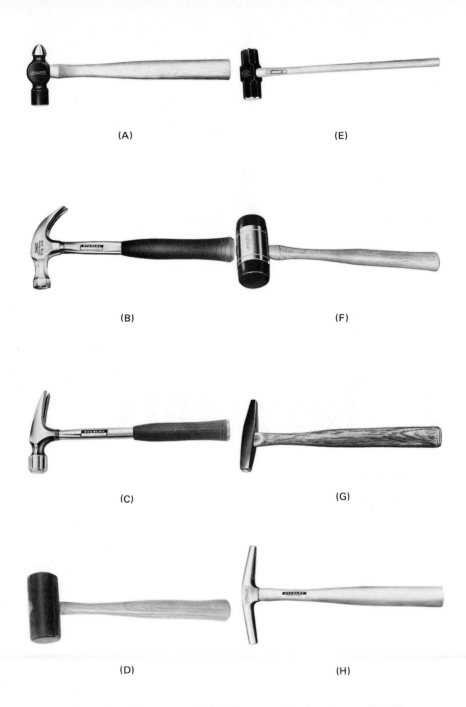

(A)

(E)

(B)

(F)

(C)

(G)

(D)

(H)

Figure 8–1 Hammers: (A) ball peen; (B) claw (curved); (C) claw (ripping); (D) rubber mallet; (E) sledge; (F) soft face; (G) tack; (H) upholsterer's.

8–1. GENERAL DESCRIPTION

Nearly everyone has a **hammer** in his toolbox, but sometimes it's not the right hammer for the job. For example, did you know that there are *two* kinds of claw hammers? Do you know why there is a ball on the ball peen hammer? And did you know that there are hammers available with interchangeable faces?

This chapter will set you straight on using the correct hammer for the job. *Ball peen, claw, mallet, sledge, soft-faced, tack,* and *upholsterer's hammers* are described. Select the hammers you need and learn to use them to their fullest extent.

The type (or types) of hammer that you need comes in a variety of weights and lengths: lightweight hammers are for small jobs and hobbies, heavier ones for general purpose, and extra-heavy hammers with long handles are used for jobs such as pounding a chisel to cut holes into masonry. Handle materials vary, too. There are steel handles, fiberglass handles, and wooden handles. Steel handles are often tubular and are filled with wood to reduce overall weight and to absorb shock in the handle when the head strikes an object. Fiberglass handles are made of straight, continuous, fiberglass filaments that are bonded with polyester resin. The fiberglass handle is assembled into the head with a strong epoxy bond and a steel wedge. Strong wooden handles are made of straight-grained white hickory that is lacquered for protection against dryness and dampness. Steel and fiberglass handles have a perforated vinyl grip on them to aid in holding onto the tool and to help eliminate perspiration; vinyl grips are not required on wood handles. Steel and fiberglass hammer handles are about the same price; wooden-handled hammers are less expensive. My experience indicates that a wooden handle is very adequate for home use.

Hammer heads are made of heat-treated carbon steel. The face, which contacts the fastener or workpiece during use, should be crowned and should have a beveled rim that prevents marring a wooden workpiece if the hammer head comes into contact with the workpiece when a nail is driven.

Select hammers that you need for your special applications. The curved claw hammer is the first hammer needed around the home. In the metal shop, your first hammer would be a ball peen hammer.

The most important factor in buying a hammer for the intended application is to get the hammer that *feels* the best in your hand. Visit your hardware store and swing hammers of different weights and sizes. The difference in a couple of ounces of head weight is in the *feel* to you. Buy one that feels *balanced* in your hand as you swing it. Buy a good hammer, too, because with reasonable care it will last you a lifetime.

8–2. APPLICATION OF HAMMERS

Grasp the hammer near the handle end opposite the head. This gives you the most control over the hammer because the head and handle length are designed for balance when the handle is held near the end. This grasping point also allows for maximum swing. Make light blows almost entirely with wrist motion; heavy blows require the use of the wrist, forearm, and shoulder. Direct the hammer blows precisely so that the hammer face is parallel to the fastener or surface being struck. Don't use the *side* of the head for striking. Don't strike the hammer against any material that is harder than the head (face) material. Striking a harder material would cause damage to the head. The handle may be gripped near the head for making light taps with the hammer.

8–3.   CARE OF HAMMERS

Use the hammer only for its intended purposes. Keep the head and handle clean by occasionally wiping it with a solvent. Occasionally apply a light coat of light oil to the head (and to the handle of steel-handled hammers). This prevents rust. If wood handles become splintered or nicked, sand the affected area smooth with sandpaper. Apply lacquer to the sanded handle and to any handle that has had the lacquer worn off. The lacquer protects the wood from dampness.

Faces of hammers should be dressed (filed or ground) as required to remove battered edges. Small burrs should be filed off; worn face surfaces should be ground. Dip the head in water often to prevent loss of metal temper by overheating during grinding. On double-faced hammers, remove the same amount of material from both sides to maintain hammer balance.

A loose handle makes a hammer dangerous to the user and to anyone or anything in the vicinity. Tighten the handle immediately by placing the hammer on a workbench with the head against the bench and the handle vertical. Using a mallet, tap the end of the handle. If necessary, drive in another *wedge* (available at hardware stores) as described in the next paragraph (except that you can't saw slots). Never use nails or screws in place of wedges.

Split or broken handles should be replaced. Cut off the old handle near the head and drive the remaining portion out of the head. In the new handle, saw two vertical slots equally spaced and a length of about two-thirds of the amount of handle that will be *inside* the head [Fig. 8–2(A)]. Fit the handle into the head, shaping it if required. Drive the head in completely. Cut the handle off flush with the top of the head. Place the hammer in the oven for an hour at 160°F to dry out the wood.

After the handle has air cooled, place the hammer handle end against the workbench with the head in the air. Place metal wedges into the slots and, with blows alternately on each wedge, drive the wedges into the handle until the head is tight [Fig. 8–2(B)]. Grind [Fig. 8–2(C)] or file the wedges flat against the head. Apply lacquer to any exposed wood on the handle; this seals it against the weather.

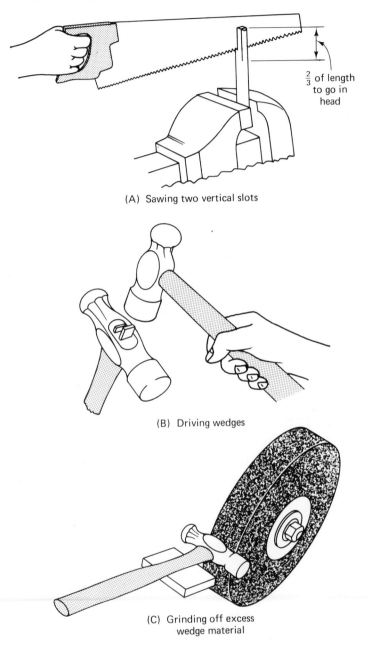

(A) Sawing two vertical slots

$\frac{2}{3}$ of length
to go in
head

(B) Driving wedges

(C) Grinding off excess
wedge material

Figure 8–2 Replacing hammer handle: (A) sawing two vertical slots; (B) driving wedges; (C) grinding off
excess wedge material.

8–4.   BALL PEEN HAMMER

Ball peen hammers are used by machine shop and auto mechanic personnel for general-purpose work such as striking punches and metal chisels (but never for driving nails), for shaping metal (peening), and for riveting. The term *peen* means to indent or compress in order to expand or stretch a portion of metal next to the indention. Peen hammer heads have two striking parts: a flat face for general-purpose hammering and a ball end for peening.

In riveting, the ball peen face is used to start the spreading of a rivet head. Once the rivet is spread open, the flat face is used to flatten the rivet out.

In addition to ball-shaped peen faces, there are also *cross* and *straight peen faces*, but these faces are generally used for special purposes. The cross and straight peen faces are shaped like chisel edges but are blunt rather than sharp. The straight peen is in line with the handle; the cross peen is in a direction *across* the handle.

Head weights vary from 2 to 28 ounces; 20 ounces is for general use. Handle lengths are between 10 and 16 inches. The peen is uniformly beveled and the peen and flat faces are hardened to reduce damage.

8–5.   CLAW HAMMER

The **claw hammer** is used to drive pointed fasteners such as nails, brads, tacks, staples, and corrugated nails into materials such as wood, wallboard, and masonry. Claw hammers are also used to remove these fasteners from materials.

There are two types of claw hammers: the *curved claw* and the *straight claw*. The curved claw hammer is for general carpentry, such as nailing and nail pulling. The curved claw is used to pull out nails. The bell face on the striking end of the head minimizes marring when nails are driven flush into wood. It also reduces nail deflection from off-angle blows. The straight claw, also known as the *ripping claw* and the *framing hammer*, is used for rough work such as dismantling. The straight claw can be forced between boards; the boards are then pried up with the claw. The ball face is the same as on the curved claw hammer.

Claw hammers are available in weights between 5 and 32 ounces. The 5-ounce weight is for light work and model use; 13-, 16-, and 20-ounce weights are for general use. Handles are from 11 to 14 inches.

In selecting your first claw hammer, select a curved claw that weighs about 16 ounces. Select a hammer that *feels* good in your hand when you swing it; the grip should also be comfortable. Ensure that the driving face is beveled and that the double-beveled nail slot for pulling nails is well machined and tapers gradually back to a thin point.

To properly drive a nail, grasp the nail near the *head* with the thumb and index finger. Holding the nail near the head helps protect your fingers if you miss the nail because your fingers won't be smashed between the hammer and the workpiece. Hold the nail to the wood or other material. Hold the hammer at the end of the handle and strike the nail head with a light blow. Ensure that the face of the hammer strikes the nail head squarely. Strike the nail with a moderate blow. When the nail can stand by itself in the material, strike it squarely with driving blows. When the nail reaches the surface, use moderate blows again until the head is flush with the surface. If you're using *finishing nails*, which are driven below the surface, use a nail set to countersink the head about ⅛ inch below the surface. In hardwoods, predrill a hole having a diameter slightly less than the diameter of the nail. This keeps the wood from splitting.

Nails often hold two pieces of material more securely if they are *toed in* or *clinched*. Toeing can be accomplished by two methods (Fig. 8–3); one method is to drive the nail in at an angle. The other method is to slightly bend or curve the nail prior to driving so that it curves in during driving. In clinching, a nail that is longer than the combined thickness of the two pieces of material is used and is driven through both pieces. One hammer is held flush against the nail head against the workpiece surface while another hammer bends the nail over in a direction along the grain of the workpiece and down into the workpiece.

A hammer can also be used to straighten bent nails. Place the

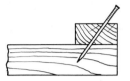

(A) Toeing by driving
the nail at an angle

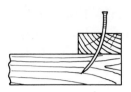

(B) Toeing by using
slightly bent nails

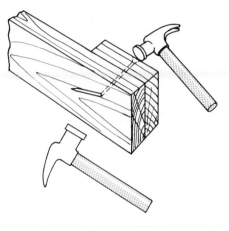

Clinching

Figure 8–3 Toeing and clinching nails: (A) toeing by driving the nail at an angle; (B) toeing by using
slightly bent nails.

nails on a flat surface such as a vise anvil and tap the nail along the
bend until it is straight.

In using the claw to remove nails, jam the claw slot around the
nail, gripping the nail just below the head for the initial pull. Holding the hammer at the handle end, pull back on the handle and ease
the nail up. To get more leverage, remove the claw and again jam
it around the nail, this time as near to the wood as possible. Again
pull back on the handle and ease the nail out. Continue in this manner until the nail is removed. You can also put a block of scrap wood

under the hammer head, which gives you more leverage for nail pulling and also prevents the surface from being marred. Remove large nails with a ripping chisel or a pinch bar.

8–6. MALLETS

There are two types of **mallets:** solid rubber and wood. The solid rubber mallet is used in garages, finishing shops, and home shops to prevent damage where hammering is required on surfaces where the finish is important. For example, the rubber mallet is used to straighten dents in metal work such as automobile bodies, for replacing hubcaps, and for driving plastic tent pegs while camping. The rubber mallet is cylindrical in shape and about 4 inches long and 2½ inches in diameter. The handle length is 15 inches long.

Wooden mallets are used by woodworkers to drive close fitting parts together, to strike wood chisels used in carving, to strike chisels used in wood cutting, and to shape metal. Most wooden mallet heads are made of beechwood. The handle is tapered so that the heads won't come off.

In use, the mallet should only strike the workpiece with sufficient force to bend the material being straightened. When used as a soft hammer, the striking force should be moderate. In using the mallet with wood-cutting chisels, lightly tap the chisels with a number of successive light blows rather than a few heavy blows.

8–7. SLEDGEHAMMER

Sledgehammers are used for heavy hammering where other hammers are just not strong enough to perform the work. For example, a light sledge may be used to hammer a metal-cutting chisel when cutting holes in masonry or mortar and when cutting metal. A short-handled sledge is used with a cold chisel to cut chain. A heavier sledge can be used with a wedge to split logs and to drive metal pegs into the ground.

Sledgehammers are double-faced and have beveled faces from 1½ to 3 inches in diameter. Head lengths are from 4 to 9 inches with handle lengths from 16 to 36 inches. Weights are from 2 to 20 pounds.

8-8.   SOFT-FACED HAMMER

The **soft-faced hammer** is used where metal parts must be driven together or where a light nonmarring blow is required to form or shape sheet metal. The soft face prevents marring of the metal from the hammer blows. The two faces of the hammer are replaceable and are usually of different materials. For example, one face may be plastic for use on iron or steel; the other face may be vinyl for use on aluminum, wood, and polished surfaces. The heads weigh between 2 and 32 ounces; handles are from 7 to 15 inches long.

Replaceable tips range in hardness from super soft to medium hard and are made from rubber, wood, hardwood, lead, plastic, vinyl, rawhide, fiber, and copper. Manufacturers often color code the tips for hardness identification. The tips are resistant to chipping, flaking, mushrooming, and common industrial solvents and acids. Heads are sometimes loaded with shot to give more driving power with less fatigue. There is also less rebound and shock.

Two other types of soft-faced hammers are the *brass hammer* and the *rawhide hammer*. The brass hammer is used to adjust and set tools on screw machines, turret lathes, and all types of turning machines. It is used to drive bushings and gears and for doing auto-body work or work on standard and automatic transmissions. It is also recommended when a tapping force is needed in fitting a bearing, as it does not chip or crack hardened bearing rings. Like the soft-faced hammer, the heads of the brass hammer are replaceable.

The rawhide hammer is used where a light blow is required to form or shape sheet metal. The hammer head is a split-head design, which permits easy replacement of the water buffalo rawhide. Other soft materials available include molded rubber, plastic, copper, babbitt, and nylon. The face diameters range between 1 and $3\frac{1}{2}$ inches; handles are approximately 14 inches long.

When using any type of soft-faced hammer, use as light a blow as necessary to accomplish the task. Never strike the faces against sharp corners because the sharpness could damage the face.

If you only have an occasional need for a soft-faced hammer, don't buy one. Instead, place a piece of soft brass, copper, lead, or hardwood against the workpiece; tap with a standard hammer.

8–9.   TACK HAMMER

Tack hammers are used to drive tacks, small brads, and small staples
into floors to hold rugs, picture frames, wires, and so on, where a
standard-sized claw hammer is too large for convenient use. One of
the two faces is usually magnetized to hold steel tacks for starting
them into the workpiece. The heads measure about 4 inches, weigh
5 ounces, and are attached to 10-inch hickory handles.

To use the tack hammer, grasp the hammer by the handle end
away from the head. If you are using a steel fastener, attach its head
to the magnetic end of the hammer head. Place the hammer head
directly over the area where the fastener is to be inserted. Strike a
light blow, keeping the face of the hammer parallel to the workpiece. Check that the fastener is straight. If it is, continue hammering with moderate blows until the fastener is secure. If a fastener is
used that is not magnetically attracted, hold the fastener between
the thumb and index finger. You can also hold the fastener with
pliers until it is properly started in the workpiece.

8–10.   UPHOLSTERER'S HAMMER

The **upholsterer's hammer** is very similar to the tack hammer (Section 8–9) except that the striking face is smaller in diameter. The
smaller face is required so that the wood surrounding the tack is less
likely to be damaged when the upholstering tacks are driven into
the workpiece. Upholsterer's hammers are used in the same manner
as the tack hammer.

measuring
and marking
tools

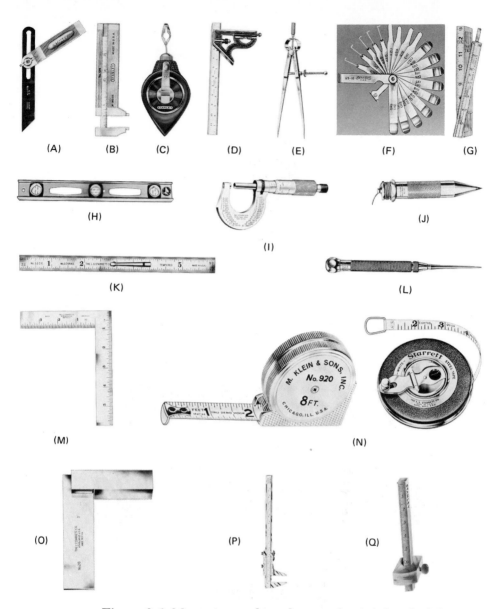

Figure 9-1 Measuring and marking tools: (A) bevel; (B) caliper rule; (C) chalk line; (D) combination square; (E) dividers; (F) feeler gauges; (G) folding rule; (H) levels; (I) micrometer caliper; (J) plumb bob; (K) pocket rules and steel scales; (L) scriber; (M) steel square; (N) steel tapes; (O) try square; (P) vernier caliper; (Q) wood marking gauge.

9-1.   GENERAL DESCRIPTION

Measuring tools are instruments used to determine the dimensions or size of a workpiece. The measuring tool selected for making a particular measurement is dependent upon the size of the workpiece and the accuracy that is required in making the measurement. The measuring tools described in this chapter cover a range of dimensions from ten-thousandths of an inch up to 100 feet. The measuring tools described are: *caliper rules, feeler gauges, folding rules, micrometer calipers, pocket rules* and *steel scales, steel tapes,* and *vernier calipers.*

Marking tools are used to make a permanent mark on a workpiece for later drilling, cutting, or whatever. The marking tools described include: *wood-marking gauges, scribers,* and *dividers.*

The other tools that are discussed in this chapter do not seem like measuring or marking tools, but they do measure angles, horizontals, and verticals, or are used as guides in marking lines. These tools are: *bevel, chalk line, combination square, level, plumb bob, steel square,* and *try square.*

9-2.   THE ENGLISH AND METRIC MEASUREMENT SYSTEMS

The **English measurement system** is a system of measures and weights in common usage in the United States, Great Britain, Canada, and several other English-speaking countries. The English system consists of units such as inches, feet, yards, ounces, pounds, and Fahrenheit. This system is known to most of us and we're content to use it. However, this English measurement system is gradually being replaced by the metric system.

The **metric system** is a system of weights and measures based on the decimal system; that is, the metric system is based on the number 10. It was introduced and adopted by law in France and subsequently has been adopted by a majority of countries, excluding the United States, Great Britain, and Canada as the common system of weights and measures. It is adopted by all countries as the system used in scientific work. There is great pressure now for the world to become standardized with one measurement system; this system is known as the *International System of Units* (SI). It is important that one world-wide system becomes a reality because of the ever-increasing trade of machines, tools, and manufactured products between countries. It is also important that you become familiar with the SI units and purchase measurement tools that are graduated in both systems.

The international system of units is a modernized version of the metric system. It is generally superior for most scientific work and is the common language for scientific and technical data. Nearly all scientific experiments in the United States as well as abroad are performed using metric units.

The chief advantage of the metric measurement system over the English system is that all units are divisible into ten parts. This enables fractional distances, areas, volumes, capacities, and weights (such as meters, liters, and grams) to be expressed as decimals. Decimals are easier to manipulate in addition, subtraction, multiplication, and division than are fractions.

In your work with hand tools in the shop, you may encounter the metric system sooner than you'd like. Hence you should become familiar with the information in the following paragraphs and the conversion factors in Appendix D.

The metric linear measurement system is based on the *meter*. The meter is further divided into tenths ($\frac{1}{10}$), called *decimeters*; hundredths ($\frac{1}{100}$), called *centimeters*; and thousandths ($\frac{1}{1000}$), called *millimeters*. The most useful conversion factors from the English system to the metric system are:

$$1 \text{ meter } = 39.37 \text{ inches } = 1.094 \text{ yards}$$
$$1 \text{ yard } = 0.9144 \text{ meter}$$
$$1 \text{ foot } = 0.3048 \text{ meter}$$
$$1 \text{ inch } = 2.54 \text{ centimeters}$$

Thus a football field (100 yards) is 91.44 meters long, a 6-foot-tall man is 1.83 meters tall, and a well-proportioned young lady is 87–58–78 centimeters!

Many of the tool manufacturers realize today that the metric system is fast upon us and are taking steps to convert. Tool manufacturers are making tools graduated in English, graduated in metric, and graduated in English and metric. You are advised to buy measurement tools that have some edges that are graduated in English and other edges that are graduated in metric. These tools will then be useful no matter which system you are using on a particular project. The descriptions of the tools contained in this chapter advise you as to the availability and use of English and metric-graduated tools.

9-3.   APPLICATION OF MEASURING AND MARKING TOOLS

To make a measurement with a linear measuring tool such as a scale, pocket scale, folding rule, or steel tape, place the tool on the workpiece along the line to be measured. The zero inch (or millimeter) end is placed against the left edge of the workpiece or on the mark from which the measurement is to be made. A reading is then taken at the end of the workpiece or the end of the area to be measured.

In making a reading with a measurement tool, look in a perpendicular direction at the mark to be measured and at the corresponding graduation on the scale. This ensures that *parallax* does not cause the reading to be inaccurate. Parallax is the apparent displacement of the reading mark or graduation on the tool scale due to a change of direction in the position of the observer. Therefore, to prevent parallax and a subsequent inaccurate reading, the observer must be directly in front of the workpiece mark and tool scale when the reading is made. This procedure also holds true when reading all other measuring tools and gauges discussed in this handbook.

With a tool scale marked in units of $\frac{1}{64}$ inch, the tool scale can be accurately read to $\frac{1}{64}$ inch (0.0156). If the mark to be measured falls between $\frac{1}{64}$-inch graduations, the reading is rounded down to the lower $\frac{1}{64}$ if the mark appears to be less than half of $\frac{1}{64}$, or is rounded up to the next $\frac{1}{64}$ if the mark appears to be half or greater than half of $\frac{1}{64}$ inch.

Metric tool scales can be read accurately to one-half of 1 millimeter. Metric scales graduated in millimeters are rounded to the next millimeter, as described for $\frac{1}{64}$-inch readings.

It is important that you measure accurately and mark accurately with a sharp pencil on wood or with a scriber on metal. Accurate measurements and markings will enable you to complete a project that looks professional.

9–4.   CARE OF MEASURING AND MARKING TOOLS

Avoid accidental scratches or nicks to the surfaces and edges of measuring and marking tools. Wipe the tools clean to remove dirt and fingerprints (moisture placed on metal surfaces from the skin can cause corrosion). Keep measuring and marking tools separated from other tools to prevent damage. Wipe scales occasionally with light oil applied with a soft lint-free cloth. Tapes that are coated with baked enamel should not have oil applied to them.

9–5.   BEVEL

The **bevel** is an adjustable tool used to lay out angles and to test the accuracy of sloped surfaces. You can transfer angles or divide angles and check mitered edges with it. It is also used as a guide for scribing lines on metal. The blade can be locked to any angle from 0 to 180°. A protractor can be used to set the angle.

The bevel handles are made of either die-cast aluminum or hardwood (less expensive) and are from 5 to 6½ inches long. The blade is accurately machined steel and is from 6 to 10 inches long. A wing nut locks the blade into position and into the handle for storage.

To transfer an angle from one location to another, place the handle against one edge of the workpiece. With the wing nut loosened, place the blade against the adjacent workpiece edge. With the handle and blade securely against the edges, lock the wing nut. Slide the handle across the edge of the workpiece to the location of the new angle. Use the blade as a guide and mark the angle.

Use a protractor to set a desired angle on the bevel. Place the handle against the protractor edge. Rotate the blade until it corresponds to the desired angle.

Prevent the blade and handle from becoming damaged. Occasionally apply a light coat of oil to the blade. Blades, handles, and piece parts are easily replaced, when required.

9–6.   CALIPER RULE

Caliper rules are used to measure outside and inside dimensions of cylinders, hole diameters, and short straight lengths. One brass jaw is permanently attached to a wooden body; the other jaw is part of a solid-brass slide. Measurement graduations are in $\frac{1}{32}$ inch.

Caliper-rule physical sizes vary from about 4 by $1\frac{3}{8}$ inches to 6 by 2 inches. The larger rules measure hole diameters from $\frac{7}{32}$ to 5 inches, outside diameters of rounds to 3 inches, and overall lengths up to 5 inches.

In using the caliper rule for outside measurements, simply pull out the sliding jaw, place it around the workpiece, and tightly close the jaw. Make the reading at the fixed jaw. Inside measurements are made similarly except that the reading is made at the reading line indicated as INSIDE.

If you need more accuracy than $\frac{1}{32}$ inch, you need the vernier caliper described in Section 9–20.

9–7.   CHALK LINE

Chalk lines are used to rapidly mark straight lines on vertical or horizontal surfaces. For example, you may snap a chalk line to make a vertical guideline when hanging wallpaper or you may snap a line across the centers of a floor of a room in preparation for the laying of floor tiles. If you buy a chalk line shaped like the line in Fig. 9–1, you may also use it as a **plumb bob** (Section 9–14), thereby negating your need for a plumb bob.

A chalk-line case is about 3 by 5 by 2 inches and has 50 or 100 feet of replaceable cotton line on its reel. Red, white, or blue powdered chalk is poured into the case. As the line is pulled out, a felt gasket hugs the line to evenly distribute the chalk coating. A hook on the end of the line is used to secure one end. A rewind handle returns the line into the case.

To mark a vertical line, hook the chalk-line hook to a nail or other fastener at the top of your intended line. Let the line out of the case until the case hangs below your lowest marking point. If your lowest point is the floor, the case must be free to swing above the floor. Let the case swing freely like a clock pendulum until it comes to rest. Take the thumb and index finger of one hand and hold the line *taut* (at the rested pendulum position) *against* the wall. Reach to a position about halfway up the line with the thumb and index finger of the other hand. Pull the line straight away from the wall about 3 inches; keep the line taut with the other hand! Now *snap release* the line and, presto, you have a vertical plumb line. If necessary, use a straight edge and pencil to extend the line on either end.

The same type of operation is required to make a horizontal line. You can place a nail at both ends if it's a long horizontal length. With the line taut, tie a knot at the end near the case. Snap the line in several places along the length. Instead of using a nail at one end, you may have an assistant hold the hook.

9–8.   COMBINATION SQUARE

The **combination square** consists of a head having 90° and 45° angles, a leveling vial, a scriber, and a slotted steel scale. The 90° and 45° angles are made between the head and the scale. The head has a machined slot in it through which the slotted scale passes. A knurled locking nut, spring, and draw-bolt assembly hold the head onto the slotted scale such that one machined side of the head makes a 90° angle and another a 45° angle with the scale. The head can be located at any position along the scale.

The combination square is used as a tool to lay out a pattern onto a workpiece. It is used in marking (with a pencil on wood or with a scriber on metal) right-angle lines (Fig. 9–2) and parallel lines. It also measures depths of holes, mortises, or tenons. It can be used to check squareness [Fig. 9–3(A)] by placing one side of the head against one side of the workpiece and sighting for light through the other side at the other workpiece edge. The 45° angle can be used as a guide for drawing 45° miter lines onto the workpiece [Fig. 9–3(B)]. The vial is used with one side of the head and indicates a *level* horizontal condition (Section 9–12). The scriber is used to scratch layout marks on a workpiece (Section 9–16).

The scale of a combination square is graduated in ⅛-, 1/16-, and

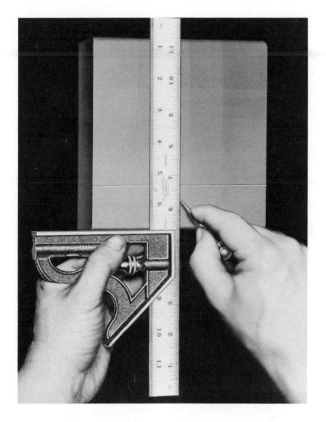

Figure 9–2 The combination square is used in layout as a guide in marking perpendicular and parallel lines. Here, the scriber is used to mark the pattern line on the workpiece.

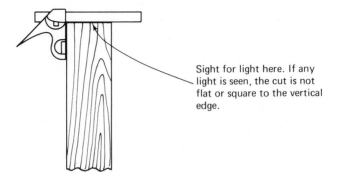

Sight for light here. If any light is seen, the cut is not flat or square to the vertical edge.

(A)

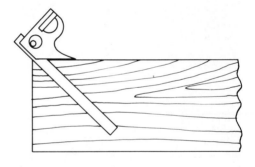

(B)

Figure 9–3 (A) Checking squareness of a workpiece; (B) drawing a 45° line.

$\frac{1}{32}$-inch increments. Some scales are available with both metric and English graduations; one side is graduated by $\frac{1}{2}$ millimeter and $\frac{1}{32}$ inch, the other side by 1 millimeter and $\frac{1}{64}$ inch. Combination square scale lengths are from 4 to 24 inches and 30 centimeters in metric. The heads are about 4 by 5 inches. Some heads have two vials, one in a horizontal direction for leveling and one in a vertical direction for plumbing.

Occasionally apply a light coat of oil to the combination square. The head, scale, scriber, and piece parts are easily replaced.

9–9.   DIVIDERS AND CALIPERS

Dividers are similar to a compass that has one metal leg and one wooden pencil leg used for making circles. The dividers, however, have two metal legs and are used for scribing circles on a metal workpiece, for dividing lines, and for measuring (in conjunction with a scale). **Calipers** (Fig. 9–4) are similar to dividers in construction except that the legs are curved (bowed) inward to obtain *outside* measurements and are bowed outward to obtain *inside* measurements. Calipers are extremely useful in obtaining cylinder-diameter measurements. Calipers are not used to divide or to scribe.

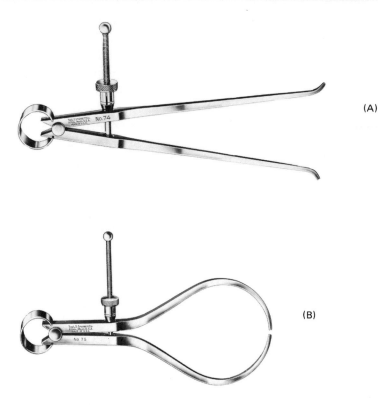

(A)

(B)

Figure 9–4 (A) Inside calipers; (B) outside calipers.

The legs of dividers and calipers are held taut by a strong flexible bow spring. A screw with a special knurled nut allows for making rapid, accurate settings of the spacing between the hardened leg points. Tool lengths are from 3 to 12 inches; 7 inches is the correct size for general use.

To set dividers or calipers to a particular dimension, place one leg firmly on the 1-inch mark of a scale. Close the other leg to a measurement about ¼ inch *less than* the desired dimension; then *back the nut off*, allowing the leg to open until it is set at the proper dimension. Operate the dividers or calipers in this way to set the legs to an unknown measurement on a workpiece or drawing. Then place one leg on the 1-inch mark on a scale and make the dimension reading where the other leg meets the scale. Subtract 1 inch from the dimension to obtain the distance between the legs.

To accurately scribe a circle or an arc on a workpiece, first make a prick-punch indentation (Section 14–7) at the circle center. Then set the dividers to the proper dimension. Place one leg point into the punch indentation. Hold the divider's knurled handle between the thumb and index finger. Slightly angle the dividers and slowly spin the dividers around to scribe the circle or arc (Fig. 9–5).

To construct a line parallel to another line, set the dividers to the required dimension between the lines. Place one point of the dividers near one end of the line. Then swing an arc in the vicinity where the parallel line is to be drawn. Using the same dimension, place the dividers near the other end of the line and swing another arc. Place a scale between the two arcs such that the scale is tangent to each arc. Scribe the required parallel line along the scale.

Keep dividers and calipers clean. Protect the points.

9–10.   FEELER GAUGES

Feeler gauges are used by auto mechanics and technicians to check valve and tappet clearances; to check and set gaps between points, relay contacts, and spark-plug electrodes; to check gear play and bearing clearances; to fit pistons, rings, and pins; and to gauge narrow slots.

Feeler gauges may be *leaves* or *wires*. The leaves are sometimes divided into two thicknesses. Each leaf and wire is marked with its

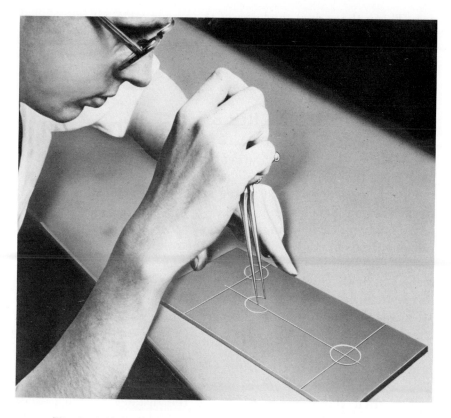

Figure 9–5 Scribing circles on a workpiece with dividers.

thickness. The leaves are used with pistons, brakes, and ignition systems. The wires are used to set spark-plug gaps.

The feeler gauge shown in Fig. 9–1 combines both leaves and wires into a single set. Leaves are from 0.010 to 0.025 inch; the wires are from 0.017 to 0.035 inch. An electrode bender is also incorporated in the set for use in bending spark-plug electrodes to the proper gaps. A knurled nut allows one or more leaves or wires to be locked into any desired position.

Feeler gauges come in sets with leaves ranging from 0.0015 to 0.200 inch. Metric units are also available.

Choose a gauge leaf which you think is less than the thickness of the opening you're planning to measure. Place the leaf into the opening. If it fits loosely, try the next thicker leaf and continue trying thicker leaves until one of the leaves fits with just a little tightness. This is the correct thickness of the opening. Do not force a leaf into the opening. (A combination of leaves may also be used.)

Keep the thickness gauge leaves free of dirt. Occasionally apply a thin coat of oil to the leaves and wires with a cloth.

9–11.   FOLDING RULE

The **folding rule** is the measuring tool used by most carpenters in most home-building and remodeling applications. It is useful where rigidity is needed, as in measuring across a window. When folded, a typical rule is 8 inches long, 2 inches wide, and ⅝ inch thick, making it handy for carrying in the back pocket. The steel joints lock the rule open and closed. Extended fully, the rule, often white or yellow, is 72 inches long and marked in black in inches and ¹⁄₁₆-inch increments on both sides. Sometimes standard stud center distances (every 16 inches) are also marked along the length of the rules. Rules are available in metric and English graduations in lengths of 1 meter, 2 meters, and 6 feet.

You should purchase a quality folding rule and one that has a *brass rule extension* in the first 7-inch hardwood stick of the rule. The extension is used to make *inside* measurements. For example, suppose that you wanted to measure the distance within a door frame. You unfold the rule to the nearest fold for the opening. You would find that your rule would be either too short or too long to fit between the door frame. You would have to make the measurement outside the door and estimate the final reading. With the brass rule extension, open the folding rule to the nearest shortest length. Place the rule between the door frame and extend the brass rule extension until the rule plus the partially extended brass rule fits the opening snugly. Read the folding rule opening. Read the brass rule length indicated at the brass end (edge) of the folding rule (at the 0-inch mark). Add the folding rule length plus the brass rule extension to get the *complete* inside measurement.

The brass extension is also handy to measure the depth of holes. As with any type of measurement reading, be sure that your eyes are directly over the mark that is to be read. This prevents parallax.

Occasionally wipe the folding rule clean. Many rules have self-lubricating joints; rules that do require a drop of light oil usually state this fact on the face of the rule.

9–12.   LEVELS

Do you need to determine if something is level (horizontal)? Or plumb (vertical)? If you do, you need a level.

Levels are constructed of solid hardwood, or of I-beam construction in magnesium or aluminum, and contain one or more single or double vials. A *vial* is a curved glass or acrylic tube nearly filled with liquid. The void in the tube is a bubble that floats to the top of the curved tube or to the *barrel*-shaped area of levels of more modern design. The tube is mounted such that the bubble is centered between marks on the tube when the level indicates a level (horizontal) position. The replaceable vials are sometimes enclosed in glass plates or brass plates. Vials may be mounted in the level (Fig. 9–6) for determining a level condition, a plumb condition, a 45° miter condition, or with a quick-turning protractor dial for determining any angle between 0 and 90° (not illustrated).

Different names are given to levels according to the function or shape of the level: *mason's, general-purpose, torpedo, pocket,* and *line.* The mason's level is the largest level and is made of mahogany. It may have up to six vials and be 42 to 48 inches long, with a body of 2½ by 1¼ inches. General-purpose levels (Fig. 9–1), used by most handymen, are from 18 to 28 inches long with bodies of about 2½ by 1 inches. General-purpose levels may be wood or metal and have three to six vials. For the homeowner's first level, I suggest a three-vial aluminum general-purpose level of 24 inches. Torpedo levels (Fig. 9–6) are hardwood or metal and are about 9 inches long, with

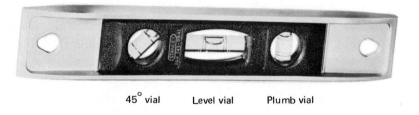

45° vial   Level vial   Plumb vial

Figure 9–6 Level vials may be positioned for determining level, plumb, and 45° conditions.

bodies of 1¼ by ¾ inch. Torpedo levels usually have three vials: level, plumb, and 45°. I suggest a torpedo level as your second level.

Pocket levels are usually hexagon-shaped aluminum cases with a pocket clip attached. There is only one vial; the overall length is 5 inches, with a hex diameter of ⅜ inch. The line level has special hooks that are placed onto a taut line. The line level can slide freely along the line for easy positioning. The bottom is flat so that the line level may also be used as a small level on other flat surfaces. It contains one vial. The line level is a ½-inch-diameter hexagonal shape and is 3¼ inches long. Pocket levels and line levels can be used to determine only horizontal conditions of levelness (plumb or 45° cannot be determined with these levels).

Levels have their top and bottom surfaces ground parallel. Some models have a grooved bottom for use on shafts, pipes, and the like. I've seen one model with a magnetic base; it is used to hold the level fast to iron and steel surfaces.

Place a level flat against a surface that is to be checked with the curved part of the vial on top, like an inverted letter U. In checking for a level condition, the level is placed horizontally. In checking plumbness, the level is held against the surface vertically. In either case, move the workpiece until the vial bubble is centered between the vial marks. You may need to shim your workpiece until the desired level or plumb condition exists.

Hang your level up when it is not in use. Prevent it from falling. If a vial is broken, it can be replaced readily.

9–13.   MICROMETER CALIPER

Micrometer calipers, more often called *micrometers* or *mikes,* are used to make a variety of *accurate* measurements with little possibility of error through misreading. Outside micrometers are used to measure the outsides of a workpiece; an inside micrometer measures holes or cavities within workpieces. Measurements may be made accurately in English units to thousandths (0.001) or ten-thousandths (0.0001) of an inch and in metric units to hundredths of a millimeter (0.01 millimeter equals 0.00039 inch). Note that all micrometer measurements are in decimal, not fractional, notation. Micrometers are useful to persons who require that a workpiece's dimensions be extremely accurate.

The following dimensions will give you a feel for small, accurate measurements: human-hair diameter, 0.0021 inch; page of a book, 0.0042 inch; paper-clip wire diameter, 0.0264 inch; and wooden pencil thickness, 0.2775 inch.

Outside micrometers are made in a variety of frame sizes to accommodate workpieces up to 24 inches or 300 millimeters. It is interesting to note, though, that the working parts of the micrometer do not move through more than 1 inch (English) or 25 millimeters (metric). Instead, frames and interchangeable anvils of various sizes are used to adapt the micrometer to the workpiece size.

Figure 9–7 illustrates the external and internal parts of outside micrometer calipers. You should become familiar with the nomenclature of the external parts: *frame, anvil, spindle, locknut, sleeve, thimble,* and *ratchet stop.* In making a measurement, the workpiece to be measured is placed between the faces of the anvil and the spindle. The thimble is rotated until the faces of the anvil and the spindle close lightly on the workpiece. The dimension of the workpiece is then read from the graduations on the sleeve and thimble.

On micrometers equipped with a *ratchet stop,* the thimble is rotated by means of the ratchet stop. When the faces of the anvil

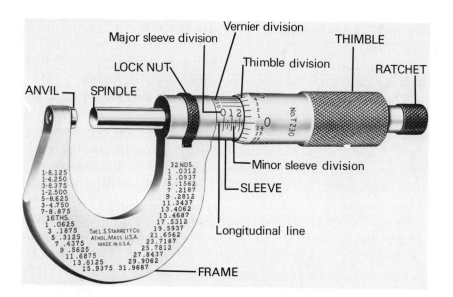

Figure 9–7 Parts of a micrometer caliper.

and the spindle close on the workpiece, the ratchet stop slips or clicks so that no additional pressure is placed on the workpiece. This ratchet assures the same consistent closing tightness on successive measurements, no matter who does the measuring. A friction thimble performs the same type of function as the ratchet stop except that the spindle will not turn when more than a given amount of turning pressure is applied. The locknut is used to lock the anvil and spindle faces to a fixed dimension. The micrometer could be used, for example, as a *go–no go* gauge (if the gauge fits over the workpiece, the workpiece is within tolerance—*go*; if it doesn't fit, the workpiece is out of tolerance—*no go*). A slight rotation of the locknut locks the spindle from moving; a slight rotation of the locknut in the opposite direction unlocks the spindle.

The spindle screw thread on English micrometers has a pitch of $\frac{1}{40}$ inch (40 threads/inch). One revolution of the thimble advances the spindle face $\frac{1}{40}$ inch (0.025 inch) toward the anvil.

Note the divisions along the longitudinal line on the sleeve of the micrometer. These divisions, called the *major sleeve divisions*, are marked from 0 (zero) to 0 (ten). This distance is exactly 1.000 inch. The distance between 0 and 1 is $\frac{1}{10}$, or 0.100, inch. Note that between the major sleeve divisions with numbers there are four smaller divisions, known as the *minor sleeve divisions*; each minor sleeve division is 0.025 inch. Therefore, the divisions (counting major and minor) along the scale are 0.000, 0.025, 0.050, 0.075, 0.100, 0.125, . . . , 0.900, 0.925, 0.950, 0.975, and 1.000 inch. As previously described, one revolution of the thimble moves the spindle 0.025 inch, which is indicated on the sleeve by minor sleeve divisions.

The beveled scale of the thimble is graduated from 1 to 25 and represents a total of 0.025 inch; the divisions are called the *thimble divisions*. The space between each thimble division corresponds to an advance of the spindle of 0.001 inch. The longitudinal line of the sleeve (previously discussed) is the reading line for the thimble.

A micrometer that is graduated in ten-thousandths of an inch has an additional group of divisions called the *vernier divisions*. There are 10 vernier divisions numbered 0 (zero) through 0 (ten); each division equals 0.0001 inch. The spacing of the vernier divisions is such that the total length of the 10 divisions fits exactly into the space of 9 of the thimble divisions. This always causes one of the vernier division lines to fall exactly opposite one of the thimble divisions. The correct vernier reading is the reading (on the vernier divisions) where a vernier division line *aligns exactly opposite* a thimble division line.

With the graduations discussed, you can now read a micrometer caliper graduated in ten-thousandths of an inch. Refer to Fig. 9–7 and read the micrometer distance measured to ten-thousandths of an inch.

Major sleeve divisions: $2 \times 0.100 \ = 0.200$

Minor sleeve divisions: $2 \times 0.025 \ = 0.050$

Thimble divisions: $0 \times 0.001 \ = 0.000$

Vernier divisions: $0 \times 0.0001 = 0.0000$

(by addition) $\qquad\qquad\qquad = 0.2500$

In the problem, the 0 thimble division aligns with the longitudinal line. Thus there are no 0.001 divisions. The vernier division line (and the 0–10 line) aligns with a thimble division line (the 3). Therefore, there are no 0.0001 divisions.

Refer to Fig. 9–8 and read the micrometer distance measured to 1 ten-thousandths of an inch. How many major sleeve divisions are there? Minor sleeve divisions? Which thimble division line most nearly aligns with the longitudinal line (the lower line is read)? Which vernier division aligns with a thimble division?

Major sleeve divisions: $2 \times 0.100 \ = 0.200$

Minor sleeve divisions: $2 \times 0.025 \ = 0.050$

Thimble divisions: $0 \times 0.001 \ = 0.000$

Vernier divisions: $7 \times 0.0001 = 0.0007$

(by addition) $\qquad\qquad\qquad = 0.2507$

Physically, the metric micrometer caliper is the same as the English micrometer caliper except that the graduations are based on the metric millimeter rather than the English inch. The spindle screw thread has a pitch of ½ millimeter; two revolutions of the

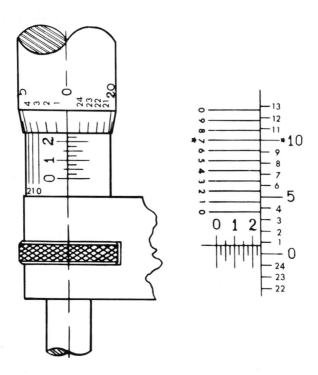

Figure 9–8 Reading a ten-thousandths micrometer.

thimble advance the spindle face 1 millimeter toward the anvil. The maximum opening between the anvil and the spindle face is 25 millimeters. Thus there are 50 threads on the metric micrometer spindle screw.

On the metric micrometer, the major sleeve divisions each represents 1.00 millimeter (mm), the minor sleeve divisions 0.50 mm, the thimble divisions 0.01 mm, and the vernier divisions 0.002 mm. The method of reading the metric micrometer is basically the same as for the English micrometer.

In use, the micrometer caliper is held in the right hand as shown in Fig. 9–9. The workpiece is held in the left hand against the anvil face. The right hand rotates the thimble or the friction thimble or ratchet stop (if available) to close the spindle face slowly against the workpiece. The measurement is not forced; a light contact pressure assures correct reading. After some practice, the correct feel that achieves accuracy in repeated measurements is developed. The use of a micrometer with a ratchet stop or a friction thimble allows for consistent readings, even from a number of persons using the same micrometer.

The workpiece should not be removed from the micrometer until the reading is taken. If it is necessary to remove the workpiece to read the micrometer, rotate the locknut to secure the spindle before removing the workpiece This procedure should be avoided, if possible, to guard against scratching the micrometer faces or the workpiece.

When measuring the diameter of a round or cylindrical workpiece, the following procedure is recommended. Hold the anvil of the micrometer firmly to the workpiece at some point. With this point as a pivot, swing the micrometer back and forth slowly; at the same time, rotate the thimble in toward the workpiece. As contact of the spindle against the workpiece is felt, decrease the swinging action until a smooth firm feel is developed between the anvil and the spindle. Read the micrometer to determine the diameter of the workpiece.

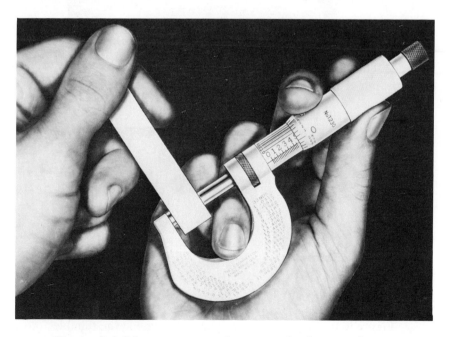

Figure 9–9 Measuring a workpiece with the outside micrometer caliper.

The micrometer caliper should be kept clean at all times. Wipe the micrometer with a soft lint-free cloth; dampen with a solvent, if necessary, to dispose of hard-to-remove dirt. Ensure that the faces of the anvil and spindle are clean. An occasional drop of instrument oil on the spindle and spindle threads assures good performance. Never use an air hose for cleaning, as the pressure could force dirt into the spindle threads. Store the micrometer in a case or box to protect it and to keep it clean.

On occasion, the micrometer may develop play or the longitudinal line may not align with the thimble 0 (zero) division when the micrometer faces are closed. To adjust for play, back off the thimble [Fig. 9–10(A)] until the adjusting nut is exposed. Insert the spanner wrench (included with the micrometer) into the adjusting nut slot and tighten just enough to eliminate play. It is better to make several

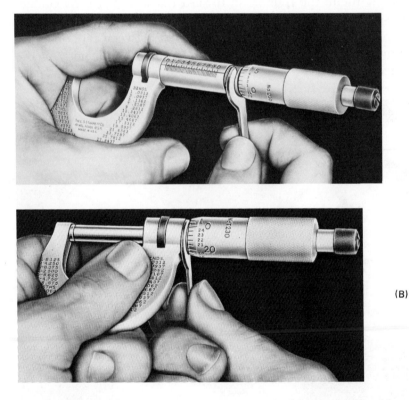

(A)

(B)

Figure 9–10 (A) Adjusting for play; (B) aligning the thimble
0 division on the longitudinal line.

small adjustments with the spanner wrench rather than one large adjustment, which could damage the threads.

To align the thimble 0 division on the longitudinal line, first ensure that the anvil and spindle faces are clean, then close the spindle against the face. Insert the spanner wrench in the small slot in the sleeve [Fig. 9–10(B)] and turn the sleeve until the longitudinal line aligns with the thimble 0 division.

It is a good habit to store the micrometer with a space of at least 0.1 inch between the anvil and spindle faces.

9–14.   PLUMB BOB

The **plumb bob** is used to locate a point exactly below an overhead point or to establish a vertical reference line. For example, you may have an existing overhead beam and you'd like to locate a floor plate (a 2- by 4-inch piece of wood) directly below it so you can nail studs and build a wall. You need a plumb bob to find the location for the floor plate quickly and accurately. Or, perhaps you want to place a 3-foot adjustable bookshelf hanger vertically on the wall. You can use a plumb bob and locate the hanger next to and parallel to the plumb-bob line.

Plumb bobs are made of steel and may be nickel-plated. They are from 5 to $6\frac{1}{2}$ inches long with diameters of from $\frac{1}{2}$ to 1 inch and weights of 5 to 16 ounces. The replaceable tips are hardened. The cap end permits attachment of braided silk line. The top of the cap has a slotted neck that assures true hanging and eliminates the need to tie knots.

In use, remove sufficient line from the cap. Place the line through the slotted cap until it *catches*. Place the other end of the line to the mark and let the plumb bob swing freely like a clock pendulum. Wait until the plumb bob comes to rest. You can then let out a little more string until the plumb-bob point touches the unknown point you've been constructing.

9–15.   POCKET RULES AND STEEL SCALES

The **pocket rule** is 6 inches long and has a pocket clip. It is a handy rule to carry for making small accurate measurements to $\frac{1}{64}$ inch and for measuring and drawing straight lines when sketching. The reverse side often lists fractions of an inch with their decimal equivalents; this reference is often very handy.

Steel scales are available in numerous models with lengths varying from ¼ inch to 12 feet and 5 centimeters to 1 meter. The scales are made of spring-tempered, semiflexible, or full-flexible steel.

Scales are graduated in either English inches, metric millimeters, or in both English and metric. Depending upon the model of scale chosen, the graduations may appear on the front top and bottom edges or both the front and the back top and bottom edges of the scale. English graduations may be in ¼, ⅛, 1/16, 1/32, or 1/64 inch, and each scale edge may use different graduations. English graduations may also be in the decimal system, graduated by 1/50 (0.02) and 1/100 (0.01) inch. The metric graduations may be decimeters, centimeters, millimeters, and half-millimeters. Combined English–metric scales may have edges graduated in 1/32 and 1/64 inch and in millimeters and half-millimeters.

9–16. SCRIBER

The **scriber** is the *pencil* used in metal work; it is used to draw (scribe) lines onto hard surfaces by making permanent scratches on the material. (The material is often covered with a dye, called layout dye, to make *layout* marks show more prominently). The scriber can be as simple as a hard, pointed metal rod or as sophisticated and expensive as a diamond-chip scriber. General-use scribers are of tool steel and are carbide-tipped. Tool steel tips are generally longer lasting than carbide tips because carbide tips will shatter when dropped on hard surfaces and the carbide tips require special grinding wheels to resharpen. Some scribers have one bent end, which is used to mark out-of-the-way places where the straight, pointed end cannot reach. The scriber shown in Fig. 9–1 has a point that is held firmly by a knurled chuck; when the scriber is not in use, the point can be reversed, telescoped into the handle, and locked by a slight turn of the chuck.

When scribing or ruling a line on a workpiece, a metal scale or bar is used as a guide (Fig. 9–2). Proper technique in the use of the metal scale and scriber results in an accurately drawn line. The point

of the scriber is placed in the corner formed by the scale and the
workpiece. The scriber is then held at a steady angle and is drawn
across the workpiece using the scale as a guide. This technique allows for greater accuracy in aligning the scale with prescribed marks
or lines. This technique also keeps the tip of the scriber from wan-
dering, causing irregular, inaccurate lines.

9–17.   STEEL SQUARE

The **steel square** (also called a framing square) is used to mark stock
for squaring and to draw parallel and perpendicular lines, and its
scales assist builders in computing angular cuts as used in framing
a house.

The longer leg of the steel square is known as the *body*; the
shorter leg is the *tongue*. Body lengths are 12 and 24 inches by 2
inches wide; corresponding tongues are 8 and 16 inches by $1\frac{1}{2}$
inches wide. Graduations are in $\frac{1}{8}$, $\frac{1}{16}$, and $\frac{1}{32}$ inch on the faces
and $\frac{1}{10}$ and $\frac{1}{12}$ inch on the back. Steel squares are made of polished
steel, blued steel, stainless steel, and aluminum.

Tapered rafter steel squares have rafter tables scaled so that
marks for rafter cuts according to rafter pitch can be made. To mark
rafter or stair stringer cuts, set the scale numbers along the edge of
the workpiece. Brace measure on octagon scales and board measure
on one-hundredths scales are also on tapered rafter squares.

9–18.   STEEL TAPES

Steel tapes are of two general sizes, a pocket size for measuring distances up to 12 feet and a larger size for measuring distances up to
100 feet. Both tapes are used in measuring linear distances or large
curved distances such as cylinder circumferences.

Pocket steel tapes are about $\frac{1}{2}$ inch wide and are usually 72
inches long, although models of 8, 10, and 12 feet are also available.
Metric and metric–English graduated tapes are also available in 2-
and 3-meter lengths. English graduations are in fractional or decimal
graduations of $\frac{1}{16}$ and $\frac{1}{10}$ inch (depending on the types of graduations desired); the first 6 inches is often graduated in $\frac{1}{32}$ inch and

$\frac{1}{50}$ inch. Metric graduations are in millimeters, centimeters, and meters. Standard stud-location marks are marked each 16 inches on the tape. A Mylar* coating over the tape provides blade protection against abrasive wear.

When tape is pulled from the case, a tape lock can be engaged to keep the tape from creeping back into the case. A push button actuates power-returned tapes.

When making inside measurements with the pocket steel tape (as inside a door frame) be sure that the tape is taut and that the dimension of the case is added to the dimension read on the tape. The tape case is usually constructed so that the case dimension is 2 inches.

Large steel tapes measure long linear and curved distances. They are available in lengths of 25, 33, 50, 66, 75, and 100 feet and 10, 15, 20, 25, and 30 meters. Combination English–metric tapes are also available in lengths of 15, 20, 25, 30, and 50 meters. The English tapes are graduated in feet, inches, and $\frac{1}{8}$ inch. Each foot is marked in a color different from the inch markings. Marks are set at each 16 inches for standard stud centers. Special tapes are available with graduations by $\frac{1}{10}$ foot and $\frac{1}{100}$ foot. Many tapes are clad in Mylar, which wears longer and resists oils, alkalies, acids, and rust. Steel tapes are used extensively in the construction and surveying fields, where large dimensions are often encountered.

In using the steel tape, the end of the pull ring is placed against the beginning measurement mark. The pull ring is a part of the length of the tape and is included in every measurement. Pull the tape taut and ensure that the tape is along the line to be measured. Measurements are made accurately to $\frac{1}{16}$ inch by rounding off. After the measurement is made, use the windup knob to wind the tape back into the case. The tool is cared for in the same manner as steel scales (refer to Section 9–15). Tapes can be replaced on some models.

9–19.   TRY SQUARE

The **try square** checks squareness and is used as a guide for marking right angles. It has an iron or hardwood handle of from 4 to 20 inches

---

*Mylar is DuPont's polyester film.

and a steel blade from 6 to 36 inches long. Some handles have a 45°
angle cut into the handle for use as a miter gauge. A level vial may
also be incorporated in the handle. Blades may be plain or may be
graduated in English or metric units.

Figure 9–11 illustrates the use of a try square in checking
squareness of a piece that is to be bolted to another workpiece. The
try square is used the same as the combination square and the steel
square (Sections 9–8 and 9–15, respectively) to check squareness and
to mark right angles.

9–20.   VERNIER CALIPER

The **vernier caliper**, most often called *vernier*, is used by toolmakers,
machinists, layout men, mechanics, and inspectors to measure outside and inside measurements of a wide variety of tools and parts.
Measurements are made to an accuracy of 0.001 inch.

The vernier caliper consists of a graduated beam with a fixed
jaw. A vernier with a second jaw slides along the graduated beam.
Clamp screws hold the fine adjustment and vernier assemblies to the
graduated beam. The fine-adjusting nut is used for the final closing
of the jaws onto the workpiece being measured.

In measuring a workpiece, the jaws are closed onto the work-

Figure 9–11 The try square is used to check squareness and
as a guide in marking right angles.

piece (or the nibs opened against a workpiece for an inside measurement) and a reading is made at the vernier. Two graduated scales are available, one for outside measurements and one for inside measurements. Some verniers have both the outside and inside scales on one side of the vernier caliper; others have the outside scale on one side and the inside scale on the opposite side. In the case of the latter, the outside scale is read left to right; the inside scale is read right to left. Some verniers have 50 divisions, others have 25 divisions. Measurements can be made accurately to 0.001 inch in the English system and 0.02 millimeter in the metric system.

Vernier calipers are made in a variety of sizes, with graduated beams of 6, 12, 24, 36, and 48 inches (60 and 72 inches or other sizes on special orders) and to 600 millimeters. Jaw depths are from approximately 1½ inches for the 6-inch vernier to 4½ inches for the 72-inch vernier. Nib widths, with the jaws closed, are from ¼ to ¾ inch.

Figure 9–12 illustrates the 50-division vernier across a portion of the graduated beam. Note the inch divisions shown as 1, 2, 3, and so on. Major beam divisions are numbered 1 through 9 and each represents 0.100 inch. Minor beam divisions, located between major divisions, are each 0.050 inch. Vernier divisions, numbered each five divisions, are 0.001 inch each.

The reading is begun at the 0 (zero) line of the vernier and is

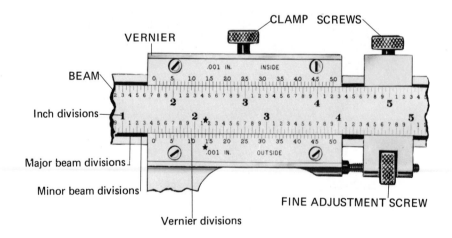

Figure 9–12 Reading a vernier caliper 50-division vernier.

the sum of the inch divisions, major beam divisions, minor beam divisions, and the vernier divisions. The vernier division line that is read is the line that is exactly opposite one of the division lines of the graduated beam; only one of the 50 division lines of the vernier will be exactly opposite one of the graduated beam divisions. This is because the vernier is constructed so that the space of 50 divisions of the vernier fits exactly into the space of 49 divisions of the graduated beam.

The dimension of the width of the opening of the jaws (an outside measurement) of the vernier caliper shown in Fig. 9–12 is

$$
\begin{array}{rcl}
\textbf{Inch divisions:} & 1 \times 1.00 \text{ in.} = & 1.00 \\
\textbf{Major beam divisions:} & 4 \times 0.100 \text{ in.} = & 0.400 \\
\textbf{Minor beam divisions:} & 1 \times 0.050 \text{ in.} = & 0.050 \\
\textbf{Vernier divisions:} & 14 \times 0.001 \text{ in.} = & 0.014 \\
(\textit{by addition}) & = & \overline{1.464} \text{ in.}
\end{array}
$$

An inside measurement is made in the same manner as an outside measurement; the difference in the position of the numbers on the graduated beam for the inside measurements is due to the measurement of the nibs, which is automatically compensated for on this type of vernier caliper.

The metric vernier is read in a manner similar to the English vernier. Centimeter divisions each equal 1 centimeter; 1 centimeter equals 10 millimeters. The major beam divisions are 1 mm each, the minor beam divisions are 0.50 mm each, and the vernier divisions are 0.02 mm each.

The vernier caliper is held for a measurement as shown in Fig. 9–13, which illustrates the use of the vernier in making an inside measurement of a workpiece. Prior to making the measurement, the clamp screws should both be loosened and the vernier slid along the graduated beam to the approximate dimension of the workpiece. The vernier nib (or jaw) opening is then compared to the workpiece and is slid to a final approximated nib (jaw) opening. The clamp screw over the fine-adjusting nut is then tightened with the fingers against the graduated beam. The fine-adjusting nut is rotated until the nibs (or jaws) firmly (but not too tightly) contact the workpiece. Then carefully tighten the vernier clamp screw and remove the vernier from the workpiece. Take the reading.

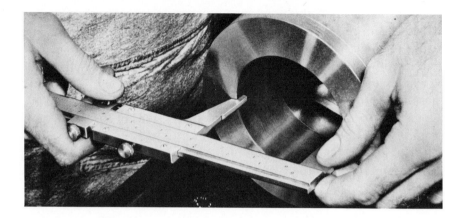

Figure 9–13 The vernier caliper is used to make accurate inside and outside measurements.

The vernier caliper should be kept clean at all times to prevent inaccuracies and for ease of operation. Wipe the vernier after each use with a clean, dry, lint-free cloth. Dampen the cloth with a solvent to remove stubborn dirt. An occasional drop of instrument oil rubbed onto the vernier and the moving jaw assembly will ensure free-running performance. Store the vernier in a case or box to protect it; the clamp screws should be loose during storage.

Handle the vernier gently but firmly. Never force it to obtain a measurement. When temporarily out of use, lay the vernier flat on the work surface, away from the edges of the work surface.

Check the vernier periodically for accuracy of the zero line. With the jaws closed, the 0 (zero) line of the outside-reading vernier scale should coincide with the 0 (zero)-inch division on the beam. If they are not aligned or if the vernier shows signs of wear, return the vernier caliper to the factory for adjustment or repair.

9–21.   WOOD-MARKING GAUGE

The **wood-marking gauge** consists of a graduated rod, a head, a thumb screw, and a fixed tempered pin. When the gauge is held at the proper angle and is drawn across the workpiece, a perfect line is scored. Hardwood gauges are used in marking wood, whereas nickel-plated steel models are used on wood and metal. The thumb screw locks the head to the desired dimension along the graduated rod.

Gauges made of wood are about 8½ inches long with dimensions graduated in ¹⁄₁₆ inch. These graduations are often inaccurate; therefore, use a scale to measure the distance between the point and the head and, after correcting the head location as required, tighten the thumb screw.

Marking gauges made of metal are more accurate and are graduated in ¹⁄₆₄ inch. Some have adjustable pins.

Grasp the marking gauge head as you would a ball. Angle the gauge such that the pin is at a slight angle to the workpiece. Hold the head *firmly* against the workpiece edge and draw the gauge toward you.

Protect the point of the marking gauge from becoming bent by properly storing it. Sharpen blunt pins with a file and oilstone. All parts of high-quality marking gauges may be replaced.

10

miscellaneous hand tools

10–1. GENERAL

This chapter contains **miscellaneous hand tools** that do not fit into any of the categories of the other chapters within this handbook, but these tools are very useful, if not necessary, for many jobs. Each tool writeup is self-contained and covers description, application, and care of the tool. It is advised that you read the introduction to each tool to determine if the tool is needed in your shop.

The miscellaneous hand tools covered in this chapter are: *abrasives, awl, glass cutter, knives (modeler's/carver's knives* and *gouges), knives (utility), nail set, nibbler, oilstone (sharpening* or *whetstone), propane torch, putty knife (scraper), ripping bar (pinch bar, pry bar), riveter, sanding blocks, scraper (wood, paint and glue), terminal (electrical) crimper, tin snips,* and *wire stripper.*

10–2. ABRASIVES

Abrasives are used to prepare wood, metal, and other materials for the application of a final finish, such as paint, varnish, or lacquer. Abrasives are also used to polish metals, stones, plastics, and ceramics to very smooth bright finishes. They are also used to remove paint and rust and to clean workpieces.

Abrasives are available with backings, as a powder, or as a

wool. Abrasives with backings are often referred to as sandpaper, although the abrasive is not sand nor is the backing always paper. For this discussion on abrasives, I have classified abrasives into *abrasive papers* and *steel wool*. The only powders mentioned are pumice and rottenstone, which are included in Table 10–2.

Abrasive Papers

Abrasives are adhered to a backing, which may be paper, cloth, fiber, plastic, or paper and cloth combined. A paper backing is usually used as the abrasive backing for hand sanding; the other backing materials are used for machine sanding. Abrasives are manufactured in both *open-coat* and *closed-coat* forms. The area of open-coat backing is covered 50 to 70 percent with abrasive; this provides less cutting, more abrasive flexibility, and prevents the abrasive from becoming clogged with residue. With a closed-coat backing, the abrasive covers 100 percent of the backing. Self-cleaning papers are used with belt sanders to remove glue from surfaces. These self-cleaning papers have soap between the grains to prevent clogging. Backings are also classified as *standard* or *wet*; residue may be washed away from the wet type of backing.

Abrasive backings are also classified by letter designations: A, lightweight; C, heavier, for hand sanding; D, heavier, for machine sanding; J; and X, which is heavier and less flexible than J.

Abrasive papers are available in sheets, belts, tapes, discs, rolls, and cylinders. Sizes vary, as shown in Table 10–1.

You may tear abrasive papers to fit a sanding block or a sanding machine as follows: fold the paper one way and crease it. Then unfold the crease and fold the paper in the opposite direction. Place the crease over a straight edge (as the edge of your workbench) and tear.

TABLE 10–1. SIZES OF ABRASIVE PAPERS

Format	Size
Sheets	9 × 11, 4½ × 5½, and 3⅔ by 9 inches
Belts	2 to 12 inches wide
Cylinders	1½ to 3½-inch diameters
Tapes	1 to 1½ inches wide
Discs	3 to 14-inch diameters

Clean clogged abrasive paper with a stiff brush, file card (Section 6–3), or wire brush. A light tapping will also remove some of the residue.

Table 10–2 lists the abrasives most commonly used by home craftsmen, hobbyists, and do-it-yourselfers. The abrasives listed are all adhered to backing, except pumice and rottenstone, which are powders.

Table 10–3 lists the grades, grit number, number sizes, and uses of the various grades of abrasive papers. The grit number is the number of openings in a screen through which abrasives can pass. The openings vary from 12 (very coarse grit) to 600 (very fine grit).

Emery cloth is used dry or with oil, primarily for light cleanup work of tools, for rust removal, and for hand-polishing nonplated metal surfaces. Emery cloth is made of grits of the abrasive mineral emery on a backing similar to other abrasive papers. Emery is actually a natural mixture of aluminum oxide and magnetite. Emery cloth is available in 9 by 11-inch sheets and grades as listed in Table 10–4. Emery cloth, once the best abrasive for use on metal, has been superseded by silicon carbide and aluminum oxide.

Steel Wool

Steel wool is an abrasive material composed of long, fine steel shavings. It is used especially for scouring, removing rust from tools, and polishing metal. Table 10–5 describes the grades and uses of steel wool.

10–3.   AWL

The **awl** (Fig. 10–1) is a handy, inexpensive tool to have in your tool box. It's shaped like an ice pick, and, in fact, if you have an ice pick, you might consider using it as your awl. I use the awl to make starter holes for small brads (as when hanging pictures), to make holes in leather and similar materials, to make pilot holes in wood for starting a drill bit, and as a scriber on wood; I misuse the awl to scribe metal, to make small holes in metal, and to scratch my initials in objects.

The awl has a wooden or plastic gripping handle and a steel spike; the overall length is about 5 inches. Keep the point sharp by

TABLE 10–2. ABRASIVES

Abrasive	Color	Description	Use
Silicon carbide	Dark gray	Hard, brittle, sharp.	Cuts soft metals and plastics. Smoothes and frosts glass (by rubbing); used in floor sanding.
Aluminum oxide	Brown	Long-lasting, fast, tough.	Used on power sanders for sanding wood and metal. Sharpens tools. Shapes and polishes metal.
Garnet	Reddish brown	Inexpensive, tough.	For hand sanding clean wood and general woodworking.
Flint	Yellow-white	Inexpensive, doesn't last long. Paper clogs easily. Soft.	For sanding painted wood or metal. For sanding gummy wood.
Emery	Black	Previously the best abrasive for metal, it has been superseded by silicon carbide and aluminum oxide.	For metal polishing (nonplated metals only).
Crocus	Red	Ferric oxide.	For polishing soft and nonferrous metals.
Pumice	Off-white	Powder. Form of volcanic glass. Cuts faster than rottenstone.	For hand-rubbed finishes. Apply with felt pad dampened with linseed oil.
Rottenstone	Off-white	Powder. Decomposed siliceous limestone.	For hand-rubbed finishes. Apply with felt pad dampened with linseed oil.
Steel wool	Silver-gray	Available in several grades.	Scouring; removing paint and rust; polishing metal.

TABLE 10–3. ABRASIVE PAPERS (EXCLUDING EMERY CLOTH)

Uses	Number Size	Grit No.	Grade
Rapid removal of surface material such as sanding old floors; removal of paint and rust.	4-1/2	12	Extra coarse
	4-1/4	14	
	4	16	
	3-3/4	18	
	3-1/2	20	
	3-1/4	22	
Removal of surface material, as new floors.	3	24	
	2-1/2	30	
	2	36	Extra coarse
Removal of rough stock; occasionally used on rough wood and for paint removal.	1-1/2	40	Coarse
	1	50	
	1/2	60	Coarse
Removal of light stock; use to sand walls before painting.	1/0	80	Medium
	2/0	100	Medium
Preparation for finish; use prior to primer or sealer.	3/0	120	Fine
	4/0	150	
	5/0	180	Fine
Finish sanding between coats of paint, lacquer, or varnish.	6/0	220	Extra fine
	7/0	240	
	8/0	280	
Used rarely for woodworking, but used for plastics, stone, metals, and ceramics.	9/0	320	
	10/0	400	
	11/0	500	
	12/0	600	Extra fine

occasionally honing the tip. If the point bends or becomes excessively dull, sharpen the point on a grinding wheel to a long conical point followed by honing. Don't let the tip become excessively hot during grinding.

In using the awl to make a pilot hole, hold the awl in the direction of the intended final hole. Push the awl into the workpiece sufficiently far to enable the next tool (or fastener) to be accurately set into the hole. Note that the awl is not a drill; therefore, it *pushes* workpiece fibers apart rather than cutting them. On thin small workpieces, this separating of fibers can split your workpiece. Therefore,

TABLE 10–4. EMERY CLOTH

Uses	Number Size	Grit No.	Grade
Rust removal and removal of mate-	3	36	Coarse
rial.	2-1/2	40	↓
	2	50	Coarse
Cleanup of work tools and rust re-	1-1/2	60	Medium
moval.	1	80	↓
	1/2	100	Medium
Hand-polishing nonplated metals.	1/0	120	Fine
	2/0	150	↓
	3/0	180	Fine

don't make your pilot hole any larger than necessary. In precision drilling of a workpiece, the correct procedure would be to make a point with the awl at the starting mark. Then drill a hole with a small drill, such as a $\frac{1}{16}$- or $\frac{5}{64}$-inch drill; continue increasing the drill size, until the desired hole diameter is reached.

10–4.   GLASS CUTTER

The **glass cutter** consists of a malleable iron handle with a ball on one end and either a tungsten steel wheel or a tungsten carbide wheel on the other end. The tungsten carbide wheel is much more expensive than the tungsten steel wheel and is only needed if you intend to do a lot of glass cutting. The wheel is used to score a line along the surface of the glass. The ball is used in some instances to

Figure 10–1 The awl is used to make starting holes for brads, drill bits, and holes in leather or similar materials.

TABLE 10–5. STEEL WOOL

Uses	Number Size	Grade
Paint, rust, soot, and dirt removal, often used with paint remover.	3	Coarse
Floor maintenance, removing soiled wax, and for preparing surfaces for refinishing.	2	Medium coarse
For kitchen use and for cleaning white-wall tires. Cleans and polishes aluminum and brass, revives surfaces, and is used for floor buffing. Removes tile stains (don't use on plastic tile).	1 0	Medium Fine
For very smooth finish and for rubbing down final coat. Also for cleaning brass, aluminum, and copper before soldering.	00	Very fine
For extra-smooth finish and for rubbing down final coat of a finish.	000 and 0000	Extra fine

tap the glass, causing it to separate at the scored line. Notches under the wheel are also used in some instances to break or nibble small pieces of glass off the glass workpiece.

   WARNING: Protective gloves should be worn while cutting glass.

Use the following steps to cut glass.

1.   Cover a large flat surface with layers of newspapers. Clean the glass to be cut and place it on the newspapers.

2.   Wipe the glass along the proposed cut line with a light oil or turpentine. Apply a drop of light oil to the wheel of the glass cutter.

3.   Hold the glass cutter vertically with the notches toward the glass. Place your forefinger on the indentation in the handle.

4.   Place the glass cutter along a straight edge of a piece of scrap wood that is used as a guide.

5.   With continuous firm pressure, draw the glass cutter

wheel along the glass so that the glass is *scored*; do not attempt to cut through the glass. Strive for a continuous line.

6.   Place a pencil or a dowel *underneath* the glass, under and along the scored line. Immediately press with your hands on each side of the scored line (or press firmly on one side and slap the other side with the open palm of your other hand). You may also place the glass over the edge of a table; hold the glass with both hands and snap down on the side over the edge.

To cut narrow strips, score the glass. Then use the ball on the glass-cutter handle and tap the glass *underneath* the scored line. For cutting off very narrow strips, score the glass. Then use pliers (duck-bill pliers preferred, Section 12–8) to break (nibble) the glass off. You can also use the notches on the glass cutter to break the glass off.

Some additional hints for successful glass cutting are: (1) never tap on the scored side of the glass; (2) retrace with the cutter wheel only over spots where the cutter missed; (3) retracing over a scored line will result in chipped, rough edges. Practice on scraps of glass before cutting the workpiece.

Use moderate pressure on the cutting wheel; too much pressure causes chipping; too little pressure results in unscored spots along the cutting line.

10–5.   KNIVES (MODELER'S/CARVER'S KNIVES, CHISELS, AND GOUGES)

Modeler's and **carver's knives, chisels**, and **gouges** are used to carve, to sculpt, to cut patterns, to make models, and to make and repair furniture. The workpiece materials may be wood, soap, linoleum, or similar materials. Knives, chisels, and gouges are available in sets (Figs. 10–2 and 10–3) or as individual pieces.

Knives, used to chip, carve, and whittle, come in varied shapes, sizes, and lengths of cutting edges. Chisels have flat blades and make a straight stabbing cut into the workpiece. Gouges have curved blades and therefore make curved stabbing cuts. One exception to this is the V- or U-shaped tool, sometimes known as a *veiner*.

Accessories that the modeler/carver may want include routers,

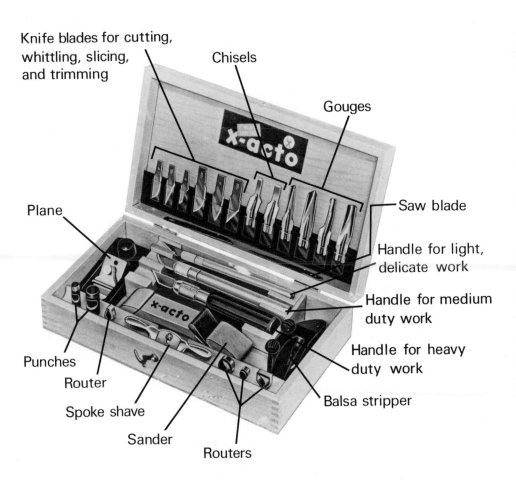

Knife blades for cutting, whittling, slicing, and trimming

Chisels

Gouges

Saw blade

Plane

Handle for light, delicate work

Handle for medium duty work

Handle for heavy duty work

Punches

Router

Balsa stripper

Spoke shave

Sander

Routers

Figure 10–2 This modeler's/carver's workshop contains knives, chisels, and gouges as well as other handy tools.

punches, sanding blocks (Section 10–14), spoke shave (Section 11–6), plane (Chapter 11), balsa stripper, C clamps (Section 4–7), oilstones (Section 10–9), and a wooden mallet (Section 8–6). Routers carve grooves or hollow the interiors of models. Punches are used to cut small pieces of round dowel, and the balsa stripper is used to guide a knife to cut thin strips of balsa wood. The wooden mallet is used to strike the handle of the gouges and chisels when deep cuts are made.

There are two basic methods to cut and carve with knives. One

Figure 10–3 Wood carving knives.

method is the thumb-push method. The workpiece is held in the left hand, the knife in the right, with the thumb on the back of the blade. The blade is pointed away from the body so that the cut is made in that direction. The left thumb is placed on top of the right thumb and pushes the knife.

The second method is the draw method. The workpiece is held in the left hand and the knife in the right. The cutting is done toward the body; the left hand supplies the power against the right fingers, which are guiding the knife. The right thumb steadies the workpiece.

Workpieces are first rough-cut to shape with a coping saw (Section 15–7). Various knives, gouges, and chisels are then used to shape the workpiece. Sanding may be performed to complete the workpiece if desired.

The most important features to look for in buying chisels,

gouges, and knives are the following. Buy tools made from a good grade of tempered steel. Buy tools with long, comfortable handles. The tools must be sharp to ensure easy, accurate cutting. It may come to you as a surprise, but new carving knives, chisels, and gouges need honing.

Sharpen your carving tools on an oilstone; use a flat oilstone for blades and chisels and an oilstone with convex and concave surfaces for sharpening gouges. Place a few drops of oil on the oilstone to be used. Place the tool bevel against the oilstone at the same angle as the manufactured bevel. Slide the tool across the stone to sharpen the edge. When the bevel is smooth and a slight burr is raised, raise the tool from the oilstone. Rub the oilstone over the burr very carefully until the burr is removed. The edge of the tool can then be stropped by carefully drawing the edge across a piece of leather.

Knives are sharpened by alternately pushing and pulling the blade edge over an oilstone in a circular motion. Test for burrs with your finger and remove them with an oilstone. Finally, strop the edge over a piece of leather.

Protect knives, gouges, and chisels from dropping or from bumping each other or other tools during storage. Wipe the steel surfaces with an oily rag occasionally to prevent rusting.

10–6.   KNIVES (UTILITY)

Two **utility knives** that find many uses around the home and shop are shown in Fig. 10–4. The lineman's or electrician's knife has three blades made of high-grade tempered steel. The length of the wire skinning blade is 2 inches, the spearpoint general-purpose blade, 2½ inches, and the screwdriver blade, which locks open, 3 inches.

The retractable blade knife (6 inches) is an aluminum handle with a latching device to hold a steel razor blade into one of three cutting positions. Blades are replaceable (spare blades are stored in the handle). This knife is particularly useful in cutting asbestos shingles, tar paper, underlayment paper, and asbestos vinyl and vinyl tiles. It is also very handy for trimming wallpaper.

To sharpen a pocket utility knife, hold the blade against a whetstone at a 30° angle. Stroke the knife forward diagonally, then turn

Figure 10–4 Utility knives: (A) lineman's or electrician's
knife; (B) retractable blade.

it over and return the stroke. Move the blade along the length of the
blade during the stroke. Sharpen the edges alternately on the stone,
followed by stropping on a piece of leather.

10–7.   NAIL SET

It is not desirable to have nail heads showing on the surface of a
piece of furniture or other workpiece that may be built. To eliminate
nail heads from showing, the craftsman uses finishing nails (Section
5–5) and countersinks the heads from $\frac{1}{16}$ to $\frac{1}{8}$ inch below the surface with a nail set (Fig. 10–5). The remaining hole is then filled with
a wood filler or putty, and the workpiece is finished.

A quality **nail set** is made from an alloy steel and hardened and
tempered for long life. It has a beveled square head that prevents

Figure 10–5 The nail set is used to countersink nail heads
below the surface of the workpiece.

mushrooming and rolling on a slanted surface. A knurled handle prevents the nail set from slipping in your hand. The nail-set point is cupped to provide a nonslip nail contact surface. Nail-set-point diameters are marked on the head and are available in $\frac{1}{32}$-, $\frac{1}{16}$-, $\frac{3}{32}$-, $\frac{1}{8}$-, and $\frac{5}{32}$-inch sizes. The body length is 4 inches with an $\frac{11}{32}$-inch body diameter.

To countersink a nail, first drive the finishing nail with a claw hammer to about $\frac{1}{16}$ inch from the surface of the workpiece. Select the proper nail set for the nail diameter. Place the nail set into the nail head and position the nail set so that it is in line with the nail. Tap the nail-set head with the hammer; before tapping again, make sure that the nail-set point still remains in the nail head. Drive the nail $\frac{1}{16}$ to $\frac{1}{8}$ inch below the surface.

10–8.   NIBBLER

The hand **nibbler** (Figs. 10–6 and 10–7) is used to nibble holes, slots, or openings of any shape in steel up to 18 gauge (0.046 inch) and

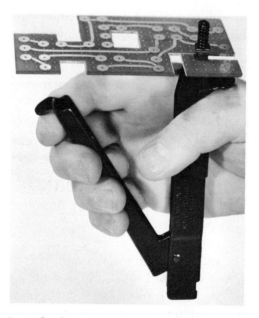

Figure 10–6 The hand nibbler is used to cut holes, slots, or other openings in plastic, vector board, and metals.

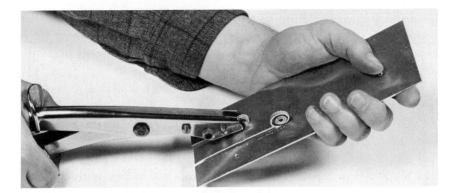

Figure 10–7 This hand nibbler is being used to cut slots in a workpiece.

in plastic, vector board, copper, aluminum, or other soft metal up to $\frac{1}{16}$ inch. The cut edges are safe, flat, and smooth. The *nibble* is a rectangle approximately $\frac{1}{16}$ by $\frac{1}{4}$ inch. The nibbler is useful in duct work, automobile body work, and in making chassis for electronic units. The nibbler shown in Fig. 10–7 can be used to cut tubing lengthwise.

In using the nibbler, first cut a $\frac{1}{4}$-inch-square hole or drill a $\frac{1}{4}$-inch hole in the workpiece to allow the nibbler punch to pass through. Insert the nibbler punch and squeeze the handles together and follow the layout pattern around the workpiece. Make the nibbler bites as close together as possible. File any rough edges.

When the nibbler punch becomes dull, it should be replaced with a new punch. Remove and replace the punch in accordance with the manufacturer's directions.

10–9.   OILSTONE (SHARPENING STONE OR WHETSTONE)

Dull tools are difficult to use, do a poor job, and are dangerous, because it takes a lot more force to make a dull tool work than it does to make a sharp tool work. **Oilstones** are used to sharpen such tools as knives, chisels, gouges, scraper blades, awl points, plane blades, spoke-shave blades, and to remove small burrs from workpiece edges.

Oilstones are made of vitrified aluminum oxide (best for all-around use) or vitrified silicon carbide. One side of the oilstone is coarse and the other side is fine. Shapes are rectangular, tapered, flat, oval, and round. Sizes range from pocket size, 3 by ⅞ by ¼ inches, to large sizes of about 9 by 1½ by ½ inches.

New oilstones should be saturated with oil. They should then be kept in a dust-free box. During use, keep the oilstone lubricated with light machine oil or machine oil mixed with equal parts of kerosene.

Loose grit and sludge should be removed from the surface of the oilstone by rubbing it with a solvent-soaked rag. Gummy residue can be removed from the oilstone by warming it in the oven, wiping off the oily sludge as it comes to the surface. The oilstone can be ground flat again by rubbing it on a silicone carbide grit and water mixture placed on the surface of a piece of glass.

Procedures for using the oilstone to sharpen various tools are described separately with each tool described in this handbook. In sharpening any tool, remember that sharp tools reflect light. When a sharp tool is held up to light, a white line means that the tool is not sharp. In honing, move the tool over the complete surface of the oilstone so that it wears evenly.

10–10.   PROPANE TORCH

You can find many uses for a **propane torch** around the home, shop, or farm. The more important uses are: to remove paint and putty; to solder copper pipes, wires, and gutters; to unfreeze pipes; to remove tile; to refinish furniture; to light charcoal fires; and in creative soldering.

The propane torch comes in a set (Fig. 10–8) and consists of a propane cylinder (which has about 15 hours of use), control valve, blowtorch head, flame spreader, solder tip, pencil flame head, and a flint spark lighter. The cylinder contains propane which is a liquid under pressure in the cylinder. When the control valve is opened, propane escapes and expands in volume 400 times. The gas is combined with air to produce an intense flame. The flame spreader spreads the flame out so that heat may be distributed over a large area. The solder tip is heated internally by the flame and is then used to solder wires or other suitable metal parts. The blowtorch head and the pencil-flame

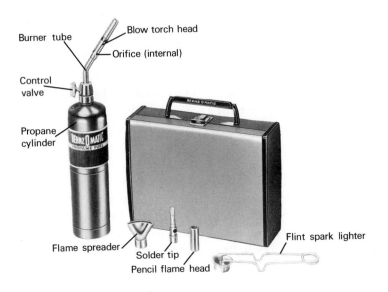

Figure 10–8 The propane torch.

head control the air mixture, hence the intensity of the heat coming from the torch is controlled. The flint spark lighter is used to light the torch.

> *NOTE:* The flame spreader is always used on the blowtorch head; the soldering tip is always used on the pencil-flame head.

The propane torch is easily assembled. First determine the head to be used and select the correct orifice to use with the head (for a pencil-flame head, use a brass 0.005 orifice; for a blowtorch head, use a nickel 0.008 orifice). Insert the correct orifice into the burner tube. Screw the head onto the burner tube hand-tight; use a wrench to turn the head just slightly tighter. Add the flame spreader or solder tip to the head, if desired; tighten the attachment screw hand-tight. Check that the control valve is fully clockwise (valve is OFF). Place the valve unit at the top of the replaceable (but not refillable) propane cylinder, insert, push in, and turn simultaneously until the burner unit is secured hand-tight to the cylinder. Do not tighten with a wrench.

> *CAUTION:* Propane is highly flammable. Keep the propane cylinder safely stored away from heat and flame. Discard empty cylinders in a safe place; do not throw them in a fire. Keep the cylinders out of the reach of children. Remove the burner from the cylinder when the torch is not in use.

To light the torch, open the control valve (turn counterclockwise) until a low hiss of escaping gas is heard (if the blowtorch head is being used, open the valve one-half turn further). Immediately ignite the torch with a spark from the flint spark lighter or from the flame of a match. Before opening the control valve further, let the burner remain on a small flame until it is hot.

Adjust the control valve for flame size. For maximum efficiency, adjust the flame from the pencil-flame head so that the blue cone at the center of the flame is $1\frac{1}{2}$ inches long; for the blowtorch head, the cone should be about $\frac{5}{8}$ inch long.

To solder with the propane torch, first tin the soldering tip in accordance with the procedures in Section 13–13. Use a small flame against the tip at all times and retin as necessary. Thoroughly clean the surface to be soldered with sandpaper, emery, or steel wool. Apply the proper soldering flux (refer to Table 10–6). Preheat the surface to be soldered with the flat face of the soldering tip. Apply the solder to the surfaces to be soldered, not to the soldering tip. Let the solder flow. Do not move the workpiece until the soldered area is cool.

You can use the flame-spreader attachment on the blowtorch head to remove cracked or broken tiles and to thaw out frozen water pipes. Warm the tiles sufficiently with the torch to soften the adhesive underneath. Using a stiff-bladed knife, putty knife, or pick, remove the tile. Again apply heat to the adhesive to warm it. Place the new tile in place and press it firmly.

In thawing out pipes, open the faucet that does not deliver

TABLE 10–6. SOLDERS AND ALLOYS

Type of solder or alloy:	Stainless steel solder and flux	General-purpose acid-core solder	All-purpose resin-core electrical solder	Aluminum brazing alloy and flux	Silver solder and flux
Apply solder or alloy when:	Solder flows freely on contact with heated metal	Solder flows freely on contact with heated metal	Solder flows freely on contact with heated metal	Flux becomes a clear liquid	Flux becomes a thin, clear liquid and forms a dull red color
Aluminum For strength in joining sheets, sections, etc.				×	
Chrome plate For trim, when on steel, brass, copper, or nickel alloys (not on die castings)	×				
Copper or bronze For electrical equipment, fittings, tubing, utensils, etc.		×	×		
Galvanized iron or steel For cans, buckets, tanks, eaves, troughs, etc.		×			
Silver and silver plate For jewelry, flatware, etc.	×				×

1	2	3	4	5	6
Stainless steel For appliances, kitchen equipment, or wherever strength is needed	×				×
Steel For utensils, pipes, sheets, tool steels, motors, etc.	×				×
Unlike metals Such as steel to brass	Unlike metals with × 's in the same vertical column can be joined. For example, copper and galvanized iron can be joined with general-purpose solder.				

water. Starting at that faucet, work back slowly with the flame until a free flow of water is restored. Do not start heating the pipe at an intermediate point. Avoid excessive heat on soldered pipe joints and on nearby studs; use an asbestos board behind the pipe to act as a heat shield.

Remove putty and paint as follows. Using a low flame, apply heat slowly along the putty to soften it. Use a scraper to remove it. Use the flame-spreader attachment on the blowtorch head to soften paint for easy removal. Aim the flame just ahead of a paint scraper, moving the flame obliquely to the surface (never at a right angle to the surface).

The torch can also be used to heat conduit for easy bending. Secure the conduit and place a piece of BX cable through it; this will prevent the conduit from creasing when it is bent. Place a piece of pipe over one end to aid in bending the conduit. Heat the conduit for several minutes with the torch by moving the flame slowly back and forth across the area to be bent. Bend the conduit, quench the heated section with water, and withdraw the BX cable.

If the torch flame is inefficient or will not light, the orifice is clogged and must be cleaned. Use a wrench to remove the head from the burner tube; be careful to check the direction of the orifice when it comes out of the burner tube. Now reverse the direction of the orifice, place it in the head, and screw the head hand-tight back onto the burner tube. Open and close the control valve rapidly several times to blow gas and impurities through the orifice. Remove the head, reverse the orifice, and reassemble the head to the burner tube. Tighten hand-tight and then use a wrench to turn the head just slightly further.

Oxidation and charring may be removed from the heads and accessories with steel wool. Store the torch in a safe place, away from heat, flames, and children.

10–11.   PUTTY KNIFE (SCRAPER)

A **putty knife** or *scraper* is a tool of many uses. Specifically, it can be used to remove paint, old gaskets, wallpaper, undercoating, and grease; it can be used to apply plaster, wood filler, putty, and automobile body filler; and it can be used to scrape furniture. In a pinch you can use a stiff-bladed putty knife to pry, to open paint cans, as a screwdriver, and as a chisel.

High-quality putty knives (Fig. 10–9) have mirror-finished high-carbon steel blades that are hardened, tempered, and ground. Blades should pass completely through shatterproof handles. Some blades are straight; others have chisel edges. Blades are available with either a *stiff blade* or with a *flexible blade*. The stiff blades are more useful for scraping; the flexible blades are more useful when applying filler and putty and removing wallpaper.

(A)

(B)

Figure 10–9 (A) Putty knife and (B) scraper.

Narrow-bladed tools are classified as putty knives; wide-bladed tools are classified as scrapers. Blade widths range from 1 to 4 inches.

Keep putty knives and scrapers clean. Sharpen chisel edges with an oilstone or, if necessary, by regrinding.

10–12.   RIPPING BAR (PINCH BAR, PRY BAR)

Ripping bars, pinch bars, and **pry bars** all have one function: to pry two objects, such as nailed boards, crates, or stuck windows, apart. The only differences between the various bars are the types of ends and the sizes (Fig. 10–10).

Pry bars are the smallest, between $\frac{7}{8}$ by 7 inches and $1\frac{3}{4}$ by $14\frac{1}{2}$ inches with one or two ends clawed for nail pulling. Pinch bars are from $\frac{1}{2}$ by 16 inches to $\frac{7}{8}$ by 42 inches and have a long, tapered end that is used as a sturdy line-up tool, with a blunt chisel tip on the other end. The ripping bars are from $\frac{1}{2}$ by 12 inches to $\frac{7}{8}$ by 36 inches and have one chisel end and one slotted claw. (Refer also to the ripping chisel, Section 3–6).

To pry two objects apart, start first with the smaller pry bar and work up to the larger pinch or ripping bar, as required. Place the clawed edge under the board or nail to be pried loose. Press on the bar. The tool leverage can be increased by placing a piece of scrap wood under the offset bend. Wedges can be placed between the partially separated pieces.

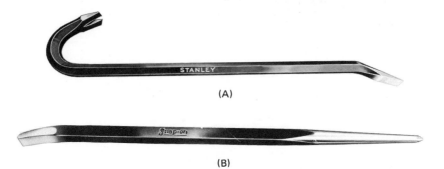

(A)

(B)

Figure 10–10 (A) Ripping bar and (B) pinch bar.

10–13.   RIVETER

Rivets are used to join together two workpieces made of thin metal, wood, canvas, leather, plastics, fiber, and other materials. The rivets replace screws, bolts, nuts, spot welds, and solder joints. They are easy to use, fast, effective, make strong joints, and are economical.

The **rivet tool** shown in Fig. 10–11 installs rivets from one side only; this is called *blind riveting*, because you don't need to see the other side of the material. This feature makes this riveter very popular for home, farm, and industrial use. The rivets used in this type of riveter have clinching mandrels through the center of the rivets. The rivet tool has two handles, which cause a pair of jaws to grip the rivet mandrel and pull the mandrel through the rivet head, flattening the head against the workpiece. The riveter is about 10 inches long.

Figure 10–12 illustrates two workpieces being joined together with rivets; note that this is a blind rivet installation. As the top of the illustration shows, a rivet with a clinching mandrel is inserted through a predrilled hole. The riveter jaws grasp the mandrel and pull the head of the mandrel against the rivet, which in turn flattens

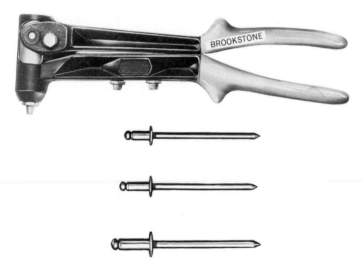

Figure 10–11 Riveter.

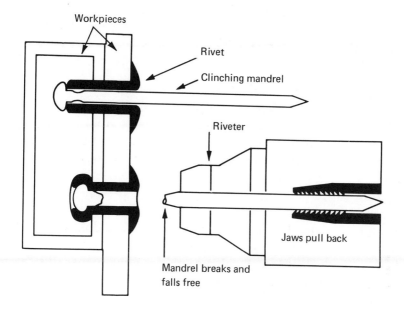

Figure 10–12 Blind rivets.

the rivet against the workpiece, making a tight joint. When the rivet and joint are tight, the mandrel breaks and falls free, leaving a neat riveted joint on both sides of the workpieces.

Rivets for the rivet tool come in several diameters, including $\frac{3}{32}$, $\frac{1}{8}$, $\frac{5}{32}$, and $\frac{3}{16}$ inch. Rivet lengths also vary; use $\frac{3}{16}$-inch-long rivets for thicknesses up to $\frac{1}{8}$ inch; $\frac{1}{4}$ up to $\frac{3}{16}$-inch thickness, $\frac{3}{8}$ up to $\frac{5}{16}$-inch thickness, and $\frac{7}{16}$-inch-long rivets for thicknesses up to $\frac{3}{8}$ inch. If you are using very thin workpieces, you can add a flat washer to the rivet to give extra thickness. The proper length of rivet is when the rivet protrudes no more than one diameter (rivet diameter) through the thickness of the materials.

To use the riveter, first select the rivets to be used. Predrill holes (with the diameters of the rivets to be used) through the workpiece. Check that the rivet fits properly. Open the riveter handles. Select the proper hole diameter on the riveter head and screw or slide (as applicable) the proper tool head into position. Place the rivet into the tool and close the handles slightly to grip the rivet. Insert the rivet into the predrilled hole and squeeze the handles. Alternately open and squeeze the riveter handles until the mandrel breaks off. Shake the mandrel free from the riveter.

10–14.   SANDING BLOCKS

Sanding blocks hold abrasive papers (Section 10–2) and provide a flat surface that distributes even pressure over the workpiece. The blocks keep softer areas in wood workpieces from being sanded below the surface of the harder fiberous areas, and the sanding block also prevents you from rounding the edges and corners of the workpieces.

You can buy a sanding block similar to the one in Fig. 10–13. A plastic body block fits into your hand comfortably. A 2- by 7-inch rubber pad under the abrasive paper makes sanding a workpiece smooth an easy task. It even dispenses its own sandpaper from a 5-foot roll stored inside. To change the abrasive paper, lift the release level, tear off the unused paper, pull out a new length, and close the lever.

Sanding blocks are available with felt pads and a metallic bottom with tungsten carbide chips adhered to the metal. These blocks

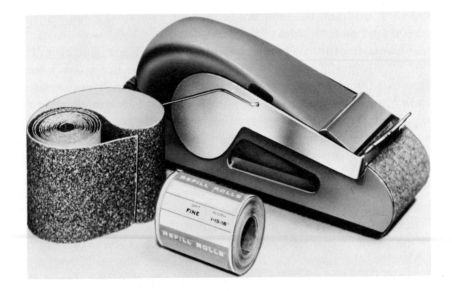

Figure 10–13 Sanding blocks may be bought or made in the shop.

measure approximately 5½ by 3 inches and are very durable. Residue can be brushed from the grits with a file brush; gummy residue can be removed with a solvent.

You can make your own sanding blocks. A convenient size is a block of ¾ by 5½ by 3¼ inches. Standard 9- by 11-inch sheets of abrasive paper can be torn into four equal pieces. The paper can be held on by hand or stapled or tacked into place along the edges. Special-purpose sanding blocks can be designed with curved or rounded edges and of various sizes for special applications.

When sanding wood with the sanding block, stroke with the wood grain unless you are doing very rough sanding when it is permissible to sand across the wood grain. Sanding across the grain leaves cuts that are sometimes difficult to remove. Sand from one end of the workpiece to the other in continuous strokes. Use coarse-grit abrasive papers followed by finer-grit papers until you attain the smoothness you desire.

10–15.   SCRAPER (WOOD SCRAPER, PAINT AND GLUE SCRAPER)

The **scraper** (Fig. 10–14) is used to scrape wood, remove paint, remove glue, remove barnacles, and to clean grease or other residue from surfaces (refer also to Section 10–11). Scrapers are available with hardwood or aluminum handles in a range of types and sizes from 6 inches long with cutter widths of 1½ inches to 10 inches long with cutter widths of 2½ inches; the smaller scrapers are handy for window sashes, windows, and work in close quarters.

Scraper blades come in many shapes. Flat, hooked, serrated,

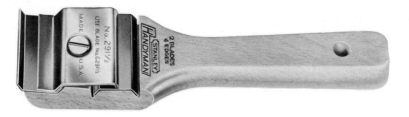

Figure 10–14 The scraper is used to scrape wood and to remove paint and glue.

two-sided, and four-sided blades are some of the types available. Many have reversible blades (the scraper illustrated has a reversible hooked blade and it also stores one blade).

Blades may be held in simply with a screw or two blades held back to back may be driven into a slot in the handle. To remove the back-to-back blades, place the handle in a vise. Use an old screwdriver and a light hammer to tap the blades out of the slot. Replace them in pairs.

Hand scrapers without handles are also available. A typical hand scraper is 3 by 5 inches in size.

In using a scraper, hold it flat against the surface to be scraped. Pull with an even pressure distributed across the blade; don't put more pressure on one side of the blade than on the other side or you'll gouge the workpiece.

Sharpen a scraper blade with a file. File at the same angle as the angle of the original bevel. Each stroke of the file should pass all the way across the blade. Remove the burr from the back edge of the blade with an oilstone.

10–16.   TERMINAL (ELECTRICAL) CRIMPER

A **terminal crimper** (Fig. 10–15) is used to crimp insulated solderless terminals to ends of wire and to make wire splices. The solderless terminals are handy for all outdoor wiring connections where power is not available for soldering, such as in automobiles. These crimpers are also very handy for wiring connections indoors to television antenna wires, antenna rotator wires, loudspeaker wiring, and so on.

The 8-inch terminal crimper shown in Fig. 10–15(A) is an all-purpose tool. In addition to crimping solderless terminals onto AWG No. 22 to No. 10 wire, it also strips No. 22 to No. 10 AWG wire, cuts solid or stranded wire, cuts 4–40, 6–32, 8–32, 10–24, and 10–32 screws cleanly without burrs or thread damage, measures wire gauges, and performs electrical and mechanical crimps.

Place wire to be cut between the cutting edges and squeeze the crimper handles until the wire is cut. Measure the amount of insulation to be stripped off using the stripping gauge on the side of the crimper. Place the insulated wire into the proper gauge stripping slot. Close the crimper handles; the stripper slots cut through the

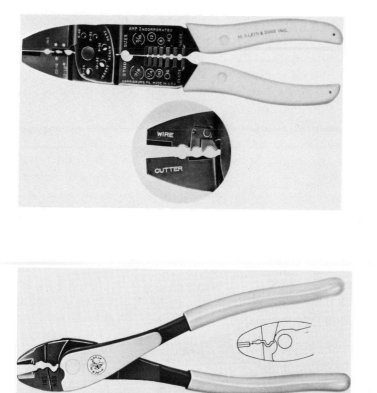

Figure 10–15 Terminal crimper.

insulation but do not cut the wire. With the handles closed, pull the wire so that the insulation is stripped off. Select the desired solderless terminal and place it over the bare wire. Place the terminal into the proper crimper grooved jaws for the gauge of wire being used. The crimper jaws are located at the top of the crimper tool.

To cut a screw or bolt, thread the fastener into the appropriate threads of the tool. The screw length exposed *plus* ⅛ inch (the thickness of one jaw of the tool) will be the length of the cut screw. Squeeze the handles together to cut the screw.

10–17.   TIN SNIPS

Tin snips are hand tools that provide a shearing force for cutting various types of sheet metal, stainless steel, and monel metal up to

18 gauge into pieces of various shapes. They are ideal to help you with rain-gutter, spout, vent, and ducting installations and to cut other sheet metals. Forged high-carbon heat-treated steel jaws cut smooth and evenly with a minimum effort. Tin-snip lengths are 7 to 12 inches; jaws cut from 1¾ to 3 inches (in one closing of the jaws).

Tin snips are divided into four types (Fig. 10–16) according to the pattern cut: regular, straight or curved, left, and right cuts. Regular-cut tin snips are used to cut straight lines and also curves in easily accessible locations. Straight- or curved-cut tin snips cut straight lines, circles, squares, or any pattern. This tin snip, often called a compound-action combination snip, is the most useful tin snip for overall metal work. Left-cut tin snips cut short straight lines or left cuts in locations where it is advantageous to keep the handles and the hand away from the metal stock. Right-cut tin snips cut to the right.

Compound-action pipe and duct snips (Fig. 10–17) are used to cut sheet-metal pipes and ducts, vinyl asbestos tile, and asbestos shingles. This snip cuts a ³⁄₁₆-inch waste strip of metal that curls out

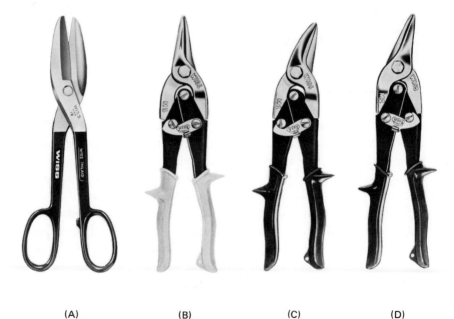

(A)   (B)   (C)   (D)

Figure 10–16 Tin snips: (A) regular; (B) straight or curved cuts; (C) left cuts; (D) right cuts.

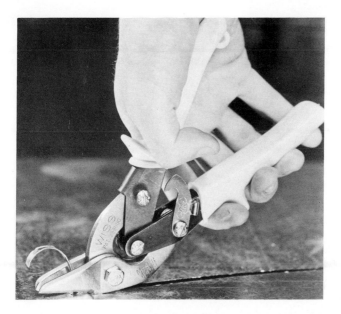

Figure 10–17 Pipe and duct snips remove a $\frac{3}{16}$ inch waste
strip from the workpiece.

of the top of the snips; this prevents injury to the operator's hands.
Pipe and duct snips can make their own starting hole.

To cut straight lines with tin snips, lay the workpiece on a bench
with the guideline extending off the bench. Hold the workpiece with
one hand and cut with the other, always holding the tin snips at a
right angle to the workpiece. The top blade of the tin snips should
cut along the scribed line. The portion of the workpiece being cut
off will bend below and out of the way of the tin snips. Keep the tin
snips as far into the workpiece as possible so that the cutting is done
from a point as near the pivot as possible. Use even pressure. Keep
the faces of the tin-snip jaws perpendicular to the workpiece to prevent the cut edge from becoming bent or burred. Gloves should be
worn to protect the hands from sharp edges and burrs.

When cutting curves, make the cut as continuous as possible.
Stopping and starting at different points causes rough edges with
sharp slivers of metal. When extra leverage is necessary, place the
tin snips on the workbench and bear down on the upper handle.

When a hole or opening is to be cut into a workpiece with tin
snips, first cut a hole into the workpiece with a small cold chisel.

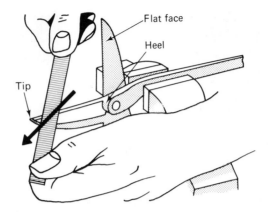

Figure 10–18 Sharpening tin snips.

Make the hole large enough to allow the tin-snip tips to enter, open, and cut.

Do not attempt to cut material heavier than the tin snips can handle. Don't use the tin snips as a hammer.

Dull tinsnips can be sharpened with an oilstone or a file. To sharpen, clamp the snips in a vise and use a file as shown in Fig. 10–18. The file is used on the beveled edges only (never on the flat face). Stroke only in the direction shown—across the full length of the edge and away from the edge. To remove the wire edge on the face of the snips (made from the filing on the beveled edge side), draw the face lightly across an oilstone from the pivot to the tip. After use, apply a light coat of machine oil to the snips.

10–18.   WIRE STRIPPER

Wire strippers are used to remove insulation from solid or stranded wires without nicking or breaking strands of the conductor wire. The wire stripper shown in Fig. 10–19(A) is inexpensive and adequate for occasional use. It is 5 inches long, has a spring to hold the cutting jaws open, and the cutting-jaw closure is adjustable for conductors of different sizes.

To set the jaw closure to the proper wire-gauge opening, loosen the screw and slide the screw, cam, and indicator until the indicator points to the gauge of the wire being cut. Tighten the screw. Place the wire into the open jaws and close the jaws tightly on the insulated wire. Pull the wire and strippers in opposite directions as the insulation is stripped from the wire. Figure 10-20 illustrates a special wire stripper for stripping insulation from coax cable (RG-59U). Three notches in the handles provide the correct jaw openings for cutting through and stripping the outside insulation, the shielding, and the insulation of the inner conductor.

Figure 10-19(B) illustrates a wire stripper for use in production work. The wire to be stripped is placed into the proper wire gauge slot, the handles are squeezed and are then released; the wire is stripped. During this operation, the tool grips the wire, cuts through the insulation, and strips the insulation off. An adjustable guide on the head of the tool can be set to remove from $\frac{1}{4}$ to 1 inch of insulation for every squeeze of the handle. The hardened jaws of this 7-inch stripper are easily replaced. Six openings handle wire sizes from No. 8 through No. 22.

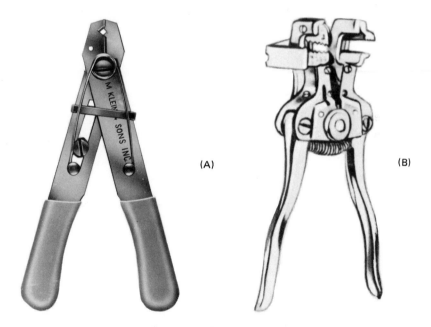

(A)   (B)

Figure 10-19 Wire strippers: (A) inexpensive model; (B) model used where extensivé wire stripping is performed.

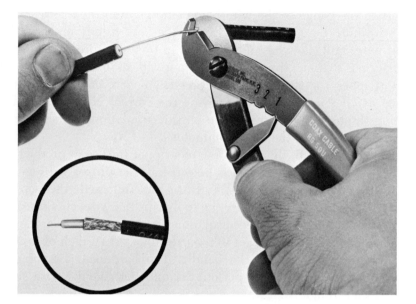

Figure 10–20 This special wire stripper is used to strip the insulation, shield, and inner conductor insulation from coax cable.

planes

Figure 11–1 Planes: (A) block; (B) jack (smoothing, fore, jointer); (C) spoke shave; (D) trimming.

11-1.   GENERAL DESCRIPTION

A **plane** is a tool used by carpenters, cabinetmakers, home craftsmen, and hobbyists to smooth, shape, trim, bevel, and chamfer a wood workpiece. The plane is especially useful in removing wood from doors, drawers, and other workpieces to ensure proper fit. The plane (Fig. 11–2) consists of a chisel-like beveled blade, cap iron, bottom, handle, knob, adjusting nut, and a lateral adjusting lever. The tempered-steel cutter blade, which has a beveled ground and honed cutting edge, is often called the *plane iron*. The cap iron clamps to the blade (plane iron) and is used to curve and break the shavings coming through the mouth of the bottom. The bottom is an iron casting that has its sides and bottom machined; the bottoms of most planes are flat, but grooved bottom planes that have less drag are available for use with green and gummy wood. The handles and knobs of larger planes are made of hardwood.

The types of planes discussed in this chapter are the planes most often used: *block, jack (smoothing, fore,* and *jointer), trimming,* and *spoke shave.* The block plane is used primarily to plane the end grain of a piece of wood. The jack plane (and associated planes) is used to plane surfaces and edges of wood to a smooth finish. The trimming plane is used usually by hobbyists, to shape small workpieces. The spoke shave is used to smooth *curved* surfaces.

Let's assume that you have a long workpiece with a wavy edge

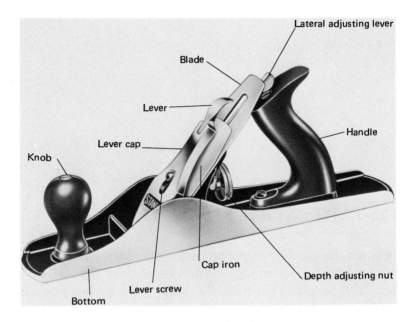

Figure 11–2 Parts of a plane.

that you'd like to shape to a smooth flat surface. Which plane should you select? You should select the plane having the longest body, because a small plane (such as a block plane) tends to ride up and down irregular surfaces. Longer planes, such as the jack, fore, and jointer planes, trim the peaks off the irregular edges. Thus the longer the plane, the better it is for trimming peaks. The jack plane is probably the best compromise in body length and is recommended as your first plane. The block plane is the second-most-needed plane.

One other tool that could be mentioned in the plane category is the *forming tool*. The forming tool consists of a holder and a blade made up of hundreds of curved teeth, which are actually miniature milling cutters. The forming tool is discussed in detail in Chapter 6.

11–2.   APPLICATION OF PLANES

The first step in correctly using a plane is to set the blade straight laterally and to the required depth. Hold the plane upside down with one hand and sight from the front into the blade. On jack, smoothing, fore, jointer, and adjustable block planes (if so equipped), adjust the lateral adjusting lever until the blade is straight. On block planes without a lateral adjustment lever, loosen the adjusting wheel and set the blade straight; on this plane, also set the blade depth and retighten the wheel. If the blade of a plane is not straight, thicker wood cuts will be taken on one side of the workpiece than on the other side.

Rotate the depth-adjusting nut to move the blade to the correct depth position. Set the blade deep for rough cuts, shallow for fine cuts. The plane can cut shavings as thin as the pages of this book.

Check that the cap iron screw is tight, causing the cap iron to be right against the blade. Also check that no wood chips are wedged between the cap iron and the blade. The cap iron should be only $\frac{1}{16}$ inch from the end of the blade for planing softwoods, less than $\frac{1}{16}$ inch for hardwoods. The cap iron breaks the curled shavings coming up through the mouth of the plane.

With the plane properly set for cutting, secure a workpiece in a vise, clamp, or other improvised holding device (refer to Chapter 4, especially Sections 4–6 and 4–17). The best height for the workpiece is just slightly above your waist. For practice, use a piece of scrap wood of the same species as your workpiece. Grasp the plane handle with one hand and the knob with the other. Place the front of the plane (the area in front of the blade) on the workpiece. Level the plane and hold it square (parallel to the floor) to the workpiece.

The plane will be moved with the grain of the wood. Start at one end of the workpiece with the blade *off* the end and push the plane across the board with a long, continuous, even stroke. Keep the pressure constant. At the beginning of the cut, a little more pressure should be applied to the knob end of the plane. When the plane is on the board, equal pressure is applied to the handle and knob. At the completion of the cut, when the front of the plane moves off the board, ease up on the pressure on the knob. The regulation of pressure to the knob at the start and at the conclusion of each stroke will keep the ends of the workpiece from becoming rounded.

One effective method in learning to plane correctly is to draw several parallel lines along the edge (along the grain) of a piece of scrap wood. Set the plane to remove very thin strips of wood. Plane along the edge and note whether you are planing straight and you are removing the same amount of material from both sides. You can also place parallel lines on the top and bottom surfaces of a workpiece near an edge of a workpiece. Plane down to the parallel lines.

You will sometimes get better cutting action if the plane is moved at a slight lateral angle, about 15°. The squareness of the cut should be checked often in all directions (refer to Section 9–8).

To chamfer or bevel the edge of a workpiece, first mark the wood as to location and angle of cut. Tip the plane to the desired angle and, holding the angle steady, plane with continuous straight strokes with the grain of the workpiece.

End-grain cutting (board edges) must be done carefully to prevent the end of the board and surface fibers of the workpiece from splitting. There are several practical methods that can be used to eliminate this splitting: (1) the edges can be beveled at 45°; (2) the workpiece can be *sandwiched* between two scrap pieces of wood and all three pieces are then planed; (3) the plane should be angled laterally at 15° as it is pushed across the end grain; (4) plane from the ends toward the center. Then plane the hump out of the center. End-grain planing is usually done with the block plane.

11–3.   CARE OF PLANES

The plane is only as good as the cutting edge of its blade. The blade has to be sharp, and this means frequent honing to renew the edge and an occasional grinding when the blade is nicked or completely dulled.

Honing is accomplished on an oilstone heavily coated with light machine oil. The blade is then held at 30° and honed. The simplest method of holding the blade steady at 30° is to purchase a honing jig that clamps the blade into place. The jig is rolled along the oilstone as the edge is honed. You can also improvise a jig by using a bolt, a nut, and a wing nut. Choose a bolt that is long enough to obtain a 30° angle. Clamp the blade between the nut and the wing nut. After honing the edge, rub the back of the edge very lightly in a figure-eight direction to remove the burr left by honing.

In regrinding, adjust the grinder tool rest, or improvise a guide, at an angle of 25°. Hold the blade firmly at the 25° angle and move the blade back and forth all the way across the grinding wheel; this method prevents wear on the wheel. Keep the blade cool by dipping it frequently in water.

When reassembling the cap iron to the blade, place the cap iron slightly back from the cutting edge of the *unbeveled* side of the blade; about $\frac{1}{16}$ inch distance is correct for planing softwoods, a little less than $\frac{1}{16}$ inch for hardwoods.

Plane blades, as well as all other plane parts, are replaceable on planes (and other tools, too) manufactured by the large, well-known, and reputable tool manufacturers.

Keep the plane blades lightly oiled with light machine oil. When a plane is not in use, lay it on its side to protect the blade. When storing the plane, retract the blade. Protect planes from being banged by other tools.

11–4.   BLOCK PLANE

The smallest plane that is used for general shop use is the **block plane**. It may be used to cut edges of small workpieces, but its main use is in cutting across the end grains of wood. The plane is constructed so that the cutter angle is low, between 12 and 21°; this low angle enables the block plane to cut end grains more easily. It can be used with one hand, but I recommend two because of the added control.

There are several styles of block planes available. The one shown in Fig. 11–1(A) has a depth-adjusting nut and a lateral-adjusting lever. In essence, the block plane illustrated is a small smoothing or jack plane (Section 11–5). Another, less-expensive type of block plane has a wheel that rotates a screw and tightens the blade within the plane frame. When the wheel is rotated to loosen the blade, the blade depth and lateral angle may be set by hand. The wheel is then rotated, clamping the blade into the desired position. Block planes are from 6 to 7 inches long, with cutter widths of from 1⅜ to 1⅝ inches. The blade is mounted with the bevel of the cutting edge *up*, toward the top of the plane.

11–5.   JACK (SMOOTHING, FORE, JOINTER) PLANE

Figure 11–1(B) illustrates the **jack plane**; it also is representative of the *smoothing*, the *fore*, and the *jointer plane*. The only difference in name is with regard to length and blade width. Plane lengths are: smoothing, from 5½ to 10 inches; jack, from 10 to 15 inches; fore, 18 inches; and jointer, from 22 to 25 inches. The jack plane blade width is 2 inches and the large plane blade width is 2⅜ inches.

These planes are for general use in surface and edge straightening and in trimming. The longer the plane, the better that plane is for cutting peaks. The jack plane is the plane most often used by the home woodworker.

The blade of the planes in this group is mounted with the blade bevel toward the *bottom* side of the plane. When storing the plane, withdraw the blade so that it does not protrude through the bottom of the plane. This protects the blade (and any object, including fingers!) that might come into contact with it.

11–6.   SPOKE SHAVE

Spoke shaves, so named because of their original use in shaving wheel spokes, are used to smooth or chamfer convex or concave curved wood surfaces. In this respect the function is exactly opposite that of a block or jack plane; the planes are designed to *remove* curves and make the workpiece flat, whereas the spoke shave is designed to *develop* and *smooth* curves. The spoke shave is grasped with both hands and is pulled or pushed along the workpiece, which is securely clamped with a vise or clamp. The spoke shave cuts only in the direction of the wood grain.

The spoke shave is about 10 inches long and has a 2⅛-inch-wide cutter. On one model the blade depth and angle are set by hand after a thumbscrew is loosened. On another spoke-shave model, two screws are provided to set the blade depth and angle.

11–7.   TRIMMING PLANE

The **trimming plane** is a small lightweight plane, usually from 3 to 4 inches in length, with a 1-inch cutter. It is used by hobbyists and craftsmen to plane small pieces of wood used in models or delicate workpieces. A single knurled nut is used to clamp the blade to the desired depth of cut.

12

pliers

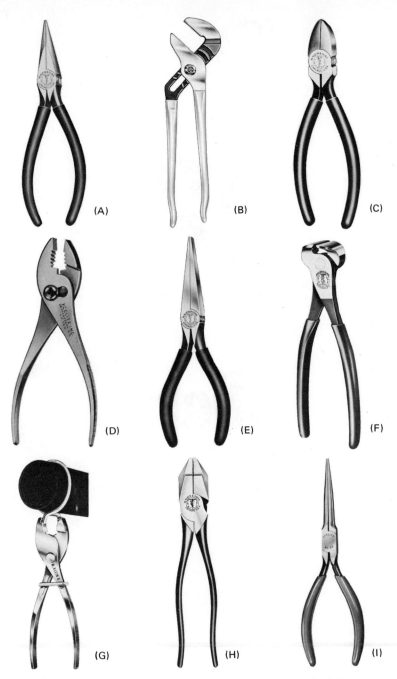

Figure 12–1 Pliers: (A) chain-nose; (B) channel; (C) combination slip-joint; (D) diagonal; (E) duck-bill; (F) end-cutting; (G) hose-clamp; (H) lineman's; (I) needle-nose.

12–1.   GENERAL DESCRIPTION

Pliers are the tools most often used for gripping, cutting, bending, forming, or holding metals or other materials. They can also be used to strip insulation from wire. Numerous types, sizes, and shapes of pliers are available, many with a very specific function. The general types of pliers most frequently used are: *chain-nose, channel, combination slip-joint, diagonal, duck-bill, end-cutting, hose-clamp, lineman's,* and *needle-nose.*

Pliers consist of a pair of milled jaws, a pivot point, and a pair of handles. Pliers are made of heat-treated tool steel and are often chrome-plated to prevent rust. Jaws are made narrow to fit tight places and some have cutting edges for cutting soft wire and stock. Handles are often knurled for a more positive hand grip, and a coil spring may be placed between the handles to hold them open. The size of the pliers is determined by the overall length, usually between 4 and 10 inches.

Midget pliers, only about 4 inches long, are used for close work, such as holding, bending, and the cutting of fine wires in electronic, radio, television, and jewelry making and repair work. Pliers 5 to 6 inches long are for general all-purpose work. Pliers 7 inches or longer are used for heavy-duty work.

For most shops, one pair each of channel, combination slip-joint, diagonal, and needle-nose pliers is sufficient. Also, I suggest a locking plier wrench (Section 17–8).

12–2.   APPLICATION OF PLIERS

To hold a workpiece with pliers, place the object as close to the pivot point as possible; this allows the gripping hand to squeeze the handles with the greatest force. If the pliers have a coil spring between the handles, hold them as shown in Fig. 12–2; if there is no spring, hold the pliers as shown but place the little finger on the inside, against the plier handle. By opening and closing your fingers, you can control the pressure at the jaws. When using pliers for electrical work, be sure to remove electrical power. As a precaution, insulate the plier handles with special rubber grips that are sold commercially and can be slipped over the metal handles; the handles may also be wrapped with several layers of electrical insulating tape.

To cut a piece of wire or stock with pliers, place it between the cutting edges of the jaws so that the wire or stock is perpendicular

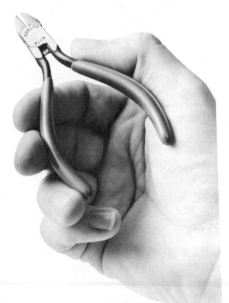

Figure 12–2 If the pliers have a spring between the handles, grasp them as shown. If there is no spring, place the little finger on the inside of the handle against the handle.

to the edges. Hold the wire or stock with one hand and place the other hand around the ends of the handles. Squeeze the handles firmly.

In bending and forming a metal workpiece, place the workpiece between the jaws as close to the pivot point as possible; ensure that no part of the workpiece comes into contact with the cutting jaws. Hold the handles closed tight and bend and form the workpiece into the desired shape.

When stripping (removing) insulation from wires with pliers, place the wire in the cutting edges or notches provided with about ¼ inch of wire extending through the pliers. If more than one notch is available, choose the proper size notch for the gauge of the wire being stripped. Lightly close the handles so that the cutting edges cut into the insulation; rotate the wire in the cutting edges to *score* the insulation. Pull the insulation-covered wire slowly, stripping off the insulation. Inspect the wire to be sure that the plier cutting edges did not damage the wire. (Special tools are available for stripping insulation. See Section 10–16.)

You can use pliers as a tiny vise, clamp, or to dissipate heat from a joint when soldering. Place a heavy rubber band or several smaller rubber bands around the handles to hold the jaws closed against the workpiece, which is secured in the jaws. If you want to protect a workpiece from damage from the serrated jaws of the pliers, wrap tape around the jaws.

Use pliers only for their intended uses. Do not try to increase the leverage of plier handles by lengthening the handles with sections of pipe or other extensions. You can slip rubber tubing over the handles to give a cushioning effect to your hands.

12–3.   CARE OF PLIERS

Damaged or worn serrated jaws may be repaired by filing. If possible, separate the jaws by removing the pivot nut and screw. Place the plier jaw in the protected jaws of a vise. Restore or repair damaged serrations by filing the jaw serrations with a three square file.

The cutters on some pliers can be reground. Before attempting to grind, however, inspect the cutter design to determine if the cutting edges will close after material is ground from the edges. Do not attempt to sharpen pliers (such as diagonal pliers) that are not designed for regrinding.

To regrind plier cutting edges, separate the pliers, if possible, and place in the protected jaws of a vise. Grind the cutting edges so that the reground bevel is parallel to the old bevel. Grind the same amount of stock from both jaws. Cool the jaws frequently in water to prevent loss of temper (loss of temper makes the cutters practically useless).

Keep your pliers clean. Occasionally wipe them with a light coat of oil. Place a drop of oil on the pivot pin and open and close the pliers several times to work the oil into the pin.

12–4. CHAIN-NOSE PLIERS

Chain-nose pliers are used for the assembly of miniature electronic parts, mechanical assembly, wire forming, and for holding small parts. A set of cutting edges to cut soft wire or stock may be located in the jaws near the pivot point. Chain-nose pliers are very similar to needle-nose pliers (Section 12–12), except that chain-nose pliers are shorter, wider, and hence stronger. Chain-nose pliers are $5\frac{1}{4}$ to 6 inches long with jaw lengths of about $1\frac{1}{8}$ inches. Some models incorporate a plated coil spring between the handles to hold the jaws open.

12–5.   CHANNEL PLIERS

Channel pliers are similar to the familiar combination slip-joint pliers (Section 12–6) except that the jaws stay nearly parallel. This is a decided advantage because the channel pliers can grip large flat surfaces such as the flats on hexagon nuts used for sink trap plumbing. The channels in one leg of the plier provide for quick nonslip adjustments. The long handles give additional leverage and reach.

In use, the jaws are positioned parallel at approximately the proper opening and are locked into place by engaging the tongue in the proper groove. The jaws do not slip even under heavy pressure.

Channel pliers, similar to those in Fig. 12–1, but with slight modifications, are known by numerous names, including power

groove, utility, arc joint, mechanic's, pump, joint, and long inter-
locking joint pliers. Lengths of the channel pliers are from 6½ to 16
inches, with maximum capacities of from 1 to 4½ inches, respectively.

12–6.　COMBINATION SLIP-JOINT PLIERS

Combination slip-joint pliers are used to hold or bend small pieces
of flat or round metal stock, tubing, bars, wires, and a variety of
other items. The slip joint allows for adjustment of the serrated jaws
to a wider opening that gives more closing force leverage to the
gripping hand. Some combination slip-joint pliers have a short set
of wire-cutting jaws near the pivot pin. The serrations on the end of
the jaws are fine; serrations at the center of the jaws are coarse. The
capacity of the jaws (the opening for insertion of the object to be
held) is approximately ¾ inch for 5-inch pliers and 1½ inches for 10-
inch pliers.

　If the pliers become loose at the pivot, tighten the pivot nut. If
the nut continually loosens, retighten it and then, using a punch and
hammer, burr the pivot threads so that the nut cannot be loosened.

12–7.　DIAGONAL PLIERS

Diagonal pliers are used to cut soft wire, small stock, and to cut cotter pins to proper length. Diagonal pliers have short jaws with the
cutting edges at a slight angle that enables the diagonals to make
close cuts. Some pliers are notched for wire stripping; the jaws are
not used for gripping. Lengths are approximately 6 inches.

12–8.　DUCK-BILL PLIERS

Duck-bill pliers are named because of the similarity of their shape
to a duck's beak. They are also similar in shape and function to needle-nose and chain-nose pliers (Sections 12–12 and 12–4, respectively). Duck-bill pliers are used for mechanical and miniature elec-

tronic assembly, wire forming, and for holding small parts. Square bends are made with duck-bill pliers, whereas round bends are made with needle-nose pliers. The lengths of the pliers vary from 5½ to 6½ inches, with jaws from 1¾ to 2¼ inches.

12–9.   END-CUTTING PLIERS

End-cutting pliers are used to cut wire, brads, and nails close to the work. They are also used to pull nails. End-cutting pliers are also known as *nail-nipping pliers* and *pincers*. The jaws are ⅞ inch long; overall end-cutting-plier length is about 7¾ inches.

In cutting off wire, brads, or nails, place the jaws around the object. Grip the pliers at the end of the handles and squeeze until the object is cut. In removing nails, lightly grip the nail with the jaws at the workpiece surface. Hold the pliers at the handle ends so that the rounded side of one of the plier jaws is against the workpiece. Push the handles downward in an arc, prying the nail out of the workpiece. If the handles are lowered to the workpiece and the nail is not completely out, open the jaws and grip the nail again at the workpiece. Continue in this manner until the nail is removed.

12–10.   HOSE-CLAMP PLIERS

If you change a number of automobile radiator hoses and have used combination slip-joint pliers to open the spring-tension hose clamps, you'll welcome **hose-clamp pliers**. Essentially, hose-clamp pliers are combination slip-joint pliers having notched jaws to keep a hose clamp from slipping. Notches are cut into the jaws for gripping the spring with the pliers in either of two positions, each 90° from each other. A slip ring that rides over notches on the plier handles permits the plier jaws to be clamped in a variety of open positions so that the clamp is open and the hose can be adjusted. Hose-clamp pliers are useful both in the installation and removal of hoses. The jaw capacity is from 0 to 1¾ inches; plier lengths are about 7½ inches.

12–11.   LINEMAN'S PLIERS

Lineman's pliers are used to grip flat materials and to bend, cut, and strip insulation from wires. The flat serrated jaws are used to twist wires together. An insulation crusher is built in. Different sizes of lineman's pliers are referred to as *electrician's* and *side-cutting pliers*; lengths vary from 4 to 9 inches.

12–12.   NEEDLE-NOSE PLIERS

Needle-nose pliers (also called long-nose pliers) are used for mechanical assembly; assembly of miniature electronic parts; wire forming; holding washers, nuts, or other small parts; shaping jewelry; and reaching into tight spaces. Some models have jaws curved to an angle of 90° from the handles. The jaws of the needle-nose pliers may also have a set of cutting edges near the pivot point for cutting soft wire or stock. Some models incorporate a plated coil spring between the handles to hold the jaws open. Plier lengths are 6 to 8 inches, with jaw lengths of from $1\frac{1}{2}$ to $2\frac{1}{2}$ inches.

In selecting needle-nose pliers, make sure that the jaws align properly when closed.

13

powered
hand
tools

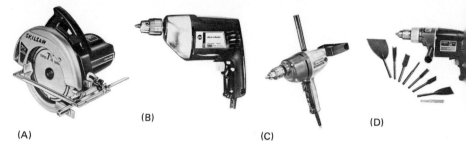

(B)

(A)

(C)

(D)

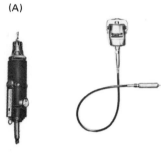

(E)

(F)

(G)

(H)

(I)

(J)

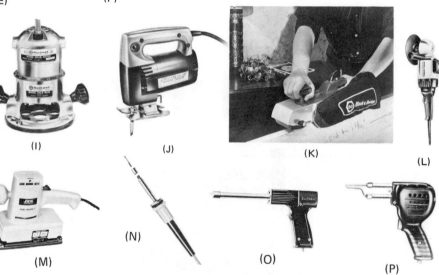

(K)

(L)

(M)

(N)

(O)

(P)

Figure 13–1 Powered hand tools: (A) circular saw; (B) electric drill; (C) heavy duty electric drill; (D) multipurpose drill; (E) modeler's power tool; (F) modeler's power tool with flexible shaft; (G) plane; (H) reciprocating saw; (I) router; (J) saber saw; (K) belt sander; (L) disc sander; (M) finishing sander; (N) miniature soldering iron; (O) pistol-grip soldering iron; (P) instant heat soldering iron; (Q) bench grinder.

(Q)

13–1. GENERAL

Powered hand tools perform many of the same functions as the hand tools described elsewhere in this handbook, but powered hand tools aid you to complete the task more efficiently, with less fatigue, and often with more accuracy. Power tools increase your range of capabilities and save you time. With practice, you can easily learn the basic functions, the capabilities, and the limitations of any powered tool that you may purchase. Once the fundamental operation of the basic tool is mastered, you can extend the range of capabilities of the tool by adding accessories.

As with any tool, the fundamental principles of operation, the use, the extent of the tool's capabilities, its limitations, safe operating procedures, and general care are only learned through practice. I want to emphasize the word *practice* and suggest that when you first encounter a tool, you should plan to spend a few hours *practicing* its use. Sit down in your easy chair and read the section of this chapter that deals with the tool first. Then read the manufacturer's instructions. Pick up the tool; learn the names of its parts. Hold the tool in position. Move its switches. Move its adjustments. Note its safety features and note any unsafe conditions. Locate lubrication points. Now it is time to move to the shop.

Clean up your shop. Make room for your new tool. Get hold of some scrap wood and secure it to your bench. Check that all adjustments on the tool are secure. Plug your tool into the power outlet and turn it on without touching the workpiece. Feel the power in your hands; respect it. Turn the power off. Place the tool to the scrap wood, apply power, and practice using the tool for its basic functions. Try more difficult operations. Extend your knowledge of the tool's capabilities and limitations by varying adjustments, changing angles, or by utilizing various cutters. Once these capabilities are mastered, add accessories to the basic tool. *Practice* with the accessories. *Practice, practice, practice*—until you are thoroughly familiar with the complete operation of the tool. Now you've accomplished something. You have mastered the tool and know its overall capabilities. You are ready to use the powered tool on a workpiece. THINK SAFETY.

The powered hand tools covered in this chapter include: *circular saw, electric drill, grinder, modeler's power tool* (and *accessories*), *plane, reciprocating saw, router, saber saw, sanders (belt, disc, finishing),* and *soldering irons.* Read over the sections describing tools that you possess. Skim the descriptions of tools you don't own because you may gain knowledge that is applicable to tools you do have. The new knowledge may well help you decide the tools you want next.

In purchasing powered hand tools, wait for a sale so that you can save money, but *buy quality tools* from reputable manufacturers. Also, be careful in buying multitools or tools with many accessories; this is usually the merchandiser's method of getting rid of those items that no one else wants. You may never use some of the accessories thrown in with the sale item.

If possible, it is a good idea to buy tools from a manufacturer that has a repair facility or representative located in your city. Know, before you buy, that you can obtain replacement parts for the tool. Also, be sure that the tool has a guarantee, and don't forget to mail it in. Finally, don't buy a tool unless a set of operating instructions, maintenance instructions, and a list of repair parts are included. These suggestions are particularly important if you are buying a used tool.

When purchasing power tools, be sure that you buy a size with a horsepower rating and speed sufficient to accomplish your jobs. Don't consider only the job at hand; consider future tasks. Tools with ball bearings outlast other tools. Motors with slip-clutch gear trains allow the motor to operate even if the drive shaft becomes suddenly jammed, which prevents gear stripping and motor burnout. (If a drive shaft stops rotating because of a jammed blade or whatever, immediately turn off the electrical power.)

For safety you should only buy power tools that are wired in one of two ways, with a three-wire grounded system or double-insulation. These features protect you from electrical shock in case of internal electrical damage. The three-wire grounded system is used with three-prong plugs. If your shop doesn't have a three-wire system, have it rewired, for *safety's sake*. When using three-wire powered tools in other parts of the home, use a properly installed adapter plug. On double-insulated tools (two-wire power), the outer shell of the tool is completely insulated from the wiring.

When you are selecting cutting blades, keep in mind that tungsten carbide blades cost a good deal more than standard blades, but they outlast the standard blades 10:1. Tungsten carbide blades have no teeth; instead, particles of tungsten carbide are fused to the blade. Tungsten carbide blades cut wood, ceramic, countertop material, slate, cement, brick, asbestos, pipe, and stainless steel.

13–2.   APPLICATION OF POWER TOOLS

The application of each of the power tools is described separately under each tool, but here are some general tips applicable to each:

1. Always be safe. Have the workpiece firmly supported and clamped. Take a safe operating position where you can reach the workpiece completely in a balanced position. Power cords should be out of the way; add an extension cord if necessary. The shop should not be cluttered and you should have ample workspace. Be aware of what to do should an accident occur.

2. It is always a good idea to experiment on a scrap workpiece. This will give you a chance to check your procedures, to adjust the tool (such as angle, depth of cut, speed, and feed rate), and may prevent you from making an error and ruining your workpiece.

3. When cutting materials, slower speeds are used for harder materials, higher speeds for softer materials.

13–3. CARE OF POWER TOOLS

The care of each power tool is discussed separately under each tool, but here are a few general tips on care that are applicable to all power tools (remove plug from receptacle before performing these steps):

1. Brush dust away from the tool after use. Occasionally use a vacuum cleaner to clean dust from around the motor (hold the vacuum nozzle close to the cooling fins of the motors and draw the dust out).

2. Remove gum, pitch, and dirt from tools and accessories with a rag dampened with turpentine.

3. Check power cords for frays, cracks, or cuts. Replace the cords in accordance with the manufacturer's instructions if there are frays, cracks, or cuts.

4. Apply oil (or other lubricant) to the tool motor and other moving parts as recommended by the tool manufacturer. Remove and replace old grease as recommended.

5. Regularly check the motor brushes for wear. Excessive sparking indicates worn brushes or springs. Remove and replace the brushes and springs in accordance with the tool manufacturer's recommendations. When new brushes are installed, contour the end of the brushes to fit against the commutator. Do this by placing a fine abrasive paper against the commutator. Lightly rub the brush against the abrasive paper. Check the commutator, too. If it is dirty, rub it with fine abrasive paper and then wipe with a rag slightly dampened with lacquer thinner. Finally, brush and vacuum out all dirt.

13–4. CIRCULAR SAW

The **circular saw** is used to cross-cut or rip wood, Masonite, fiberboard, and similar materials into two or more parts. In addition, it is used to cut mitered joints, to dado, and to bevel edges. It cuts along straight lines only. The circular saw is primarily used to make rather rapid cuts that may be slightly rough, but if care and proper procedures are used, it can make smooth, accurate cuts. A circular saw is almost a necessity if you plan to frame a cottage, add a new room, or remodel an existing room. Its light weight and small size make it portable.

A circular saw is labeled by the size of the blade it uses. Thus a 7¼ circular saw uses a blade that has a diameter of 7¼ inches. Circular saws are available in 6½-, 7¼-, and 8-inch sizes. They are also characterized by the horsepower (hp) and revolutions per minute (rev/min) of the motors, which typically are from 1 to 2½ hp and 4700 to 5200 rev/min.

A 7¼-inch 1½-hp 5200-rev/min saw is more than adequate for most home-building uses. The important items to be concerned with in determining the size you need are the depths (thicknesses of wood) that a saw will cut to at 90° and 45° angles. These are listed in Table 13-1.

Nearly all circular saws have the same features incorporated in them, so your selection is really a personal preference as to manufacturer and style. The features in circular saws include a trigger-grip on–off switch, sawdust ejection through (or around) a retractable blade guard, an adjustable rip fence with an indicating scale, a cut-off guide, a vertical adjustment to control the depth of cut, and a tilting shoe (base) with a graduated scale for making bevel cuts.

Prior to plugging the circular saw cord into an electrical outlet, install the correct blade for the material to be cut (blades are subsequently discussed), set the depth adjustment, the bevel adjustment, and the rip fence (cutoff) guide, if the guide is to be used. To install a blade, use a box wrench (usually provided with the saw) to remove the arbor bolt. Place the blade on the arbor such that the teeth at the front of the saw are pointing upward. When you look directly at the mounted blade, the blade will turn counterclockwise during operation [Fig. 13-1(A)]. Reinstall and tighten the arbor bolt. Loosen the

TABLE 13-1. DEPTH OF CUT OF CIRCULAR SAW

Saw Size (in.)	Depth of Cut at 90° (in.)	Depth of Cut at 45° (in.)
6½	2¹⁄₁₆	1¾
7¼	2⅜	1⅞
8	2¹³⁄₁₆	2¼

depth adjustment; grip the saw shoe and pull it down from the saw. Set the saw so that the depth of the blade and cut will be ¼ inch greater than the thickness of the material to be cut. Tighten the depth adjustment securely. If a bevel cut is to be made, loosen the bevel adjustment; grip and tilt the shoe until the required angle is indicated on the bevel scale. For accurate work, set the angle with a protractor. Tighten the bevel adjustment. If you are making an end cutoff or are ripping a board, loosen the rip-guide adjustment, set the guide to the proper dimension, and retighten the adjustment.

Check carefully that all adjustments are proper and tight. Plug the power cord into an electrical receptacle. Grip the circular saw knob with the left hand and the handle with the right hand (sorry, I haven't seen left-handed circular saws for us lefties). The index finger grips the trigger on–off switch. Momentarily squeeze and release the trigger. Note that the saw blade is traveling in the proper direction. If all is well, you're ready to cut, but first read and understand the following sawing procedures:

1. Firmly support the workpiece. Sawhorses (Section 4–14) are used for this purpose. Position the workpiece with the *best surface facing down to the floor* because the circular saw blade cuts up into the workpiece. With the workpiece positioned in this manner, wood splintering will occur on the rough or back side rather than on the best surface. The scrap to be cut off should be to your right.

2. If necessary, mark the cutting line; no line is required if you are using the rip-fence guide.

3. Position your body out of the line of the cut; keep to the left of the cut.

4. Place the front of the saw shoe flat onto the workpiece with the saw on the part that you are cutting. Don't place the saw on the scrap wood.

5. Slide the saw so that the rip-fence guide is along the edge of the workpiece (Fig. 13–2), parallel to the cut to be made. Note that this guide is only usable for cuts about 6 to 8 inches wide. If the guide isn't to be used, locate the blade so that it is just to the right (in the scrap area) of the cutting line.

6. Pull the trigger and let the saw reach full speed before you start cutting.

7.   Holding the saw with the shoe level on the workpiece (Fig. 13–3), push the saw along the saw line (or hold the rip-fence guide along the edge). Note that as the saw starts into the cut, the blade guard retracts.

8.   Keep the blade on a straight line. Don't twist the saw and bind the blade. This can cause the saw to *kick back*. Hold the saw firmly. Cut as fast as the blade will cut. Don't force the saw sufficiently to appreciably slow the speed of the saw.

9.   When the saw-line cutting guide runs off the end of the workpiece, it is no longer useful. Watch the blade for the last inch or so of cutting. Hold the saw steady as the scrap falls off.

The following hints provide you with additional information for making accurate saw cuts:

1.   To make accurate straight cuts, clamp a piece of straight-edged scrap wood to the workpiece. Run the saw (left side of the saw) along the edge. This technique may be used for making cross, rip, miter, or combination (mitered *and* beveled angle) cuts.

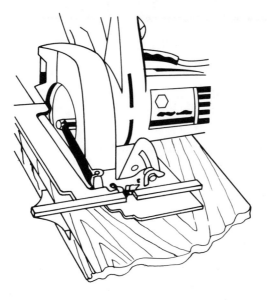

Figure 13–2 Use the rip fence guide as a cutting aid in sawing straight lines.

Figure 13–3 Keep the circular saw shoe flat against the
workpiece.

2.   Tilt the shoe to make bevel cuts (Fig. 13–4). For accurate
      bevel angles, check the shoe with a protractor.

3.   To make a shallow cut (not completely through the
      board), raise the blade and secure it in position. Check
      the depth of cut on a scrap piece of wood before cutting
      the workpiece.

4.   To make a dado cut (a groove), make several shallow cuts.
      You can use a number of cuts to clean out the groove or
      you can use a chisel to remove the wood between several
      shallow cuts.

5.   If you want to cut a notch in a workpiece, remember the
      saw kerf. One surface of the workpiece is cut more than
      the other surface because of the round blade. Finish the
      notch cut with a hand saw.

6.   Plunge cuts can be made into the center of a workpiece.

Secure the workpiece. Start with the saw blade out of the wood. Firmly place the front of the saw shoe against the workpiece. Hold the back of the saw in the air. Manually retract and hold the blade guide. Start the saw. When it is at full speed, lower the back of the saw slowly and carefully into the workpiece. When the blade has passed through the workpiece, release the blade guard and let it snap into position. Continue your cut.

7.   Use sawhorses to support large workpieces.

It goes without saying that a properly selected sharp blade is required for safe, accurate, efficient cutting. *All-purpose* blades (Fig. 13–5) are used for all-purpose wood cutting—cross-cuts, miters, and ripping. *Planer* blades are used for very smooth cuts in all cutting directions. *Cutoff* blades are used for cross cutting, and *rip* blades are used for rip sawing. Special-purpose blades are available to cut plywood and special materials such as countertopping, metal, and masonry.

One attachment that is worth noting is a miter-arm attachment. Two types are available; one is portable. The other is a stationary model that adapts your hand circular saw to a radial-arm-type saw. The circular saw slides accurately along metal tracks. Miter cuts to 45° left or right can be made.

Figure 13–4 Adjust the circular saw bevel adjustment for bevel cuts.

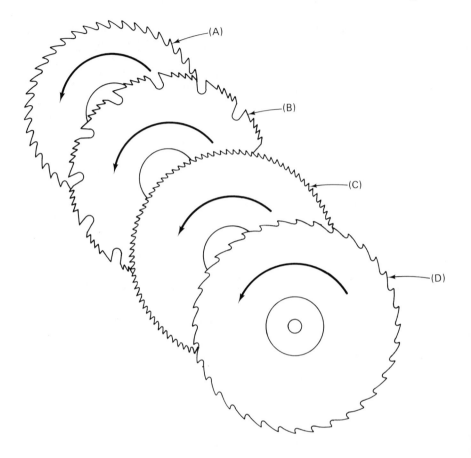

Figure 13–5 Circular saw blades: (A) all purpose; (B) planer; (C) cut-off; (D) rip.

Ensure that your blades remain sharp. Dull blades can be re-sharpened by a professional saw sharpener. Refer to SAWS—SHARPEN-ING AND REPAIRING in the Yellow Pages of your telephone directory.

Occasionally wax the bottom of the shoe. This will reduce the friction of the shoe as it slides across the workpiece.

13–5.   ELECTRIC DRILL

The **electric drill** is the first power tool that should be purchased for use in the home. It was originally named a drill because it did just that; it drove bits that drilled holes. But today, this versatile tool is used as a driving unit and is coupled with other accessories to become a disc or drum sander, grinder, buffer, wire brush, saw (reciprocating, hack, and circular), screwdriver, hole cutter, rasp, paint mixer, paint sprayer, and nut driver.

Electric drills are named by the maximum capacity of the chuck. Drills are available in ¼-, ⅜-, ½-, and ¾-inch sizes; the ¼- and ⅜-inch sizes are used in the home; the ½- and ¾-inch sizes are primarily for industrial or construction uses. Larger drills must run at slower speeds because more torque is required; hence the greater the drill capacity, the slower the drill operates. Drill speeds are fixed on some models, have two speeds (slow and fast) on others, and are variable on newer models. Motor horsepower increases with size, too, because it takes a larger motor to provide the driving torque. Drill size capacity, speeds, and horsepowers are summarized in Table 13–2. The maximum variable speed indicated is the approximate speed of a fixed drill.

The standard pistol-grip style of drill [Fig. 13–1(B)] is the most popular because its design lends itself to a majority of job applications. On pistol-grip drills with capacities of ½ inch or over, extra hand holding power is required to keep the drill from twisting during operation. A removable bar located at 90° to the chuck end is attached when the drilling operation requires it. The need for additional forward pushing power and holding control by the operator during heavy drilling operations has necessitated the installation of a permanent handle grip located at the back of the larger drills [Fig. 13–1(C)]. The multipurpose drill [Fig. 13–1(D)] is used with the appropriate accessories to drill, hammer-chisel, hammer-drill, and for other uses that are described subsequently within this section.

The major parts of a drill are the motor, gear drive, housing, on–

TABLE 13–2. DRILL CAPACITIES, SPEEDS, AND HORSEPOWER

Drill Capacity (in.)	Revolutions per Minute	Horsepower
¼	0 to 2250	⅙ to ¼
⅜	0 to 1200	⅙ to ¼
½	0 to 600	¼ to ¾
¾	250 and 475, not variable	1 to 1½

off trigger switch and variable-speed control, trigger lock, reversing switch, and chuck.

Drills are turned on and off with a trigger switch. On drills that feature variable speed, the speed is increased as the trigger is squeezed. A trigger lock locks the trigger, and therefore the speed, at any desired speed. Variable-speed drills are versatile; they provide high speeds for drilling wood, sanding, and buffing, and slower speeds with more torque for drilling metals, threading holes, and driving screws. This feature allows you to match the speed to the job.

Many drills incorporate a reversing switch. When placed in the reverse position, the drill spins in the opposite direction. This feature is useful in cleaning out drilled holes, in removing jammed drills, and in removing screws (screwdriver bit in chuck).

The drill chuck is a three-jaw attachment that is used to grip an infinite range of round drills and accessory shafts up to the maximum capacity of the drill (actually of the drill chuck). The three-jaw configuration has the ability to always hold the shaft within the center line of the drill. A tee-handled wrench, called a *chuck key,* is inserted into the side of the chuck to tighten and loosen the chuck jaws against a shaft.

The drill chuck has to be removed sometimes to install accessories. Chucks are generally screwed onto the drill shaft using right-hand threads. To remove the chuck, secure the drill in a vise using wooden blocks to protect the drill housing. Using a strap wrench assembled to the chuck, strike a sharp blow to the wrench handle in the direction for unscrewing the chuck. After loosening, unscrew the chuck and screw on the accessory.

To sum up drill characteristics, I recommend that a good all-purpose one-drill workshop would be a ⅜-inch variable-speed reversing drill with an infinite-speed locking feature.

When using the drill for *any* purpose, maintain a good hand hold on the drill (Fig. 13–6) as well as a good footing on the floor. Injuries very often occur when a drill jams in a workpiece and the drill twists out of the operator's hands. If possible, secure the workpiece in a vise or with clamps. When using a ½-inch drill in hard materials, two men should control the drill at all times. Refer to Sections 2–2 and 2–12 for discussions of drilling techniques.

Here are some additional tips on drilling. Read them over before you begin your first drilling operation:

Figure 13–6 Maintain a good hand hold on the electric drill during all operations.

1. Before inserting a drill or accessory into a drill chuck, and again after removal, inspect the shaft for burrs. Remove any burrs with a file.

2. Insert a drill or accessory shaft into the chuck. As you hand-tighten the chuck, rotate the shaft to insure that the shaft seats properly in the chuck. Then use the chuck key to tighten the chuck. Ensure that you remove the chuck key from the chuck. Momentarily squeeze and release the trigger and check that the drill or accessory is spinning in the center line of the drill (that is, that the drill or accessory has been properly seated in the chuck; this procedure is especially important when you are using small-diameter drills).

3. So that you won't misplace the chuck key, tape the tee handle to the electric cord of the drill.

4. Use the correct drill speed and feed while drilling or using accessories. Always let the tool do the work. Remember, it might seem slow, but it's a lot faster than doing the work by hand.

5. Appendix N provides decimal equivalents of number and letter drill sizes.

The following accessories are available for use on electric drills (the major accessories are illustrated in Fig. 13–7): speed reducer, screwdriver attachment, a device to limit the depth of cutting of a drill, drum sander, drum rasp, disc sander, disc rasp, extension drill, polishing wheels, grinding wheels, wire brushes, shaping/router bits, circle cutters, plug (wood) cutters, right-angle drivers (handy for drilling through rafters), jig-saw (reciprocating) attachment, circular-saw attachment, paint stirrer, flexible 40-inch shaft, carbide-impregnated cutoff discs, and a hacksaw attachment. Drill press stands are also available; the electric drill is clamped into the stand, thus becoming a bench drill press.

The multipurpose drill operates in three modes of operation: *drill/drive, hammer-chisel,* and *hammer-drill* [Figures 13–1(D) and 13–8]. With the appropriate drill, screwdriver, or chisel bit installed, it can drill, drive screws, hammer-chisel, hammer-drill, scrape paint, chip putty, chisel wood, chisel floor tile, edge, channel, gouge, shape, and slot.

In the drill/drive mode of operation, the multipurpose drill chuck revolves at a variable speed of from 0 to 850 rev/min; it is also reversible and performs the same functions as the electric drill (Section 13–5). In the hammer-chisel mode, the chuck moves in an in-and-out direction at a varying rate of 0 to 33,750 blows/min. This mode is employed when the tool is used as a chisel. In the hammer-drill mode of operation, the chuck moves in a combined circular motion *and* an in-and-out motion. The hammer-drill mode is especially effective when using masonry bits to drill holes in masonry.

The multipurpose drill is driven by a ⅓-hp motor and is double-insulated. It has ball-and-thrust bearing construction and has dou-

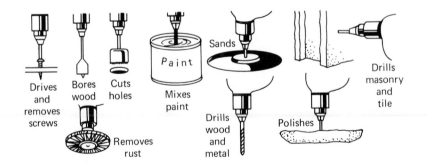

Figure 13–7 Many accessories are available to extend the use of the electric drill.

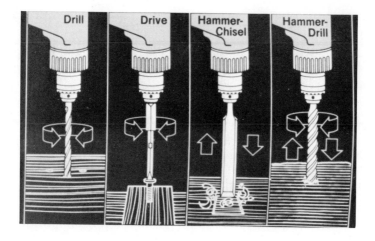

Figure 13–8 Modes of operation of the multipurpose drill.

ble-reduction gearing for added torque. The chuck takes up to a ⅜-inch bit shank.

To use the multipurpose drill in the drill/drive mode, operate the tool in the same manner as described previously. To change to another mode of operation, simply rotate the collar and change the bit. In the hammer-chisel mode, hold the tool in position before applying power. With power applied, move the chisel bit carefully along the workpiece to prevent splitting and the removal of excess material. In the hammer-drill mode, hold the masonry bit to the marked hole location (it's a good idea to start a tiny hole by tapping the hole center point with a nail head-and-hammer combination) and turn the tool on. Press lightly against the tool as it makes the hole.

13–6.   GRINDER

The **bench grinder** cannot be considered as a powered *hand* tool. However, it has many applications in the shop with regard to hand tools. It is used to sharpen knives, hatchets, drill bits, chisels, lawn mower blades, garden tools, and other shop tools. It grinds off burrs and mushroomed tool heads. With the use of various wheels, it is also used to remove rust, clean, and polish.

In buying a bench grinder, you should ensure that you buy a

grinder that incorporates two important features: wheel guard covers and eye shields. These features protect the operator from flying metal pieces and sparks. Grinders should also incorporate tool rests that are adjustable as to distance from the wheel and the angle of the rest with respect to the wheel.

Grinder sizes are specified by the size of the grinder wheels; thus a 6-inch grinder uses a 6-inch grinding wheel. Grinders of 5 to 7 inches with $\frac{1}{4}$- to $\frac{1}{2}$-hp motors are adequate for home use. These grinders run at 3400 to 3500 rev/min.

Good grinding wheels have metal bushings that fit tightly onto the grinder spindle. The shaft locknuts should be tightened only enough to secure the wheel. After installing a wheel, brush, or polishing cloth, stand aside and run the grinder a few minutes to check it out. Turn the power off.

Adjust the tool rest at the desired angle and $\frac{1}{8}$ inch from the wheel. Ensure that the area behind and around the grinder is clean. Cover your eyes with safety goggles before operating the grinder. Also check the wheel for cracks before applying power; if cracked, replace the wheel. Never use a grinding wheel at a speed faster than the speed marked on the wheel.

When grinding, remove as little material from the workpiece as is required. Keep the workpiece cool by frequently dipping it in water. In renewing a straight edge, pass the workpiece laterally across the grinding wheel (Fig. 13–9). The workpiece edge must always be parallel to the grinding wheel.

If the grinder tool rest will not tilt to the desired grinding angle, make a jig to hold the workpiece at the proper angle rather than trying to grind a workpiece by hand.

Grinding wheels are made of abrasive grains bonded together. These grains are usually aluminum oxide or silicon carbide. Aluminum oxide is used to grind high-tensile-strength materials such as high-speed steels and carbon steels. Silicon carbide is used on low-tensile-strength materials, such as brass, bronze, gray iron, aluminum, and copper. Wheel grits are categorized as coarse (No. 12 to No. 24), medium (No. 70 to No. 120), and fine (No. 150 to No. 600). Hard wheels are used to grind soft materials; soft wheels are used to grind hard materials. A medium wheel is for general use.

Wire brushing wheels are used to remove rust, paint, and to polish. They are available with fine, medium, and coarse wire bristles.

Figure 13–9 A safe grinder has wheel guards, eye shields,
and adjustable tool rests.

Buffing discs are used to polish metals such as aluminum, brass,
and stainless steels. These discs are made of lamb's wool or sewn
cotton laminates.

The surface of a grinding wheel often becomes filled with particles of metal, rust, and paint. This results in degraded performance
from the wheel. The filling of the wheel with particles is known as
loading and requires that maintenance be performed on the wheel.
The loading, as well as dull grinding grits, are removed from the
wheel with the use of a star wheel dresser.

> **WARNING:** Be sure to support the star wheel dresser against
> a support during use. Always wear protective gloves and a
> full face mask to protect yourself from flying particles.

A star wheel dresser consists of a holder and a series of hardened star-shaped discs. The discs rotate freely against the grinding
wheel during use.

Construct a support for the star wheel dresser and place it at a
height approximating the grinder shaft (Fig. 13–10). Secure the support (and the grinding wheel if not already secure). Start the grinder
and allow the wheel to reach full speed. With protective gloves on
both hands and a face mask in place, grasp the dresser with both

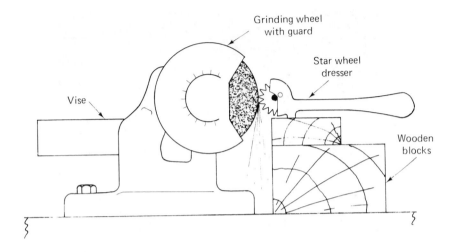

Figure 13–10 A star dresser is used to dress a grinding wheel.

hands and rest it firmly on the support to keep the dresser from being thrown by the force of the spinning wheel. Slowly advance the dresser toward the grinding wheel until contact is made against the wheel. Keep the dresser disc edges parallel to the wheel face and move the dresser back and forth across the wheel in a straight path parallel to the wheel surface. Continue this motion until the wheel is renewed. Ensure that grooves are not formed in the wheel from the dresser discs.

13–7.   MODELER'S POWER TOOL (AND ACCESSORIES)

Modeler's power tools are virtually miniature power shops. With the numerous accessories available, the modeler's power tools cut metal, saw wood, engrave, drill, polish, grind, deburr, buff, rout, and clean. The power tools can be hand-held, can be mounted in stands, or can be carefully clamped in a vise if protection is provided for the case.

Two types of modeler's power tools are available. One is the hand-held model [Fig. 13–1(E)], which can be bench-mounted; the other is the flexible-shaft type [Fig. 13–1(F)]. Both styles have valuable features and the selection is left to your individual preference. The same tool accessories can be used with both types.

The hand-held modeler's power tool is available with or without a built-in variable-speed control. On models without the speed control, an on–off switch is located on the end opposite the cutter. Always mount or hold the tool so that this switch can be readily reached in any emergency. On variable-speed models, a dial is provided to select the power-off position or a variable speed between 5000 and 25,000 rev/min. A variable-speed feature is essential for maximum efficient use of the miniature power tool. If this feature is not available on your model, you can purchase an external variable-speed control that mounts on your bench (and you can use it not only for this tool but for other tools as well).

Accessories are held in the hand-held modeler's power tool by means of a *chuck cap* and *collet* (various sizes of collets are used for accessory shafts of different diameters). To change tools, remove the power cord from the electrical receptacle, and depress and hold the *chuck lock pin* located at the shaft end of the tool. *Manually* rotate the chuck cap until the lock pin snaps into place and stops the chuck cap from turning. Continue to depress the lock pin and with the chuck wrench supplied with the tool, loosen the chuck cap. When the chuck cap is loose, pull the accessory shaft from the collet. If a different-sized accessory shaft is to be used, remove the chuck cap and replace the collet with the correct size collet. Replace the chuck cap. Insert the accessory shaft as far as it will go into the collet. With the chuck lock pin still depressed, use the wrench to tighten the chuck cap. Once tight, remove your finger from the chuck lock pin and ensure that the spring-loaded pin has come out of the locked position. *Do not apply electrical power while the chuck lock pin is depressed.*

The flexible-shaft modeler's power tool is available in a hang-up model or in a bench model. Foot-operated or manually operated variable-speed controls are available to control speeds during operations. Various interchangeable handpieces provide for speeds up to 35,000 rev/min.

Accessory shafts are held in the flexible-shaft modeler's power tool by means of a three-jaw chuck. A tee-handled chuck key is inserted into the side of the flexible-shaft chuck to tighten and loosen the chuck jaws against a shaft.

Figure 13–11 The drill press stand allows you to drill accurate holes to specified depths.

Figure 13–12 The universal stand holds the tool at any angle.

The hand-held modeler's power tool can be mounted in one of two fixtures. The drill-press stand (Fig. 13–11) is useful for drilling accurate holes. The motor can be raised or lowered on the column for different-sized workpieces, but is held in a fixed position when in use. The *table* is raised or lowered by another adjustment to drill a hole to the desired depth. A depth lock is also provided. The universal stand (Fig. 13–12) is useful for holding the tool during grinding, buffing, and polishing operations. An adjustment wing nut lets you set the tool to a convenient position. A mounting hole enables the stand to be mounted to a bench.

The router attachment (Fig. 13–12) allows you to use the tool as a miniature router. An adjustment on the attachment sets the depth of cut. The router can be used freehand or with a supplied guide that

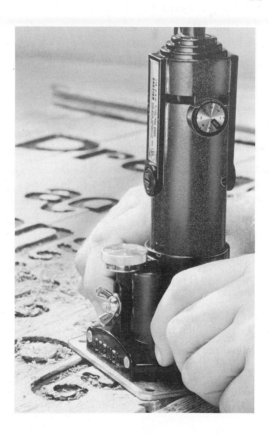

Figure 13–13 The router attachment is a pleasure to use.

is run along the workpiece edge, enabling you to make perfectly straight cuts.

Modeler's power tools perform their work through the use of high speed rather than high torque. Therefore, use light pressure against the workpiece. In this way you avoid unnecessary tool marks and you avoid overheating the tool. You also maintain accurate control of the tool.

Never stall the motor or even slow it down near the stalling point. A sudden stall could overload the motor and possibly break or kink the flexible shaft on the flexible-shaft model.

Modeler's power tools are so small that you may overlook safety. But remember, the shafts of these tools are traveling at up to 35,000 rev/min. Handle them with care. Wear safety glasses or goggles at all times when grinding or routing.

Figure 13–14 illustrates some of the accessories available for use in the modeler's power tool. Typical uses of the various types of accessories are described in Table 13–3 and are shown in Figs. 13–15 through 13–19.

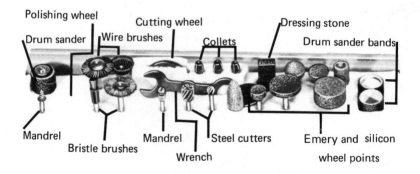

Figure 13–14 These are some of the accessories available for the modeler's power tool: drum sander; polishing wheel; wire brushes; wrench; cutting wheel; collets; dressing stone; drum sander bands; emery and silicon wheel points; steel cutters; mandrels; bristle brushes.

TABLE 13–3. TYPICAL USES OF MODELER'S POWER TOOL ACCESSORIES

Accessory	Typical Uses
High-speed steel cutters	Cutting grooves and countersinking in soft metals. Internal carving of plastic. Routing in wood. Carving and hollowing soft and hard woods. Slotting and grooving woods and plastics.
Tungsten carbide cutters	Removing flash or unwanted details from cast-metal models. Engraving in metal dies and shop and garden tools.
Small engraving cutters	Adding detail to ceramics, wood carvings, and jewelry castings or settings. Working on printed circuit boards, Bakelite, and soft metals.
Emery wheel points	Sharpening. Grinding flash from castings and molds. Smoothing welded joints. Deburring. Shaping.
Silicon grinding points	Engraving and drilling holes in glass, ceramic, and other hard, brittle materials. Grinding and shaping hard steels.
Polishing wheels	Polishing metal surfaces. Removing surface scratches and polishing plastics. Polishing jewelry.
Drum and disc sanders	Rough shaping, sanding, and smoothing.
Wire brushes	Removing rust and corrosion. Polishing cast or machined metal surfaces.
Bristle brushes	Cleaning and polishing.
Cutting wheels	Cutting rods, tubing, light bar stock. Cuts hose clamps and frozen bolts.
Steel saws	Slotting or cutting wood, plastic, or soft metals. Cutting thin-shell fiberglass molds.
Router bits	For routing, inlaying, and mortising in wood and other soft materials.
Dressing stone	Dress emery points.
Mandrels	Used to mount polishing accessories, cutting wheels, sanding discs, and polishing wheels.

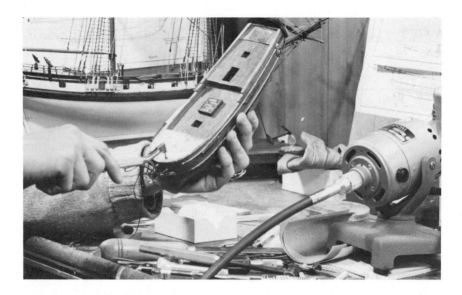

Figure 13–15 Shaping a surface of a wood model.

Figure 13–16 Sanding.

Figure 13–17 Carving.

Figure 13–18 Polishing.

13–8.   PLANE

A powered **plane** is used to rough plane flat surfaces prior to finish sanding or for cutting rabbets. High-speed tungsten steel cutters turning at up to 25,000 rev/min are used on wood, plastic, composition, and aluminum workpieces. Cuts of thicknesses from paper-thin to $\frac{3}{16}$ inch may be made on stock as wide as 2 to $2^{13}\!/_{16}$ inches. Motors range up to $\frac{1}{2}$ horsepower.

Three types of planes are available: *block planes, full-sized portable planes,* and *plane attachments to router motors.* The block

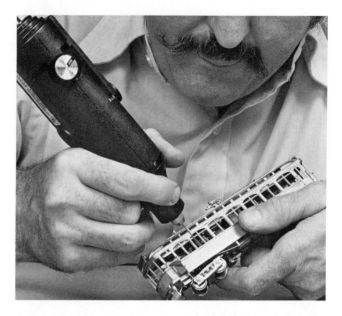

Figure 13–19 Removing unwanted details from a cast model.

plane shown in Fig. 13–1(G) planes up to $1^{13}/_{16}$ inches wide (a dressed
2- by 4-inch edge thickness) and from paper-thin to a depth of $1/_{64}$
inch. It fits into the palm of the hand and is especially useful in planing end grains. A removable steel fence is used to guide the plane for
90° cuts; a bevel planing-fence attachment allows accurate bevel
planing from 0 to 45° angles.

The full-sized plane (16 inches) can cut stock up to $2^{13}/_{16}$ inches
wide and $3/_{32}$ inch deep on a single pass. Chip disposal is provided.
An adjustable rip fence allows bevel cutting from minus 15° to plus
45° angles.

A plane attachment for a router allows you to get double duty
from your router. If you have only an occasional need for a plane,
you should consider this approach because the plane is probably
the least needed powered hand tool for the home shop. The plane
attachment has a 60° bevel planing range (minus 15 to plus 45°),
chip disposal, depth-of-cut adjustment, and trigger switch control.

To use the plane, first tightly secure the workpiece in a vise or
other clamping method. Then, before plugging the electrical cord
in, grab the plane with two hands, one on the trigger-switch handle
and the other on the motor or forward knob. The block plane can

be used with one hand, but two hands give you better control. Set the depth for the desired cut; it's better to take a number of shallow cuts than to take one deep cut. The first cut, however, should always be shallow until you get the feel of the plane's cutting action on your workpiece. Loosen the fence bevel adjustment and set the fence to the desired angle of bevel. Tighten the bevel adjustment. Now, you're ready to apply power.

Set the front of the plane on the workpiece edge with the cutters remaining off the workpiece. Press the trigger switch and let the motor come up to full speed before you begin to cut. Hold the plane parallel with the workpiece edge and hold the fence firmly against the workpiece (Fig. 13–20). Using a forward and sideward pressure to hold the fence against the workpiece, make a continuous stroke from one end of the workpiece to the other end. At the end of the stroke, lift the plane off the workpiece and return it to the starting position for the second and subsequent strokes.

Power plane blades are quickly and easily removed for replacement and sharpening. Take the blades to a professional for sharpening. Wrench and blade setting guides are included with the plane.

Figure 13–20 Using a forward pressure and a sideward pressure, make a continuous stroke from one end of the workpiece to the other end.

13–9.   RECIPROCATING SAW

The **reciprocating saw** is a heavy-duty all-purpose saw similar to the saber saw (Section 13–11) except that the blade movement is horizontal rather than vertical. Blades up to 12 inches can be installed into the reciprocating saw for cutting fenceposts, pruning trees and shrubs, cutting logs up to 13 inches in diameter, cutting bar stock, steel pipe, metal conduit, wood, plastic, and composition board. The saw is ideal for pocket cuts, roughing in, for scroll work, and for rip or cross sawing. In structural or remodeling work, it can be used to cut completely through a wall.

The removable 3- to 12-inch blades stroke from $\frac{3}{4}$ to $1\frac{1}{4}$ inches. The blades are driven by a $\frac{1}{5}$-hp motor. Motor speeds are either two-speed (1600 strokes/min for steel, aluminum, and brass, or 2000 strokes/min for wood, plastic and composition) or variable speeds from 0 to 2400 strokes/min. A removable handle is kept in place for large cutting jobs.

As you can gather from the uses of the saw, the reciprocating saw is of little use to the homeowner, but it's a real workhorse for the carpenter, electrician, plumber, or remodeler.

A multiposition foot at the front of the saw can be put in three different positions for use in flush cutting, rip and cross cutting, and for scroll work. Saw speed selection is made with a variable control at the trigger on–off switch. Blades are removed and replaced by using an Allen setscrew wrench. Use the shortest blade possible for the task.

To saw with the reciprocating saw, place the foot firmly against the workpiece. Set the saw to the desired speed range. Hold the saw with both hands and squeeze the trigger on–off switch. The blade reciprocates back and forth, cutting on the backstroke.

When cutting holes for pipes, first bore a hole to allow the blade to pass through. Plunge cuts can be made when short blades are in the saw by firmly holding the lower part of the foot (the part below the blade teeth) on the workpiece with the blade point stretched out ahead. Start the motor (at a slow speed) and start the cut. As a groove is made, gradually raise the saw, causing the blade to penetrate the workpiece.

WARNING: Be sure that there are no electrical wires, conduits, water lines, or gas lines in the path of the blade.

Figure 13–21 illustrates some of the blades available for reciprocating saws. The number of teeth per inch range from 3½ to 32; blade lengths range from 3¼ to 12 inches. Remember that the fewer teeth per inch, the rougher the cut is. Blades with 3½ to 6 teeth/inch are used for sawing wood; blades with 6 to 10 teeth/inch are used for general-purpose sawing; and blades with 10 to 18 teeth/inch are used for cutting metal.

13–10.   ROUTER

The **router** is the hand-powered tool with which you can show off your most creative workmanship; it's a lot of fun to use and it can produce artistry in wood, plastics, and compositions. It doesn't have a lot of practical application for the homeowner or do-it-yourselfer, but it does have a number of worthwhile applications for the carpenter.

For the artistic craftsman, the router is used to produce intricate

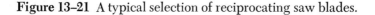

Metal cutting

Wood scroll cutting

Multi-purpose

Metal scroll cutting

Plaster cutting

Wood roughing-in

Knife blade

Double edge

Pruning

Figure 13–21 A typical selection of reciprocating saw blades.

contours in wood, multicurved moldings and edges, relief panels, trim work on cabinets and bookshelves, sign engraving, and delicate grooves for intricate inlays. The more serious advanced craftsman and do-it-yourselfer uses the router to make rabbet and dovetail joints as well as many other types of joints, and dados, grooves, and bead moldings. The carpenter uses the router on a production basis to plane edges, mortise doors for hinges, and trim countertopping.

Incidentally, just buying a *router* doesn't buy you much. You need a good selection of various bits and often need an additional attachment for your particular job. Unfortunately, routers are rather expensive—their expense is not apparent immediately, but when you add the sum of the pieces of the basic router plus the bits, straight and curved guides, power plane, hinge mortising template kit, dovetail kit, slot and circle cutting attachments, and veneer trimming guide, you have quite an expensive tool. Thus, if you only have occasional use for the router, I suggest borrowing it from a friend or renting it. And maybe you can con your spouse into giving you a router for Christmas and you can buy the individual bits and attachments as you need them. The router, by the way, is one power tool that's often on sale.

In selecting a router, look for construction that utilizes bearings and a large high-speed horsepower motor; the greater the work load, the greater the horsepower needed. Motor sizes from $\frac{3}{4}$ to $1\frac{1}{2}$ hp and speeds of 18,000 to 35,000 rev/min are available. A $\frac{3}{4}$-hp motor at 22,000 rev/min is sufficient for home use, whereas 1 to $1\frac{1}{2}$ hp at 22,000 to 25,000 rev/min is used commercially.

Prior to using the router, a bit must be placed into the router collet and the depth of cut adjusted. Before doing either, remove the router electrical plug from the power source. Then secure a bit of your choice into the router collet by precisely following the manufacturer's instructions. It is extremely important that the bit be installed securely because of the high speed. Most routers use either a lock nut and a collet nut to secure the bit or have a locking device to keep the shaft from rotating while the collet nut is tightened.

Next (with the electrical plug still disconnected), set the depth of cut. Calibrations are usually in $\frac{1}{64}$-inch increments from 0 to $1\frac{1}{2}$ inches. Place the router on a flat surface and loosen the height lock knob. Turn the height-adjusting knob until the bit just touches the surface. Now, position the bit so that it can be projected below the base to the desired setting. Rotate the height-adjusting knob to set the bit in the desired position. Tighten the locknut.

The power off–on switch may be located on the motor or may be a trigger switch in one of the guide handles. Where trigger handles are utilized, a locking button may be incorporated to hold the trigger switch on. Further pressure and a releasing of the trigger unlocks the spring-loaded lock.

Observe the workpiece and plan how you will use the router. If you have more than one similar workpiece, plan to do the same cutting on similar workpieces consecutively. Secure the workpiece firmly by use of a clamping device such as a vise, clamp, or jig. Remember that the clamping device must be thinner than the workpiece so that the router can pass over it.

Unless you are planning to perform freehand routing, clamp a guide (Fig. 13–22) or template to the workpiece. Attach any accessories needed.

Ensure that a sharp bit is secured in the router before connecting the electrical plug into power. Once the bit is checked, connect

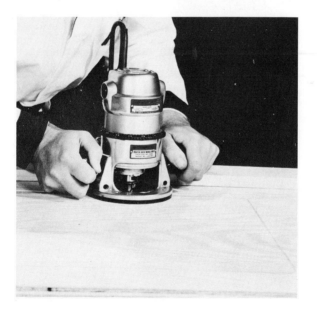

Figure 13–22 Use a piece of straight scrap wood or a template to guide the router.

the plug to the power source. Grip the router firmly at all times and especially during turn-on because of the initial starting torque (Fig. 13–23). Press the on–off switch to ON and let the router motor come up to full speed before you begin cutting. Hold the router against the guide and let the bit cut into the workpiece, feeding left to right as the router is moved across the workpiece. Feed the router at a moderate speed; too slow a feed may burn the wood and heat up the bit, causing a loss of temper in the bit metal; too fast a movement slows the motor and causes the motor to overheat. Keep both the motor and the bit from overheating. If the motor slows down too much, decrease the depth of cut and make two or more passes.

The average cut should not exceed a depth of ¼ inch per pass (Fig. 13–24) when large cutters are used. In cutting hardwoods, two or three passes should be used. Two or three passes are more practical than risking damage to the motor or cutter.

When cutting straight cuts, keep the router against the clamped down guide. The edge guides that come with the router can be used

Figure 13–23 Grip the router firmly at all times. Here, a dado is being cut with a mortise bit.

Figure 13–24 The average cut should not exceed ¼ inch depth per pass. Here, a Roman ogee bit is used to cut a decorative edge.

for cuts close to the edge. In cutting circles or arcs, the edge guide is pinned down.

Template guide work is accomplished by the use of special guides in the router base. Dovetail joints are cut using a special jig and dovetail bit. In laminate trimming work, the router base is replaced with a special veneer-trim kit.

Freehand cuts are used for special designs and for inlay work. Mark the pattern first. On inlay work, set the router depth so that the cut depth is slightly less than the inlay material.

As mentioned previously for other tools, practice first on scrap wood of the same species as the workpiece. This gives you the feel of the router on the workpiece material (Fig. 13–25).

Accessories that are used with the router include bits (Fig. 13–26), dovetail template, butt hinge template, laminated plastic trimmer attachment, alphabet and numbers template, pantograph template (the original size is traced with a stylus; one-half size is made), and a router table, used to convert the router into a shaper.

Figure 13–25 Practice on scrap wood first. Here a bead is
being cut.

Two types of cutter bits are available: one-piece and a screw-on
bit that allows different cutters to be mounted on one shaft. Only
high-speed steel cutters or carbide-tipped cutters should be purchased; other types just do not hold up. Carbide-tipped cutters are
for use on laminates, plastics, and plywood.

Keep the cutters sharp and clean. During operation, prevent
the workpiece, the cutters and the motor from overheating.

To resharpen a bit, grind only the inside of the cutting edge. Be
sure to grind the clearance angle the same as that originally fur-
nished. Never grind the outside diameter of the bits, because they
are specially ground for proper clearance. If you're not experienced
in sharpening, I suggest you have a professional regrind your bits or
purchase new bits when required.

Inspect the bit shafts for burrs prior to installation into the
router and upon removal from the router. Remove burrs with an
oilstone. Pitch and gum can be removed with kerosene. Keep a light
coat of machine oil on the bits when storing them, and store them
so that they do not hit each other or other tools.

Straight—for general stock removal, slotting, grooving, rabbeting

Veining—for decorative freehand routing such as carving, inlay work

Sash bead—for beading inner side of window frames

Sash cope—for coping window rails to match bead cut

Core box—for fluting and general ornamentation

Dovetail—for dovetailing joints. Use with dovetail templet

Corner round—for edge rounding

Bead—for decorative edging

Cove—for cutting coves

45° bevel chamfer—for bevel cutting

Mortise—for stock removal, dados, rabbets, hinge butt mortising

Rabbeting—for rabbeting or step-cutting edges

Roman ogee—for decorative edging

Panel pilot—for cutting openings and for through-cutting

Pilot spiral (down)—for operations where plunge cutting is required in conjunction with templet routing, using the pilot guide

Straight spiral (down)—for through cutting plastics and non-ferrous metals; also for deep slotting operations in wood

Straight spiral (up)—for slotting and mortising operations particularly in non-ferrous metals such as aluminum door jambs

V-groove—for simulating plank construction

Spiral—for outside and inside curve cutting

Bits for trimming plastic laminates. Solid carbide or carbide-tipped bits for flush and bevel trimming operations Solid carbide self-pivoting flush and bevel trimming bits

Solid-carbide combination flush/bevel trimming bit

Carbide-tipped bevel trimmer bit

Carbide-tipped ball bearing flush trimming bit

Carbide-tipped 25° bevel trimmer kits

Carbide-tipped combination flush/bevel trimming bit

Carbide-tipped 15° backsplash trimmer—with $\frac{5}{16}$″ diameter hole

Figure 13–26 Router bits.

Occasionally clean and wax the base of the router so that there is less friction between the base and the workpiece during operation.

13–11. SABER SAW

The **saber saw** (also called a jig saw) is a reciprocating saw used to cut thin-gauge metals, bars, angles, fiberglass, plaster, tile, wood, plastic, composition, and pipe. It is especially useful in cutting square, circular, irregular, intricate cutouts in sheet materials, walls, and air ducts. Capacities are approximate; softwood, 1⅝ inches; hardwood, 1 inch; aluminum, ¼ inch; and mild steel, ¼ inch.

The saber saw is available with three types of speed control: fixed-speed, two-speed, and variable-speed. The fixed-speed saw operates at about 3000 strokes/min. The two-speed saw has a rate of about 3200 strokes/min on high speed and 2700 on low speed. Speed selection is controlled by a two-position switch located on the handle. The variable-speed saw has a speed range of from 0 to approximately 3500 strokes/min and is controlled by a trigger type of switch. Motor ratings are from ¼ to ½ hp.

The two-speed and variable-speed saber saws have been developed, like the electric drill, to further increase the range of applications of the saber saw. The high speeds are used with materials such as wood and compositions; the lower speeds are used to cut metal and plastic. The variable-speed saw lets you select the proper speed for the job; the harder the material, the slower the speed. It also lets you slow down to cut curves.

The main items on the saber saw are a case, a trigger switch, a blade chuck, a saw blade, a shoe plate, and a sawdust blower (not available on all models).

Most saber-saw blades are fixed in one plane of operation with the blade moving up and down; to turn the saw blade around, the complete saw has to be turned. One manufacturer, however, has a blade that can be rotated without turning the saw itself and without removing power from the saw. To turn the blade, pressure is applied (in a downward direction) to the top handle over the blade; the blade can be locked in a straight position in any of four 90°-angle positions.

The cutting action of the saber saw is in an upward direction, toward the bottom of the shoe plate. This upward cutting action pulls the shoe plate tightly to the workpiece during cutting and relaxes its pull when the blade is moving away from the shoe plate. Therefore, it is important that the workpiece is placed with its good side down (rough side up); the feathered and splintered edges will then appear on the rough side of the workpiece.

The up-and-down action of the blade imparts a high vibration factor to the saw during its operation; firm and steady downward pressure during sawing tends to cancel some of the vibration, as does clamping of the workpiece. The calibrated shoe plate is adjustable with respect to the blade through a range of 0 to 45° left or right for cutting bevels. A single screw located on the angle protractor is used to adjust and lock the shoe plate to the required angle (Fig. 13–27).

Saber-saw blades are available in a wide range of styles to meet specific applications. The determining criteria in blade selection are: the material to be cut and the type of finish to be left by the blade. The finish or type of cut is classified as rough, medium, and fine. Narrow blades are used for curved work and wide blades for straight work. Choose the shortest blade for the job.

Blade lengths are from 3 to $4\frac{1}{4}$ inches long. The longer blade lengths are usually for cutting wood. Two forms of blade teeth are available for most general work, the stagger-tooth blade and the wavy-tooth blade. The stagger-tooth blade has teeth that are set in

Figure 13–27 The tilting shoe is set for making bevel cuts.

an alternating pattern of right, left, right, left. This blade is most often used on soft materials such as wood, plastics, and aluminum. The wavy-tooth blade is used to cut ferrous metals up to ¼ inch thick and nonferrous metals up to ⅛ inch thick. Blades vary in number of teeth from 3 teeth per inch, used in cutting soft materials, to 32 teeth per inch, used in ferrous metal cuttings. Figure 13–28 is included as an aid in selecting the correct blade for the material to be cut.

The blade chuck is a slotted collar located at the end of the output shaft of the saw. Generally, there are two screws (or hex setscrews) located on this collar, one in the front and the second on the side, 90° from the front. These screws align and lock the blade to the output shaft.

To install a blade in the saber saw, first disconnect the power plug from the outlet. Then loosen both screws in the blade chuck until the shank of the blade can be inserted and bottomed. With the blade bottomed, turn the front screw in until it lightly contacts the blade. Turn and tighten the side screw firmly against the blade. Return to the front screw and securely tighten it.

To make a cut with the saber saw, hold the saw firmly in one hand and place the shoe plate firmly on the workpiece with the blade not touching the workpiece. Start the saw and let the motor run up to speed. Move the saw onto the workpiece and begin cutting (Fig. 13–29). Feed the blade into the workpiece at a moderate feed and speed. Don't force the saw; let the blade do the cutting.

To saw thin metal, you should use a backup piece of either plywood or Masonite behind the metal, or sandwich the metal between two pieces. This backup piece aids in cutting clean edges on the workpiece, and it also aids to dampen vibration, which is the biggest source of blade breakage.

In sawing thicker metal workpieces, such as ⅛- or ¼-inch sections, ample support should be supplied. To eliminate vibration when sawhorses or other support is used, always keep the area of the workpiece being cut as close as possible to the support.

The saber saw has the ability to make a plunge cut into a workpiece. A plunge cut is a cut through some inner part of the workpiece without cutting in from the edge and without drilling a hole for the blade. To make a plunge cut, angle the saber saw onto the forward edge of the shoe plate (Fig. 13–30) with the teeth to the surface.

Blade type	Description of blade and use	Type of cut	Speed of cut	Blade length	Teeth per inch
Flush cutting	Hard or soft wood over $\frac{1}{4}$" thick.	Rough	Fast	3"	7
Plaster cutting	Special V-tooth design provides constant abrading action which is most effective in cutting plaster, masonry and high density plastics.	Rough	Fast	$3\frac{5}{8}$"	9
Double cutting	Most wood and fiber materials. Tooth design allows for cutting in both directions with equal speed.	Rough	Fast	3"	7
Double cutting	Cuts most wood and fiber materials. Tooth design allows for cutting in both directions with equal speed and quality of cut.	Medium	Medium	3"	10
Skip tooth	Cuts most plastics and plywood. Special tooth design with extra large gullets provide extra chip clearance necessary for cutting plywood and plastic.	Rough	Fast	3"	5
Wood cutting coarse	Cuts soft woods $\frac{3}{4}$" and thicker. Canted shank provides built-in blade relief, thus helping to clear the saw dust and cool the blade.	Rough	Fastest	3"	7
Wood cutting fine	Cuts soft woods under $\frac{3}{4}$" thick. Canted shank provides built-in blade relief, thus helping to clear the saw dust and cool blade. More teeth per inch allows for finer quality of cut.	Medium	Medium	3"	10
Wood cutting hollow ground	Hard woods under $\frac{3}{4}$" thick. Hollow grinding provides no tooth projection beyond body of blade, thus imparting an absolutely smooth finish. Canted shank for blade clearance.	Smooth	Medium	3"	7
Metal cutting	For cutting ferrous (iron) metals $\frac{1}{16}$" to $\frac{3}{8}$" thick and nonferrous (aluminum, copper, etc.) $\frac{1}{8}$" to $\frac{1}{4}$" thick.	Medium	Medium	3"	14 to 32
Hollow ground	For cutting plywood and finish materials $\frac{1}{2}$" and thicker where fine finish is desirable. Hollow ground for very smooth finish on all wood products. Provides the longest life woodcutting blade possible.	Fine to medium	Medium	$4\frac{1}{4}$"	6 to 10
Knife blade	For cutting leather, rubber, composition tile, cardboard, etc.	Smooth	Fast	3"	Knife edge
Fleam ground	For cutting green or wet woods $\frac{1}{4}$" to $1\frac{1}{2}$" thick. Fleam ground provides shredding type cutting action which is most effective in sawing hard, green or wet materials. Provides longest cutting life possible.	Smooth to coarse	Medium	4"	10
Scroll cut	For cutting wood, plastic and plywood $\frac{1}{4}$" to 1" thick. Set teeth and thin construction allows this blade to make intricate cuts and circles with radii as small as $\frac{1}{8}$".	Smooth	Medium	$2\frac{1}{2}$"	10
Wood cutting coarse	Cuts most plastics and wood up to 4" thick. Special tooth design with extra large gullets provide extra chip clearance for fast cutting in thicker materials.	Rough	Fast	6"	3

Figure 13-28 It is important to use the proper saber saw blade for the job.

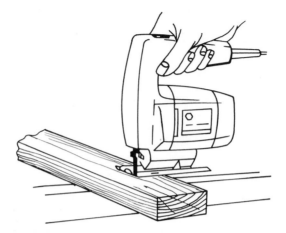

Figure 13–29 Hold the saber saw firmly.

Turn the motor on at a slow speed and begin the cutting. As the blade cuts a groove, slowly lower the back of the saw, causing the blade to cut deeper, until it finally plunges through.

The rip fence and circle guide are two accessories used with the saber saw, to make straight cuts using a reference edge and to cut circles, respectively. The rip fence and circle guide insert into the slot in the shoe of the saber saw and can be locked at any setting. The rip fence guides the saber saw in cutting strips parallel to a workpiece edge (Fig. 13–31).

When cutting circles, the combination rip fence and circle guide

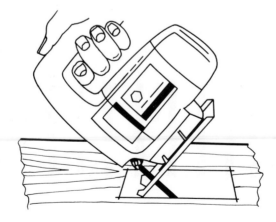

Figure 13–30 Making a plunge cut.

Figure 13–31 Use the rip fence guide for making cuts parallel to the edge of the workpiece.

is removed and reinstalled with the cross bar edge up. The required radius is then set between the pivot hole and the blade. This position is then locked. By placing a pin through the cross bar into the center of the required circle, the blade can be inserted into a predrilled hole or slot and the circle cut out using the pin as a pivot point.

Saber-saw blades are expendable and should be replaced when they become dull.

13–12.   SANDERS (BELT, DISC, AND FINISHING)

If there is one job that I dislike, it's sanding the workpiece. However, as you well know, it's the sanding that turns the workpiece into a professional-looking job. The three **sanders** described in this chapter (belt, disc, and finishing), will aid you in finishing a workpiece and will save you many hours of time and energy.

Belt Sander

The *belt sander* is used to remove paint, stains, and varnishes; to sand rough lumber and round edges; and to smooth badly scarred surfaces. It is used where a lot of material is to be removed with speed. It can sand flush to vertical surfaces.

The belt sander uses a continuous abrasive-coated belt that rides over two drums and a sanding plate. The rear drum is powered, whereas the front drum is an idler that is adjustable for tension and for true tracking of the belts across the sanding plate (4 by 6 inches) and drums. A dust-pick-up bag is provided. The belts are driven by motors of from ¾ to 1½ horsepower at approximately 1200 to 1500 feet/min.

The size of the belt sander is determined by the belt width. Most home belt sanders are 3 inches wide.

Belts are changed rapidly by means of a quick-releasing lever or by pushing the forward drum toward the rear. Note the direction of travel marked on each belt and mount the belt over the drums in the correct direction. Press the drum release and let the front idler drum go back into place. Adjust the travel knob to alter the angle of the front drum so that the belt tracks perfectly. Make several momentary power on–off tests to check the trueness of the belt on the drums. The final trueness adjustment can be made with the belt running.

Secure the workpiece. Grip the belt sander firmly with two hands and turn it on. Let the motor get up to speed before contact is made with the workpiece. Place the sander to the workpiece and begin sanding, keeping the sander moving; failure to keep the sander moving at all times will cause excessive material to be removed from one area. To cut rapidly, move the sander at a 45° angle across the workpiece. Keep the sander flat at all times and only bear down hard enough to cut. Make long, straight, continuous sanding strokes. Do not use too much pressure. Do not tilt the sander as you move it off the workpiece or you'll have rounded edges.

Disc Sander

The *disc sander* is excellent for paint and rust removal from boats and cars and as a polisher. It is used extensively by auto-body repair shops and occasionally in the home shop. It is most often used on curved surfaces.

The disc sander size is the size of the sanding disc used. These are usually 5 or 7 inches. The sanding discs are mounted onto a rubber or fiber backing pad. The sander motors range from ⅞ to 1½ hp and speeds of up to 5000 rev/min; two-speed models are available with speeds of approximately 2400 and 4700 rev/min. Polishing is usually done at the lower speeds.

Two types of disc sanders are available. One is an in-line model that looks like a drill, and the other is an offset model [Fig. 13–1 (L)]. You can reach better with the offset model.

Apply power to the disc sander and let it reach maximum speed before touching it to the workpiece. Hold the sander with two hands (Fig. 13–32) and tilt the disc slightly against the workpiece. Apply just enough pressure to bend the rubber backing. Keep the sander moving so that an excessive amount of material is not removed from one area. The main criticism against the disc sander is that it digs into the workpiece if not controlled and kept moving. It does not give as good a finish to a workpiece as do the finishing and belt sanders.

Finishing Sander

The *finishing sander* is a finishing tool used for fine-finish sanding of wood, metal, and plastic workpieces. With the properly selected abrasive papers (Section 10–2), it is also good for sanding rougher

Figure 13–32 Tilt the disc sander slightly against the work-piece.

work. Because of its flat, square base, it can be worked directly into a corner and provides a better-finished sanding job than can be done by hand.

There are three types of finishing sanders: *orbital, straight-line,* and a combination *orbital/straight-line.* The orbital/straight-line sander costs a little more than the other two but is well worth the price. The rectangular base, called a *platen,* of the orbital finishing sander moves in an orbital path of about $\frac{3}{16}$-inch diameter at about 4000 orbits/min. This orbital action is for fast, tough sanding, removal of old paint and varnish, and for initial final sanding operations. Straight-line sanders are for fine hand-sanded-like finishes. Straight-line sanders operate at approximately 14,000 strokes/min. Motors are about $\frac{1}{6}$ hp.

The combination orbital/straight-line sander provides both types of finishing sander actions in one machine by converting the orbital motion of the platen into a back-and-forth straight-line motion. Selection of either action is performed by moving a lever (or rotating a screwheaded cam) between the motor housing and the platen.

The sanding platen or pad is lined with a rubber or felt face to add a firm flexible backing to the sanding sheets during use. The sanding platens are made in two popular sizes, $3\frac{5}{8}$ by 9 inches and $4\frac{1}{2}$ by 11 inches. The smaller dimension of each of these two sizes is the width of the sanding paper, but the longer dimensions are not, since they include an extra length that is needed for clamping the sheet at each end of the sander platen.

Attaching the sanding sheet to the platen is accomplished by several methods. Some employ a spring-clamping device, whereby one end of the long length of the sheet is rolled around the end of the platen and clamped. The second clamp is employed after stretching the sheet taut over the platen. A second method involves the use of a split-ratcheted cylinder located at each end of the pad. To secure a sanding sheet to the pad, insert one end of the sanding sheet into the slotted front cylinder (opposite the handle). Draw the opposite end of the sheet taut across the platen and insert its end into the slotted ratchet cylinder. Using a screwdriver or tool supplied, tighten this cyinder until the sanding sheet is taut.

After the type of action (orbital or straight-line) has been selected, install the abrasive paper onto the sander as previously

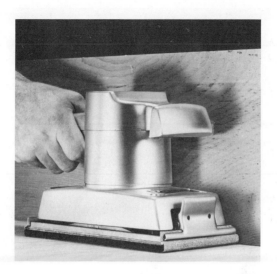

Figure 13-33 The finishing sander can be purchased with a combination orbital/straight-line action.

described. Plug the sander electrical cord into the power receptacle, and holding the sander in one hand, turn the sander on. Now, place the sander onto the workpiece and move the sander with the grain of the wood. (The orbital action should be selected first, followed by straight-line sanding). Although the sander can be held in one hand (Fig. 13-33), it is better to use two hands to guide it. Do not apply pressure with the hands; let the weight of the machine provide the pressure.

The soft felt platen is adequate for most work. However, on wood workpieces that have both soft and hard grain in them (such as fir), it is recommended that a piece of hardboard be placed between the sandpaper and the felt pad; this will cause all the grain to be cut at the same level rather than the softer grain cut faster and hence deeper than the harder grain.

Figure 13-34 illustrates a small finishing sander that is handy for use on curved surfaces.

Keep abrasive papers clean. Remove dust from them by rubbing the paper with a stiff brush. Brush and vacuum the exposed surfaces of sanders on a regular basis. Wipe the exposed surfaces with a rag dampened with turpentine.

Figure 13–34 This small finishing sander is useful on curved
surfaces.

13–13.   SOLDERING IRON

Soldering irons are used to solder metal pieces together. You'll probably use the soldering iron most frequently to solder electrical connections for repair of electrical appliances and for use in soldering
wires and components in electronic kits that you may construct.
Soldering irons usually take one of four forms: miniature soldering
iron, pistol-grip soldering iron, instant-heat soldering iron [Fig. 13–
1 (N, O and P, respectively)], and as an attachment to the propane
torch (Section 10–10).

The miniature soldering iron is used almost exclusively in the
electronic industry for soldering wires, transistors, integrated circuits, printed circuits, and other electronic components. It is avail-

able with interchangeable thread-in heating elements from 10 to 50 watts. Tips are also interchangeable thread-in units and are available in a number of shapes, including chisel, offset chisel, pyramid, pencil, long-taper chisel, and spade. This iron is plugged in and left on while it is in use.

The pistol-grip iron features a 75-watt sealed nichrome element. A replaceable copper tip is used for the soldering tip. This iron is plugged in and left on while it is in use. It is for heavy-duty electronic soldering such as soldering ground lugs to chassis.

The instant-heat soldering gun is a heavy-duty gun (100 to 140 watts) that reaches the melting temperature of solder about 3 seconds after the trigger is pulled. The tip is easily replaced by removing two hex nuts. A spotlight on the housing lights up the work area. The iron is for heavy-duty wiring.

Section 10-10 lists the various solders and solder fluxes (flux is a substance used to promote fusion of the solder and the wires or components) to use for various soldering applications. A multicore resin-type solder is always used with electronic equipment—never acid-core solder, because it will eventually eat away the component leads.

Upon receiving a new soldering iron or tip, the first thing you must do is to *tin* the tip. You should follow the manufacturer's specific instructions for accomplishing this task; basically, it involves heating the tip for a predetermined time period, applying a bit of solder to the tip, wiping the tip clean, and repeating this process one or more times until the tip is tinned. A tinned tip enables the solder to flow from the heated tip to the connection being soldered.

To properly solder, you must first heat the soldering iron to its operating temperature. Then, wipe the tip across a damp sponge or cloth to clean it and apply a small amount of solder to the tip. Place the flat part of the tip against the junction or connection to be soldered. Remember, heat rises; locate your tip accordingly. Let the tip heat the junction. Apply solder to the junction and let the heat of the junction melt the solder. When the solder flows into the junction, remove the iron and let the junction cool and solidify before moving the parts of the soldered area. A bright soldered junction indicates a good joint. A silver-gray junction indicates a *cold soldering joint* that must be corrected; reheat and apply a small amount of additional solder.

punches

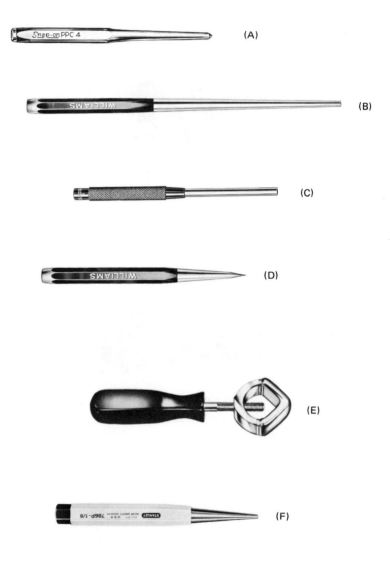

Figure 14–1 Punches: (A) center; (B) long taper (aligning);
(C) pin; (D) prick; (E) punch and chisel holder;
(F) solid (starter).

14-1.   GENERAL DESCRIPTION

Punches are used to punch indentations in metal and other materials for later drilling of holes, to mark metal for layout, to drive straight or tapered pins, and to align holes in two workpieces. The types of punches most often used in the home shop, by maintenance personnel, and by technicians are the *center punch* and the *solid* (starter) *punch*. *Pin punches* are used in applications where a large number of pins are removed. *Prick punches* are used in laying out patterns on workpieces; and long taper (aligning) punches are used in heavy assembly work, where two workpieces are to be aligned for assembly.

A *punch and chisel holder* is available for use in holding tools in tight spaces.

Punches are made from hardened-tool-steel stock. One end is shaped for the job application; the other end, called the *anvil*, is struck with a ball peen hammer. You should purchase only quality punches with tempered anvils. The tempering keeps the anvil from *mushrooming* and fracturing, which can cause accidents from flying splinters of metal.

14-2.   APPLICATIONS

To use a punch, grasp the selected punch lightly in the fingers of one hand. Place the punch flat against and in a direction that is perpendicular to the workpiece. Strike the anvil lightly with a light ball peen hammer. If additional strikes are required, check before each blow to ensure that the punch is still perpendicular and flat against the workpiece. Hold the punch in the punch and chisel holder when you are working in tight spaces.

Always use the proper size punch. In removing pins from a hole, the correct punch size is that size which just fits into the hole. Hold the punch in direct line with the pin.

Protect yourself from flying pieces of metal by wearing safety glasses or goggles. Protect others by placing a protective booth or portable screen around your work area. Repair mushroomed anvils, as required.

14–3.   CARE OF PUNCHES

Long taper, pin, and solid punch points should be kept flat. If necessary, grind the points flat [Fig. 14–2(A)] and at right angles to the center line of the punch. Adjust the grinder tool rest so that the end of the punch is opposite the center of the wheel [Fig. 14–2(B)]. Place the punch on the rest and rotate it as it is fed against the wheel. Keep the point cool by dipping it often in water.

Prick and center punch points are ground to 30° and 60° conical points, respectively. Adjust the grinder tool rest for the proper angle [Fig. 14–2(C)]. Place the punch on the tool rest and grind as described for the long taper punch.

If the punch anvil becomes *mushroomed* with burrs, file or grind the burrs off. Keep the anvil cool by dipping it often in water.

14–4.   CENTER PUNCH

The **center punch** is used to punch a conical-shaped indentation into a metallic workpiece as a starting point for a twist drill point. The point of the chisel, and hence the shape of the conical indentation, is 60°, which is the same as the tip of twist drills. The formation of the conical indentation in the surface of the workpiece allows for the direct drilling of a hole without the fear that the bit will *walk* over the surface, causing an inaccurately drilled hole. On workpieces

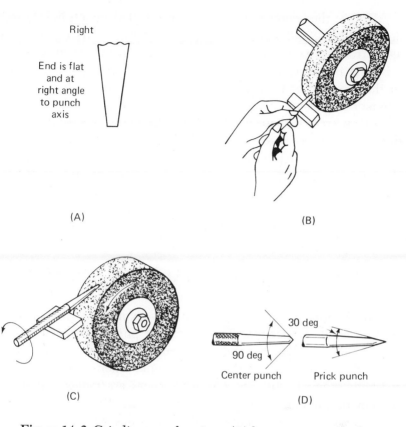

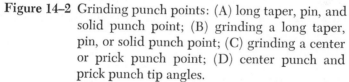

Figure 14–2 Grinding punch points: (A) long taper, pin, and solid punch point; (B) grinding a long taper, pin, or solid punch point; (C) grinding a center or prick punch point; (D) center punch and prick punch tip angles.

where accurate layouts are required, hole centers are punched with a prick punch prior to punching with the center punch.

The center punch is sometimes used to mark alignment points or to otherwise identify pieces that are disassembled from each other. The center punch may be used to make indentations in very hard woods for drill-point centers; in softer woods, the awl is used.

A typical center punch is made of from ¼- to ¾-inch hardened-tool-steel stock and is from 3½ to 7 inches long. The punch tapers to a point of ⅛ inch. It is easily identified from other punches by the short conical-pointed 60° end.

To use the center punch, hold the selected punch lightly in the fingers of one hand and slant the punch with the striking end (anvil) away from yourself. Hold the punch point to the layout point and raise the punch to a vertical (perpendicular) position with respect to the workpiece. Firmly strike the punch anvil with a ball peen hammer to make an indentation in the surface of the workpiece.

If an error is made in the exact placement of the punched indentation, correct it as follows. Place the punch in the indentation and slant the punch with the point toward the original mark. Tap the anvil until the punch point and the workpiece fractured metal move over to the original mark. When the punch point is in line with the original mark, raise the punch to a vertical position and strike the anvil to enlarge the indentation.

14–5.   LONG TAPER (ALIGNING) PUNCH

The **long taper punch** is used to align workpieces so that holes line up for installing fasteners. The long taper punch is especially useful for engine installations and replacement of springs. In use, the tapered punch is placed through one hole where two holes in two workpieces are to line up. The workpieces are moved slightly. On alignment, the long taper punch will drop into the aligned hole.

Long taper punches are available in stock sizes of from $\frac{3}{8}$ to $\frac{3}{4}$ inch with lengths of from 8 to 16 inches; point diameters are from $\frac{5}{32}$ to $\frac{3}{4}$ inch.

14–6.   PIN PUNCH

The **pin punch** is used to drive straight, tapered, spiral, roll, dowel, cotter, and shear pins out of items such as lathes, outboard motors, guns, rifles, and other applications in which two pieces of metal are joined together by pins. The pin punch may also be used to drive bolts out of metal or wood. The pin punch is recognized by its straight shank (no taper) and flat end. Punch diameters from $\frac{3}{32}$ to $\frac{3}{8}$ inch in lengths from $4\frac{1}{2}$ to $6\frac{1}{4}$ inches are available. Pin-punch shanks are from $\frac{1}{4}$ to $\frac{1}{2}$ inch.

To remove a pin from a hole, use a solid, or starter, punch first. Using a light ball peen hammer with light blows, drive the pin out with the solid punch until the taper diameter of the solid punch nearly equals the hole diameter. Then use the largest-diameter pin punch that fits into the hole to complete the pin driving. In the case of tapered pins, carefully measure both ends of the hole to determine which is the smaller diameter; apply the pin-punch tip to the smaller end directly against the pin. The pin punch should not be used to start a pin out, because a sharp blow with the hammer to *unfreeze* the pin could bend or break the narrow shank of the pin punch.

14–7.   PRICK PUNCH

The **prick punch** is used as a starting tool in the layout of metal work-pieces. It is used to punch small conical-shaped indentations in the workpiece surface to permanently mark points of a line, the intersections of lines and circles or arcs, and the centers of circles and holes. The small indentations are also used for the leg of a divider. A typical prick punch is made of $\frac{3}{8}$-inch hardened tool steel and is from $4\frac{1}{2}$ to 6 inches long; it has a long, tapered shank, terminating with a conical point.

Use the prick punch in the same manner described for the center punch in Section 14–4.

14–8.   PUNCH AND CHISEL HOLDER

The **punch and chisel holder** is used to save bruised knuckles. It is especially useful for holding a punch or chisel in hard-to-reach spaces.

To use the holder, insert the punch or chisel into the holder and tighten the handle that forces the tool against the plastic-coated head. Hold the holder and tool in one hand in position against the workpiece; tap the tool with a ball peen hammer. Check proper alignment of the tool to the workpiece before each successive tap with the hammer.

14–9.   SOLID (STARTER) PUNCH

The **solid punch**, also called a *starter punch*, is used as the starting
punch in driving out straight, tapered, spiral, roll, dowel, cotter, and
sheer pins, and bolts and rivets that have had the heads removed.
Because of its tapered shank, the solid punch cannot be used to drive
pins completely out. In these cases, drive the pin the rest of the way
out with a pin punch (Section 14–6). Always use the largest solid
punch size to fit the hole. Place the punch solidly against and in line
with the pin. Tap the punch anvil with a ball peen hammer and drive
the pin out until the diameter of the solid punch is approximately
that of the hole. Then use the pin punch. Solid punches are made
of stock from $\frac{1}{4}$ to $\frac{9}{16}$ inch and lengths from $4\frac{1}{2}$ to $7\frac{1}{4}$ inches; point
diameters are from $\frac{3}{32}$ to $\frac{1}{2}$ inch.

15

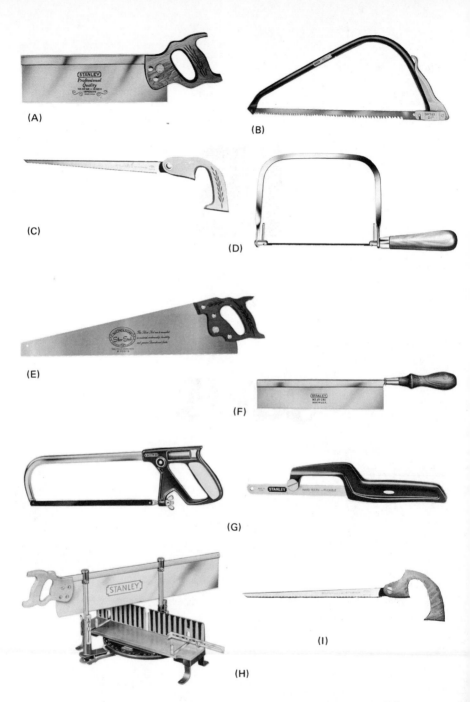

Figure 15–1 Saws: (A) back; (B) bow; (C) compass; (D) coping; (E) crosscut and rip; (F) dovetail; (G) hacksaws; (H) miter saw and box; (I) keyhole.

15–1.   GENERAL DESCRIPTION

Saws are used to cut a workpiece into one or more pieces, to cut an opening in a workpiece such as for cables, wires, or pipes, or to make cuts such as tenons and mitered joints for joining workpieces together. Workpieces may be made of wood, metal, plastic, or other materials. Each type of cut is made with either a different type of saw and blade combination or with a different technique, such as a slower speed.

Before describing a particular saw's characteristics, it is necessary first to define some general saw features and terms. The *butt* of a saw blade is the widest end and is the end where the handle attaches. The *tip* of the blade is the end away from the handle. The *points* are the teeth. The coarseness of the blade is determined by the number of teeth; 5 points to the inch is considered *coarse*, 10 points to the inch is considered *fine*. *Alternately* set teeth have every other tooth set to *opposite* sides, one to the left, the next to right. The *kerf* is the cut made by the saw in a workpiece.

Quality saws cut faster and with less effort because the teeth are precision-ground. More teeth cut with a smoother finish; fewer teeth cut faster but leave a rougher finish on the workpiece. Blades are made of steel or of stainless steel. Some are coated with a coating of Teflon-S*, which is self-lubricating and has a high abrasion re-

---

*Teflon-S is DuPont's registered trademark for its stratified non-stick and self-lubricating finish.

sistance. The coating helps the saw to cut smoother; it also prevents rust.

Saw handles are made of solid hardwood, laminated hardwood, or unbreakable molded plastic.

Probably the three hand saws used most often are the *cross-cut saw*, the *hacksaw*, and the *coping saw*. These saws should be among the first in your shop. Other saws that you may consider which are discussed in this chapter are: *back, bow, compass, dovetail, keyhole,* ings, is also covered in this chapter.
and *rip*. The *miter box*, which has wide application in cutting mold-

15–2.   APPLICATION OF SAWS

Nearly every saw is used in a slightly different manner. Some cut on the push stroke, others on the pull stroke, and still others on both strokes. Hence general sawing techniques are discussed here and details are contained under each saw description.

One of the most important considerations in any sawing operation is the supporting of the workpiece, both the actual workpiece and the scrap being cut off. It is nearly impossible without adequate support to make an accurate cut with any saw. The support depends on the workpiece size. In cutting material from a piece of 4- by 8-foot plywood, sawhorses or substitutes such as chairs or tables are used. Smaller pieces may be held in special jigs or in wood vises. Metal pieces may be held in a machinist's vise that has its jaws protected to prevent marring of the workpiece surface.

After the workpiece is supported, place a pencil mark completely across the workpiece where the saw cut is to be made. Place the saw to the *scrap* side of the mark at a 45° angle. Place the first knuckle of the thumb of your other hand against the blade edge. Using the butt part of the blade and your thumb as a guide, pull back on the saw and make a slight notch. Repeat until there is a small groove. Then take longer cuts, the length of the blade. Let the saw cut at its own speed by letting the *weight* of the saw do the cutting. Don't push down on the saw; take your time. Keep the saw at an angle of about 45° for the most efficient cutting (the ripsaw is an exception; it should be held at 60°). Be sure to hold or support the scrap when the scrap is ready to separate from the workpiece. Failure to hold the scrap will cause the end to split. Also, slow the speed and the length of the stroke near the end of the cutting.

If your job is to trim off only a *slice* of material from the workpiece, clamp a piece of scrap against the workpiece and cut off both pieces. If your job is to make a long straight cut, clamp a piece of straight scrap along the marked cutting line and use the scrap as a guide for your blade. To cut at an angle, again clamp on a piece of scrap wood, but clamp it *parallel* to and at the proper distance from the marked line to cut the required angle. In this application, tilt the blade against the scrap and start the saw into the wood at the mark. Continue to guide the saw along the marked line and against the scrap.

If the blade swerves away from the cutting line slightly, bend the blade slightly to bring it back onto line. Avoid sharp bends. If you go off the guide line quite a bit, return the saw to the point where you started to go off and saw straight. You can use a plane later to smooth off the miscut.

On long cuts, the saw may bind in the kerf. To alleviate this binding, wedge a piece of wood into the kerf. Move the wedge along the kerf, as required, to prevent binding.

To ensure that you are holding your saw square to the workpiece, use a try square against the workpiece and upward to the saw blade. Check your sawing occasionally and straighten the saw as required.

15–3.   CARE OF SAWS

After the use of a saw and prior to placing it in storage, apply a light coat of oil to the blade. Keep the handle bolts tight at all times.

If a saw blade becomes clogged with sawdust or pitch, wipe the blade with a kerosene-soaked rag. If this doesn't remove the sawdust or pitch, soak the blade in kerosene. Follow the soaking by wiping the blade with a rag or, if necessary, by scraping.

Saw-blade teeth can generally be resharpened four or five times with a file before the teeth need resetting. Generally, file sharpening is left to the professionals and you can locate one in the Yellow Pages of your telephone directory under SAWS—SHARPENING AND REPAIRING. Blades of bow, compass, coping, hacksaw, and keyhole saws are replaced rather than resharpened. Specific procedures for sharpening cross-cut and ripsaw blades are discussed in Sections 15–8 and 15–13, respectively.

15–4.   BACKSAW

Backsaws are used in the workshop to cut wood joints and to make straight cuts in molding. The backsaw is used most often as the saw in a miter box (Section 15–12). It has a rigid substantial back that prevents the blade from flexing. Straight cuts are made with the backsaw; it is never used for curved cuts.

The teeth of the backsaw are finer than the teeth of either the cross-cut saw or the ripsaw. This gives it the ability to cut either across or with the grain of the wood. The blade is rather thick, with teeth that are bevel-filed and set; when a cut is made, the teeth should cut just to the outside of the cutting line in the scrap wood so that the workpiece is accurate in length.

Backsaws are from 10 to 30 inches long; the smaller lengths are used for general straight cuts where the workpiece is held in a wood vise or clamp. Saws used with miter boxes are from 22 to 30 inches long. The width of the blade under the back is from 2½ to 3½ inches for the shorter saws and from 4 to 6 inches for the longer saws. There are 11 to 13 points to the inch.

The backsaw should be used in a miter box (Section 15–12) if available and if the workpiece fits into the miter box. When a miter box is not used, clamp the workpiece in a vise or clamp it in some other manner. Start the cut with the saw at about a 45° angle and pull rearward until a starting cut is made. Then proceed back and forth, holding the blade at 45°. When you near the bottom of the cut, straighten the saw and cut straight.

15–5.   BOW SAW

The **bow saw** is a lightweight tubular frame saw used primarily to cut trees and logs, but it can also be used to make rough cuts on large pieces of wood such as posts, two by fours, and planks. It is the ideal saw for cutting firewood in camp; it is much superior to an axe. Blades are from 21 to 30 inches long and are easily replaced.

Support the piece of wood to be cut. In camp, place another log crosswise under the log to be cut and place your foot on the log to clamp it tight. Keep your foot a safe distance from the blade. Hold the saw with one hand on the tension clamping lever and frame. Place the other hand on top of the tubular frame at a comfortable distance from the end. Place the blade at the cutting mark and draw the saw toward you and push it back only a few inches until the blade begins its cuts. Then take long strokes, the length of the blade. Keep the blade flat and straight; keep it from twisting. Let the saw do the cutting; no extra force is required. The teeth cut on both the push and the pull strokes and clear out the saw dust, leaving a clean blade kerf.

Keep a light coat of light oil on the blade to prevent rusting caused by outdoor dampness. If a blade breaks, replace it as follows: pull the tension clamping lever out from the handle and around the pivot point 180 degrees. Remove the blade from the pin. On the other end, remove the sheet-metal screw or bolt that holds the blade. Replace the blade and reverse the procedure to install the new blade.

15–6.   COMPASS SAW

Craftsmen, electricians, plumbers, and carpenters use the **compass saw** to make cutouts of curved and straight shapes in wood or plywood. It is often used to make openings in floors and walls for cables, pipes, and electrical boxes. Its chief advantage is that it can start cutting from a small bored hole through the floor or wall where the opening is to be cut. Its heavy-duty blade permits the cutting of wood and light metal.

The compass saw is from 12 to 14 inches long; there are from 8 to 10 points per inch in the blade. The blade tapers from about 1½ inches at the laminated hardwood handle to about ¼ inch at the tip. Some compass saws come with a *nest* of blades of different lengths and with different numbers of points per inch. Other models have a pistol grip, with an index-finger hole for a firm saw grip.

In using the compass saw, be sure that the blade cut is kept just to the outside of the pattern line in the scrap area. This is necessary because the heavy-duty blade makes a rather wide cut. If necessary, as in removing material for an electrical outlet box, first bore a hole of about ½-inch diameter. Using the saw tip, make vertical strokes to get the blade cutting along the pattern. Then tilt the saw to a 45° angle and continue at this angle until you are close to completing the cutout. Then return to the use of straight strokes.

Lightly oil the blades to prevent them from rusting. Remove and replace the blade by removing and reinstalling the screw-type fastener in the handle.

15–7.   COPING SAW

The **coping saw** is used by carpenters, home craftsmen, and hobbyists to cut otherwise impossible curves and angles in wood, plastic, and thin metal. Small-diameter curves can be cut because of the thin, narrow blade. It is the only hand saw that is used to cut intricate scrollwork. The coping saw is about 12 inches in length with a spring-steel rounded-edge frame that provides a throat opening on different models of from $4\frac{1}{2}$ to 7 inches; a wider throat will permit cuts to the center of larger workpieces. Blade lengths are $6\frac{1}{2}$ inches, with widths of from $\frac{1}{6}$ to $\frac{1}{8}$ inch. There are from 10 to 20 points/inch in the high-carbon-steel replaceable blades. Because blades are inexpensive, they are replaced rather than sharpened.

The angle of the blade is adjustable so that it can be rotated in the frame to allow the saw to do coping work over a larger work area. As can be seen in Fig. 15–1, the blade is mounted between two pin-shaped handles that are perpendicular to the blade. To rotate the blade, loosen the hardwood handle by unscrewing it in a counterclockwise direction. When the blade is relatively loose, rotate the pin handle at the far frame end either clockwise or counterclockwise to the desired blade angle. Rotate the pin at the handle end. Hold this pin in position and tighten the handle until the blade is tight. On some models, the pin at the frame end is part of a notched stud that provides about 25 blade positions. These notches act as locks to hold the blade in position.

The blade is normally placed in the coping-saw frame with the teeth pointing away from the handle. In this position, cutting is accomplished on the push stroke. However, there are times when you may desire to pull the saw toward you to cut; in this case, the blade is turned around. The blade is replaced or turned around by unscrewing the handle until it is very loose. Remove the blade from the blade slots. Note that there is a tiny cross pin on each end of the blade that holds the blade into the saw frame. Place the new blade (or the reversed blade) into the slots. Rotate the pin handles to the desired angle and tighten the handle.

When using the coping saw, support the workpiece in a vise or clamp it to a work surface. Place the blade on the cutting line and begin the strokes. The coping-saw blade cuts only in one direction (the blade cuts on the push stroke when the blade is inserted with the teeth pointing away from the handle). The beginning strokes should be short. After the blade has started, take full strokes along the pattern line on the workpiece. Keep the blade perpendicular to the work and follow the curved or straight lines of the pattern. If the blade is sufficiently into the workpiece so that the frame comes to the workpiece, loosen and rotate the frame by way of the pin handles around the blade to the side of the workpiece to clear the frame. It is not necessary to remove the blade from the workpiece. Retighten the handle.

To cut interior cuts within a workpiece, bore a ¼-inch hole through the workpiece. Remove the blade from the frame, place the blade through the hole in the workpiece, and replace it into the frame. Tighten the handle and proceed to cut.

15–8.   CROSS-CUT SAW

The first hand saw that you should purchase is the **cross-cut saw**. It is used to cut *across* the grain of wood, and can also be used to cut *with* the grain, but less efficiently. The cross-cut saw is always used on plywood, regardless of the direction of the grain shown on the top or bottom ply. Cross-cut saws are available in lengths from 16 to 26 inches; the most popular sizes are 24 and 26 inches. Widths of blades are from 6½ inches at the butt to 1½ inches at the tip. Blades are available with different numbers of points, from 5 points/inch (coarse cut) to 10 points/inch (fine cut). The teeth are alternately set (bent) to the left and right; this causes the sawdust to be cleared from the cut and also causes the cut to be slightly wider than the thickness of the blade. The teeth cut on both the forward and the rearward strokes.

To cut a piece of wood, draw a full line across the workpiece at the cut mark. Support the wood firmly for cutting. Place the saw blade on the *scrap* side of the cutting line at an angle of 45°. Using the butt part of the blade and the first knuckle of your thumb (of the hand not holding the saw) as a blade guide, pull the saw and make a small starting notch. Repeat until a small groove appears. Then start to take longer cuts. Let the saw cut at its own speed by letting the *weight* of the saw cause the teeth to cut. Don't push on the saw; take your time. Keep the saw at a 45° angle for greatest efficiency.

You should leave the sharpening of cross-cut saws to a professional, but if you want to try it, here's how.

The cross-cut points can be filed four or five times before it is necessary to reset the points. If resetting is required, however, it is done prior to filing. Place the blade between two pieces of hardwood the length of the saw and clamp the wood and saw into a vise. The wood should be ⅛ inch below the gullets of the points. Stroke a flat file across the top of the points to flatten the teeth points. These flats act as guides in sharpening. Next, use a *saw set* to alternately bend each tooth to the left and right. The alternate teeth on one side are set first, followed by the teeth on the opposite side.

With the tip of the saw blade to your left, find the first tooth on the left end which is pointed toward you. Place a triangular file into the gullet to the left of this first tooth, position the file at 45° [Fig. 15–2(A)], and file until one-half of the flat at the top of the tooth is gone. Continue alternately with every other tooth until you reach the handle. Reverse the saw in the vise and in the same manner, file the other alternate teeth [Fig. 15–2(B)] until the other half of the flat is removed.

15–9.   DOVETAIL SAW

The **dovetail** saw is also known as a *hobby* saw and as a *cabinet* saw. It is similar in appearance, function, and operation to the backsaw, except that the dovetail saw is smaller in size and the handle is round rather than a handgrip design. This smallness makes the dovetail saw a favorite with hobbyists and modelers for use in intricate dovetailing, tenoning, dadoing, and rabbeting.

As with the backsaw, the dovetail saw makes straight, true, and smooth cuts. The dovetail blade leaves a narrow kerf. The dovetail

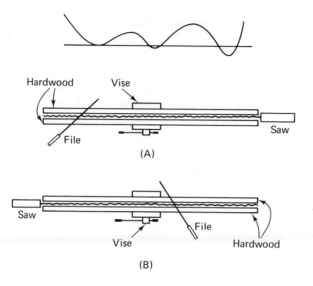

Figure 15–2 Filing crosscut saw blade points.

saw is used in the same manner as the backsaw (Section 15–4) except that it is not used in a miter box.

The dovetail saw is about 10 inches long overall from the hardwood handle to the blade tip. The blade is 25-gauge polished steel and has a rigid back; the width under the back is about 1½ inches. Typical blades have 15 points/inch.

15–10.   HACKSAW

A **hacksaw,** consisting of a frame, a grip, and a blade, is used to cut metal sheet, iron pipe, tubing, screws and bolts, steel bars, brass, bronze, copper, and other metals. The frame provides tension on the blade. Most frames are adjustable to accommodate both 10- and 12-inch blades, have notched studs to hold the blade in four positions, and have unbreakable plastic grips. The throat depth is from 3 to 4 inches. A wing nut and tension wheel adjust the blade tension. The blade is mounted with the teeth forward to cut on the forward stroke. A minihacksaw that uses regular hacksaw blades or broken blades is used where the regular hacksaw cannot reach. The minihacksaw is 9 inches long (without blade).

Hacksaw blades are available in 14, 18, 24, and 32 teeth/inch. The 18-teeth/inch blade is recommended for general all-purpose work. The 14-teeth/inch blade is used for most metals with sections of 1 inch or more thickness; 18 teeth/inch for steel bars, brass, and copper ¼ to 1 inch thick; 24 teeth/inch for iron pipe and medium tubing ⅛ to ¼ inch thick; and 32 teeth/inch for thin metal sheets and tubing up to 18 inches thick. In general, then, fine teeth are used for thin stock, coarse teeth for thick stock. A good rule to follow is that if the proper blade is chosen, two teeth should be able to rest simultaneously on the workpiece (and the wall of a tube). If two teeth cannot be put on the material, tilt the hacksaw. Various blade widths are available for cutting slots of different sizes, such as slots in bolt heads. There are also two teeth sets; *wavy* for thin work and *regular* for general-purpose work.

There are high-speed and standard blades. Blades classified as high-speed, shatterproof, and flexible provide a balance between toughness and flexibility which assures safety and cutting efficiency. Blades made of molybdenum are hard, long-wearing, straight-cutting, and preferred by toolmakers for cutting rigidly clamped material. The blade is also ideal for general machine-shop use. Tungsten blades cut the toughest materials. Tungsten blades are also used on tool and die steels and abrasive materials.

Standard flexible blades for general-purpose cutting have only the teeth hardened; the back remains flexible to minimize breakage. This type of blade is economical for the inexperienced or occasional user under a variety of conditions. Flexible blades are also used in cramped areas without a vise.

Special unbreakable standard blades are balanced, safe, tough, flexible, and are used for miscellaneous cutting. The blade is hardened throughout and is then made flexible. This results in hard, sharp teeth with a semihard back to withstand the twisting that reduces blade breakage and tooth strippage.

The standard all-hard blade is used by the skilled technician. It is used for workpieces that can be held in a vise. The standard all-hard blade gives exceptional uniformity and cutting ability. It is important that the workpiece being cut is held rigid to prevent breakage of the blade.

Two special blades are available for the hacksaw. A tungsten-carbide-tipped blade is used to cut ceramic, steel, and glass; it is *not* used for soft metals. A spiral-toothed blade enables the hacksaw to be used like a coping saw.

Place the workpiece firmly in a vise or other holding jig. Use a file to make a small starting nick on the workpiece. Then hold the saw firmly with one hand on the grip and place the thumb of the other hand at the guideline. Place the blade on the guideline and against the thumb. Use light pressure and slow, short strokes as the hacksaw is started on the guideline on the workpiece. Take short strokes of 1 to 2 inches; a light downward pressure should be made on the forward stroke. There should not be any pressure on the rearward strokes, as the blade does not cut in the rearward direction, and pressure in this direction only causes dulling of the blade. After the cut has been started, remove your thumb and place it on the saw (Fig. 15–3). Increase the stroke length of 6 to 7 inches. Do not twist the blade, as this may cause the blade to break. When the cut is nearly through the workpiece, use light pressure and slow, even strokes until the workpiece parts. If the workpiece is larger than the

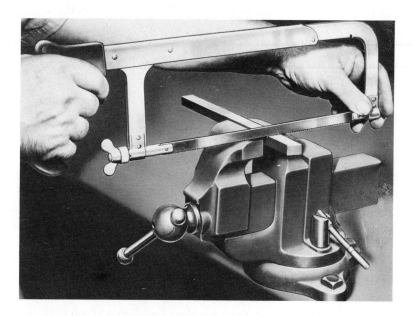

Figure 15–3 Proper use of the hacksaw.

throat of the frame, loosen the tension wheel and wing nut and rotate the blade to the side or bottom to continue the cut. For overhead cuts, many users invert the blade. Lubricants or coolants are generally not used. In cutting pipe or rod, the workpiece will sometimes close on the blade, causing strain. Brace the cut open (as with an old screwdriver), as required. When cutting thin sheet metal, sandwich the metal between two pieces of wood and cut through the entire sandwich. To cut thin-walled tubing, insert a dowel into the tubing.

Use the proper blade for the workpiece being cut. Whenever possible, grip the workpiece in a vise; when this is not possible, use a flexible blade. Keep the blade from becoming excessively hot during use. Replace dull blades.

15–11.   KEYHOLE SAW

The **keyhole saw** is similar to the compass saw (Section 15–6), except that it is physically smaller in size and its blade is narrower; therefore, the keyhole saw can cut smaller diameters than the compass saw. The keyhole saw cuts holes for electrical cables, water and gas pipes, and fixtures in walls and floors. Keyhole saws are from 10 to 12 inches long and have 10 points/inch. The keyhole saw is used in the same manner as the compass saw.

15–12.   MITER BOX

The *miter* is an abutting surface or bevel on either of the pieces joined in a miter joint. A *miter joint* is formed when two pieces of identical cross section are jointed at the ends, and where the joined ends are beveled at equal angles. A **miter box** is used to cut these miters. Miter boxes can be made of hardwood and cost only a couple of dollars, or they can be made of metal with many features to assure accuracy and can cost over $100. Obviously, your needs determine the type of miter box you'll choose. For home use, one made of hardwood is adequate; a craftsman making handcrafted picture frames and moldings may choose the more accurate model.

Figure 15–4 The wooden miter box is used by the homeowner to make accurate miter cuts in molding
and picture frame woods.

The wooden miter box (Fig. 15–4) is made of ¾-inch kiln-dried
oak, rock maple, or other hardwood. A typical box is from 11 to 16
inches long and has a cutting depth and width of 1¾ and 3½ inches,
respectively. It has saw-blade guide slots cut into it at 45° and 90°.

The backsaw (Section 15–4) is used to cut wood placed in the
miter box. Locate the miter box on your bench with the lip extending
over and tight against the edge (Fig. 15–5). Place a piece of scrap
wood on the bottom of the box to protect it and to raise the workpiece toward the top of the box. Place the workpiece on top of the
scrap and against the back of the box. Place the marked cutting line
in a position with the slots such that the blade will cut just outside
the mark. If possible, use a clamp and another piece of scrap wood
to clamp the workpiece tight against the back of the box. Otherwise,
hold the workpiece tight against the back with your hand. Place the
saw into the appropriate miter-box slots and against the workpiece
with the handle tilted slightly upward. Start with a pull stroke. As
the saw goes slightly deeper, level the saw blade until it is parallel
to the workbench. Take long strokes and let the weight of the saw
do the cutting. Go slow and easy at the completion of the cut.

Figure 15–1(H) illustrates a miter box and backsaw used by
professionals. It is made of malleable iron. The positive saw guide
controls the saw blade and also holds the blade up so that the workpiece can be positioned in the miter with both hands. The rear blade
guide pivots about an index plate that is graduated in degrees. The

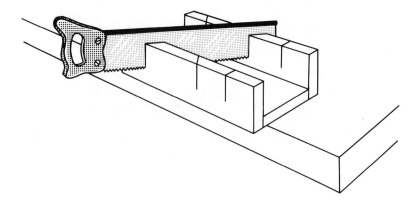

Figure 15–5 The miter box is used to cut mitered joints in
moldings and other decorative pieces.

plate is also marked for 4-, 5-, 6-, 8-, or 20-sided figures. A spring-
loaded pointer stops at the most used angles.

Adjustable stock guides are used to hold the wood against the
back of the miter box. An adjustable-length stop is used to set up a
standard workpiece length for duplicate pieces. Stops are also provided for sawing to a given depth and to prevent sawing below the
baseboard.

The capacity of the width of the workpiece is related to the
angle cut. For example, the maximum *width* of a workpiece that can
be cut with a 26- by 4-inch backsaw at 90° is 8⅝ inches; at 45°, 6
inches; and at 30°, 4 inches.

More practical, all-metal miter boxes for the home craftsman
are available. A sliding key secures the saw guide at the proper angle
as well as the desired depth of cut. The saw guide may be set at the
most used angles of 90, 60, 45, and 30°.

To use the metal miter box, raise the backsaw to the top. Set
the box to the desired cutting angle. Place the workpiece against the
back and clamp it with the stock guides. Adjust the length stop
guide if you're planning to cut more than one workpiece. Lower the
backsaw carefully to the workpiece. Begin the cut with a pulling
stroke. Continue the cut with long strokes until the workpiece is
parted.

All parts of high quality metal miter boxes can be replaced with new replacement parts.

15–13.   RIPSAW

The **ripsaw** is the hand saw used to cut (rip) with the grain of the wood. The teeth of the ripsaw are shaped like tiny chisels with their edges crosswise to the saw. The teeth are alternately set to the left and right to clean out the sawdust. The ripsaw cuts only during the push stroke and operates most efficiently when it is held handle upward at an angle of 60°. A typical ripsaw is 26 inches long and has 5½ points/inch.

To identify an unknown saw blade as a rip or a cross-cut blade, carefully examine the teeth and remember this mental gimmick. Ripsaw teeth are shaped the same as the angle formed at the bottom of a capital letter R, standing for Rip (Fig. 15–6).

In cutting with the ripsaw, support both the workpiece and the scrap piece. Hold the saw with the handle upward at an angle of 60° with the blade tip against the workpiece and against the first knuckle of the thumb of your other hand at the cutting line. Make sure that the blade is going to cut just to the outside of the marked line in the scrap wood. Make a few short strokes to get the saw started (remember that the teeth only cut on the push stroke). Then continue with strokes the length of the saw. It may be necessary to place a wedge of scrap wood into the saw kerf to prevent the workpiece from binding the saw. For long ripping cuts, you can clamp a length of straight scrap wood along the cutting line. Saw along the scrap wood, using it as a guide.

Figure 15–6 Rip and cross cut blade teeth patterns.

The sharpening of ripsaw blades should be left to a professional, but if you want to try it, here's how.

Proceed in exactly the same manner as for the cross-cut blade (Section 15–8), except hold the file straight across the blade. File every other tooth; then turn the saw around and file every other tooth not previously filed. This procedure of turning the saw around prevents you from removing more metal from one side of the blade than from the other side.

16

screwdrivers

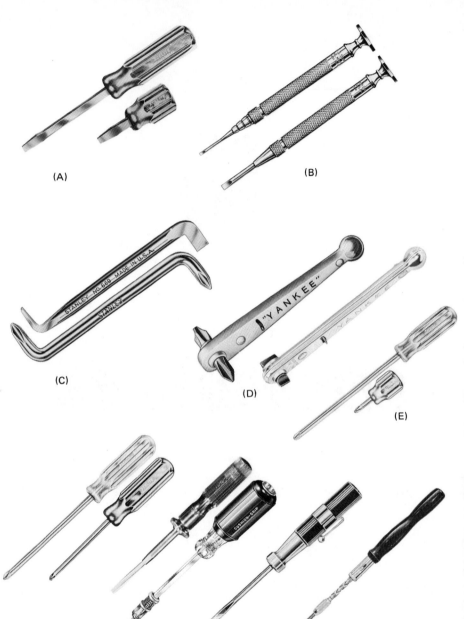

Figure 16–1 Screwdrivers: (A) conventional; (B) jewelers';
(C) offset; (D) offset ratchet; (E) Phillips head;
(F) Reed and Prince; (G) screw holding; (H)
spark detecting; (I) spiral ratchet.

16–1. GENERAL DESCRIPTION

Screwdrivers are tools for driving or withdrawing screws or slot-headed bolts. The screwdriver blade tip is inserted into the screw-head slot and is rotated to drive (usually clockwise) or withdraw (usually counterclockwise) the screw or bolt. Screwdrivers are named, by the type of tip, as *conventional* (for slotted screws), *Phillips head*, and *Reed and Prince*, or, by shape or function, as *off-set, jewelers', offset ratchet, screw-starting, spark-detecting*, or *spiral ratchet*.

Screwdriver blades are made of tempered alloy steel and are available with chrome plating to retard rusting. The tip end is cross-ground and the sides are hollow-ground. The blade is anchored deep in a shockproof, breakproof, plastic handle. Wide flutes on the handle provide a firm gripping surface.

Screwdriver bits for use in braces are also available. This type of screwdriver is particularly useful for installing a large number of screws or for installing screws where a large amount of torque is required (refer to Section 2–4).

16–2. APPLICATION OF SCREWDRIVERS

A screwdriver is a simple tool, and therefore its proper selection and use are often overlooked. In selecting a screwdriver, select the longest bladed screwdriver that is convenient and has the proper size tip for the job. The longer length allows for added pressure and control of the screwdriver on the screwhead. The width of the conventional tip should equal the length of the screw or bolt slot, and the tip thickness should equal the width of the screw or bolt slot. Undersized screwdriver tips will cause damage to the fastener or the screwdriver tip, and the tip may slip out of the fastener and mar the workpiece. Oversized tips will also mar the workpiece when the screw or bolt head becomes flush with the workpiece. The Phillips head and Reed and Prince tips should fill the fastener slots.

In use, the screwdriver is gripped firmly by the handle; the blade is steadied and guided in the screw or bolt slot with the other hand. Always keep the blade in the center of the screw or bolt head and apply turning pressure straight through the blade.

Tiny screwdrivers may be held between the thumb and index finger (Fig. 16–2).

Use screwdrivers only for their intended purpose. Never use a screwdriver to pry or chisel. Never use pliers on the blade of the screwdriver; if additional torque is required, use a square bladed screwdriver with a proper-sized wrench to fit the blade. Also, never hammer the end of a good screwdriver, because you may damage the tip. If you need to remove paint or rust from a screw slot, use an old screwdriver and angle it in the slot. Lightly tap the handle.

Figure 16–2 Tiny screwdrivers used in model work or equipment repair are held with two or three fingers.

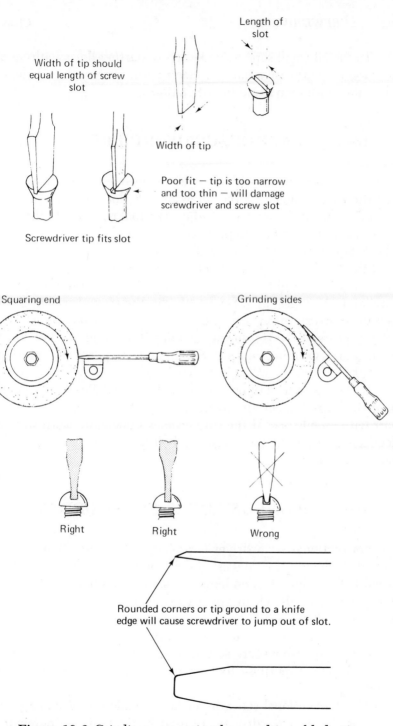

Width of tip should equal length of screw slot

Length of slot

Width of tip

Poor fit — tip is too narrow and too thin — will damage screwdriver and screw slot

Screwdriver tip fits slot

Squaring end

Grinding sides

Right

Right

Wrong

Rounded corners or tip ground to a knife edge will cause screwdriver to jump out of slot.

Figure 16–3 Grinding conventional screwdriver blade tip.

To install small screws, make screw-starting holes with an awl. For larger screws, use a hand or electric drill. Screw threads may be lubricated with soap to aid in installation.

16–3.   CARE OF SCREWDRIVERS

If the tip of a conventional screwdriver becomes worn or nicked so that the tip no longer fits the screw or bolt slot, the tip must be reground. When using a grinder, adjust the tool rest to hold the screwdriver against the wheel to produce the desired shape. Use an emery wheel. Square the tip (Fig. 16–3); then grind both sides of the tip until the tip is the required thickness. Keep the blade thick enough to make a fairly tight fit in a screw slot. The sides should be nearly parallel. During grinding, frequently dip the screwdriver into water to prevent overheating, which can cause a loss of temper. If a blue color appears at the tip during grinding, the metal has lost its tempering, and grinding beyond this area is required for maximum strength.

If the tip of a Phillips head or a Reed and Prince screwdriver becomes burred, place the blade in a vise and carefully remove the burr with an oilstone. If the tip becomes sufficiently worn so that it does not properly fit the screw- or bolt-head slots, the screwdriver must be replaced.

16–4.   CONVENTIONAL SCREWDRIVER

The **conventional screwdriver** is probably the most often used tool around the house. It is suggested that you buy one quality set to use properly for tightening and loosening screws and bolts only, and also buy some 8- to 10-inch inexpensive conventional screwdrivers. You can use the inexpensive ones to open cans, pry, tighten eye bolts, chip, and so on, without the fear of ruining your good screwdrivers. Keep an inexpensive spare screwdriver in your glove compartment, too, as a general-purpose tool for use in making emergency automobile repairs.

The conventional screwdriver has a blade 4 to 12 inches long; short, or stubby screwdrivers are used in tight spaces. Screwdriver blades may be round or square; a wrench may be used on the square blade to enable you to apply more torque to the screw or bolt. Conventional screwdrivers are sold in sets with blade tip widths, blade lengths, and handles proportioned for the most common screw and bolt sizes.

16–5.   JEWELERS' SCREWDRIVER

Jewelers' screwdrivers are for delicate, fine work. They are especially suited for the model railroader, other hobbyists, and fathers who have occasion to repair children's toys. Precision jewelers' screwdrivers are used by watch and clock makers, jewelers, opticians, and toolmakers. Series of different-sized jewelers' screwdrivers are available in sets, but the occasional user should buy a set that consists of one body with four or more interchangeable screwdriver blade bits. A typical set includes four blades with conventional tips from 0.025 to 0.050 inch plus one Phillips head blade tip. Each

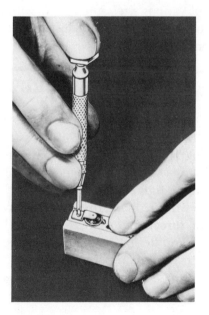

Figure 16–4 The jewelers' screwdriver is used for screws and bolts on models, small toys, or for precision work such as watch repairing and toolmaking.

blade is notched or keyed so that it fits into the body and locks so that it won't rotate during use; a knurled chuck tightens the blade into the body.

Select the desired blade and insert it into the chuck. Rotate the blade until you feel the blade notch slip into place. Tighten the chuck. Place the blade into the screwhead, press your index finger on the concaved swivel knob, and rotate the body to tighten the screw (Fig. 16–4).

16–6.   OFFSET SCREWDRIVER

The **offset screwdriver** is used to drive or withdraw screws or bolts that cannot be aligned with the axis of the conventional or Phillips head screwdrivers because of space limitations, such as when mounting an electrical box to a wall. The offset screwdriver is also used where high torque is required to tighten or loosen a screw or bolt. Offset screwdrivers are made in a variety of sizes with conventional and Phillips heads of various sizes. On models with four tips, two tips are offset at 90° and two tips at 45°. This offset allows for quarter- or eighth-revolution torquing.

16–7.   OFFSET RATCHET SCREWDRIVER

Like the offset screwdriver, the **offset ratchet screwdriver** is used where space limitations prevent the use of a straight-drive screwdriver and where high torque is required. However, this type of offset screwdriver has the added advantage of having a ratchet, which allows for the complete tightening of a screw without the necessity of removing the screwdriver blade tip from the screw. A lever allows ratcheting in either direction for tightening or loosening. Models are available with two different-sized tips in either conventional or Phillips head or with combination conventional and Phillips heads. Sets may also be purchased that have an offset ratchet handle with various-sized slotted, Phillips head, hollow-head setscrew, cap screw, and bolt adapters.

16–8.   PHILLIPS HEAD SCREWDRIVER

A **Phillips head screwdriver** is distinguished by the tip, which is designed to fit into Phillips head screws or bolts. The tip has about

30° flutes and a *blunt* end. The screwdriver tips are made in four sizes, to match Phillips head screws as follows: size 1 for No. 4 and smaller screws, size 2 for Nos. 5 to 9, size 3 for Nos. 10 to 16, and size 4 for No. 18 and larger. Blade lengths vary from 1 to 18 inches.

The tip of the Phillips head screwdriver is similar to the tip of the Reed and Prince screwdriver (Section 16–9). The Phillips *screw* has beveled walls between the slots, whereas the Reed and Prince screw has straight, pointed walls. The Phillips screw slots are not as deep as the Reed and Prince. You may check that you are using the proper screwdriver for a given screw as follows. Hold the screw in a vertical position with the head up. Place the screwdriver tip in the head; if the screwdriver tends to stand up unassisted, the screwdriver is probably of the proper type and size.

16–9.　　REED AND PRINCE SCREWDRIVER

The **Reed and Prince screwdriver** is similar to the Phillips screwdriver except that the tip is defined as a cross-point tip. The tip has 45° flutes and a *sharp* pointed end. The outline of the end of the Reed and Prince screwdriver is close to a right angle. This type of screwdriver is used on *Frearson screws.* Blade lengths vary from 3 to 12 inches (refer to Phillips head screwdrivers, Section 16–8).

16–10.　　SCREW-HOLDING SCREWDRIVER

Screw-holding screwdrivers are used to hold and start slotted screws in a workpiece. This allows the starting to be done with one hand and also allows the starting of screws in confined spaces. Different screw-holding arrangements, including steel jaws and wedgelike split-tip screwdrivers, are available. The steel-jaws model has a set of clamped jaws that slide down the bit and grasp the screw (or bolt) under the head. The clamp holding the jaws is spring-loaded and thus holds the screwhead slot against the blade tip. The split-tip screwdriver wedges the blade firmly into the screw slot when the sliding sleeve is slid into position. Screw-holding screwdrivers are made in several sizes and must be matched to the size of the screw to be driven.

16–11.   SPARK-DETECTING SCREWDRIVER

The **spark-detecting screwdriver** is useful to the home automobile mechanic. A tough, composition handle contains a neon tube, which glows when the screwdriver tip is touched to a high-frequency circuit such as in an automobile ignition system. Blade lengths are from 5 to 9 inches with tips from $\frac{9}{64}$ to $\frac{1}{4}$ inch wide.

16–12.   SPIRAL RATCHET SCREWDRIVER

The **spiral ratchet screwdriver** is used by craftsmen in applications where a large number of screws must be driven by hand. A spring keeps the interchangeable blade in the screwhead and automatically returns the handle to the driving position after each stroke. The screwdriver is operated by pushing on the handle; the spiral ratchet drives the screw.

A lever on the screwdriver selects either right-hand spiral ratchet drive for tightening, left-hand spiral ratchet drive for loosening, or a rigid setting that allows you to lock the spiral-drive mechanism. The rigid setting allows the screwdriver to act as an ordinary screwdriver, for final torquing of a screw or bolt.

Spiral ratchet screwdrivers are usually sold with two screwdriver bits: a conventional bit and a Phillips head bit. Various-sized models are sold for special applications: light duty for small-parts assembly, all-purpose regular duty ($\frac{7}{32}$- or $\frac{1}{4}$-inch conventional bit and a No. 2 Phillips head bit), and heavy duty.

Spindles and chucks, shell and handle tubes, shifters, springs, and small parts of the spiral ratchet screwdriver can be purchased and replaced without special tools or procedures.

17

wrenches

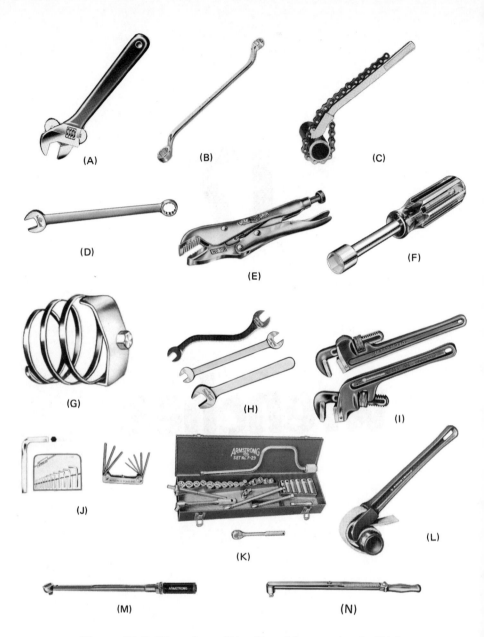

Figure 17–1 Wrenches: (A) adjustable open end; (B) box; (C) chain pipe; (D) combination; (E) locking plier wrench; (F) nut driver; (G) oil filter; (H) open end; (I) pipe; (J) setscrew; (K) socket; (L) strap; (M) torque limiting type torque wrench; (N) deflecting beam - converging scale type torque wrench.

17–1.   GENERAL DESCRIPTION

One variety of **wrench** is used to tighten or loosen fasteners such as bolts, nuts, headed screws, and pipe plugs. Another variety of wrench is made to grip round stock, studs, and pipe. There are also special wrenches, such as locking plier, torque, and setscrew wrenches: the locking plier wrench is used for a multitude of jobs; a torque wrench is used to tighten square or hex-headed fasteners to a specified force; and setscrew wrenches are used to tighten special hex setscrews.

There are many types of wrenches and many sizes for various applications. You should select and purchase those wrenches most applicable to your needs. For example, if you're a beginning home-owner, you might select an adjustable open-end wrench and a locking plier wrench as your first tools. They can do a multitude of jobs for you. If you're a beginning mechanic, you'd probably select a socket wrench set and a set of combination wrenches. An electronic technician would certainly want a set of nut drivers among his tools. And the home automobile do-it-yourselfer would want an adjustable open-end wrench, an oil-filter wrench, and a socket wrench set in his tool box. The hobbyist would select miniature wrenches. Purchase only high-quality wrenches for your tool box or shop. Cheap ones slip, bend, and their corners become rapidly rounded.

Wrenches are made of hardened and tempered steel. Many

are chrome-plated to prevent rusting. On fixed nominal-opening wrenches (such as open-end, box, combination, and sockets), the size of the opening is stamped near the opening; sizes are available in English units and metric units. The openings are from 0.005 to 0.015 inch larger than the sizes marked on the wrench so that the wrench fits easily over the nut or bolt.

This chapter describes the following wrenches: *adjustable open-end, box, chain pipe, combination, locking plier, nut-driver, oil-filter, open-end, pipe, setscrew, socket, strap,* and *torque.* Determine your needs, purchase the wrenches, and learn to use them properly.

17–2.   APPLICATION OF WRENCHES

In selecting a wrench for a particular job, consider the type of work to be done, the space limitations, and the number of fasteners. There are not any fast and hard rules as to which wrench should be used for a particular job, but there are some general guidelines. When a wrench cannot be used *over* a fastener head, an open-end wrench of either the fixed or adjustable type is used. The open-end wrench is used on nuts of fuel, oil, and hydraulic lines; clutch and transmission control rods; brake rods; and cable ends. A box wrench is used where the wrench *can* be placed over the fastener head. Many advanced technicians prefer combination wrenches; they use the open end to spin the nut down and the box end for the final torquing.

Select the proper size wrench for the nut, bolt, or other fastener to be loosened or tightened. Use of a wrench of the wrong size will cause the points of the nut or bolt to be rounded, making it very difficult to further tighten or to remove. Always use adjustable wrenches so that the pulling force is applied to the fixed jaw, never to the adjustable jaw. Do not use a pipe or other device to extend the length of the handle of a wrench; instead, get a wrench with a longer handle. Do not strike wrench handles with a hammer to tighten or to loosen a bolt or nut.

If a rusted nut, bolt, or other type of fastener is to be removed, apply penetrating oil or a mixture of kerosene and lubricating oil and allow time for the oil to penetrate before attempting to turn the fastener with a wrench. Pull on the wrench (instead of pushing), whenever possible, to keep from skinning your knuckles if the wrench slips. Do not exert a hard pull on a pipe wrench until it is firmly attached to the workpiece.

17–3.   CARE OF WRENCHES

To protect wrenches from becoming damaged, *always* use a wrench of the proper size. Ensure that adjustable open-end, pipe, chain pipe, strap, oil filter, and locking plier wrenches are adjusted for proper fit; this protects the wrench and the workpiece.

Always keep wrenches free of oil, grease, grit, and dirt. After use, clean them with a rag saturated with kerosene. Avoid getting grit into the working parts of ratchets, chains, and adjustment nuts. Remove grit at once; a few particles can score your tools deeply.

The knurled nuts of adjustable open-end and pipe wrenches should occasionally be lubricated with graphite. Occasionally apply a drop of light oil to the moving parts of all wrenches. This will prolong the life of the wrenches and will assure better operation.

17–4.   ADJUSTABLE OPEN-END WRENCH

An **adjustable open-end wrench** is used to tighten an infinite number of English- and metric-size nuts, bolts, headed screws, and pipe plugs. It is normally used when the proper size of open-end, box, or combination wrench is not available. The adjustable open-end wrench has one fixed jaw and one movable jaw and is shaped such that the jaws form four sides for firm gripping of hex nuts or bolts. The wrench head is thin and angled from the handle for use in tight areas, and its jaws are smooth; this makes it popular for use in tightening and loosening chrome-plated fittings. This angled head has proved very useful and therefore the adjustable open-end wrench has taken over the functions of the monkey wrench to such a degree that there are few monkey wrenches available today. The adjustable open-end wrench is also known as the *Crescent wrench*, named after its first manufacturer.

The movable jaw of the adjustable open-end wrench is adjusted by rotating a knurled nut. Some models include a locking device in the form of a push rod to hold the adjustment. Typical wrench han-

Apply force in direction
indicated

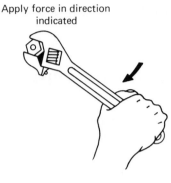

Figure 17–2 Fitting and using the adjustable open end wrench.

dles are from 4 to 16 inches long with jaw capacities of approximately ½ to 1¾ inches. Longer handles provide the best leverage.

Always place the adjustable open-end wrench on the nut or bolt to be tightened or loosened so that the force used is applied to the fixed jaw as shown in Fig. 17–2. After placing the wrench into position, tighten the knurled adjustment nut until the jaws tightly fit the nut or bolt. If the jaws do not fit tightly, the wrench will slip and the corners of the nut or bolt will be rounded; your knuckles may also be skinned. Press the locking device (if available on your wrench) to hold the wrench opening at the proper adjustment. In tight areas, the wrench can be flipped over repeatedly to give you a better turning advantage on the fastener.

17–5.   BOX WRENCH

Box wrenches completely *box* the nut or bolt to be tightened or loosened and hence are safer tools than the open-end wrenches. The box opening contains 6 or 12 points; the 12-point end allows the wrench to be used for $\frac{1}{12}$ turns (30°) in close quarters. The box wrench is usually a double-ended wrench with different-sized openings in each end. The openings range from ¼ to 2¾ inches and 8 to 32 mm. Midgets are available from $\frac{3}{16}$ to $\frac{11}{32}$ inch. The height of the box is correctly proportioned for all nut sizes and series. Handle lengths vary from 4½ to 18 inches; longer lengths provide greater leverage. The handle may be straight, but it is often offset 15° from the box opening to allow for hand clearance. Sometimes the box end is offset.

Ratchet box wrenches are also available but are recommended only for mass production operations.

Always select the proper size of box wrench (Fig. 17–3) for the nut or bolt to be turned. The box wrench does not slip off and hence is preferred over the open-end wrench. Repeated swings in arcs of 30° (a 12-point wrench) are sufficient to completely tighten or remove a nut or bolt. Remove the wrench completely from the nut or bolt and then replace it when repositioning the wrench for another partial turn. This method is slower than with an open-end wrench, but the box wrench enables you to make tighter fittings or to remove already-tight fittings. Thus it is often desirable to rapidly *spin down* a nut or bolt with an open-end wrench and then set it tight with a box wrench. For this reason, many homeowners and mechanics prefer the combination wrench (Section 17–7).

17–6.   CHAIN PIPE WRENCH

The **chain pipe wrench** is a unique wrench in that it can be used on stock of any shape—square, hexagonal, irregular, or round (Fig. 17–1

Figure 17–3 Always use the proper size box wrench.

shows the chain pipe wrench encircling a round workpiece). It can also be used in close quarters such as around a pipe that is against a wall or under a sink and can't be gripped with a pipe wrench. It is used to tighten, loosen, or grip various sizes of stock, pipe, nuts, and plugs from ½ to 6 inches, depending upon chain length. It can also be used to remove automobile oil filters. However, do not use this wrench on surfaces that you do not want marred; the serrated gripper can cause damage. Homeowners, mechanics, plumbers, electricians, steamfitters, and maintenance men will find many uses for this tool.

In using the chain pipe wrench, tightly place the curved surface (an arc that is just below the serrated gripper) against the workpiece. Wrap the sprocket chain around the workpiece as tightly as possible and lock the chain sprocket in the slot behind the serrated gripper. Pull the wrench such that the workpiece is forced between the serrated gripper and the chain. Apply a leverage force to the wrench handle so that the gripper bites into the workpiece and the wrench turns the workpiece. Some models have a double set of serrated gripper edges which allow use of the wrench in either direction without removing it from the workpiece.

Keep the chain well lubricated with oil during storage to prevent rust.

17–7.   COMBINATION WRENCH

The **combination wrench** has an *open-end* wrench at one end of the handle and a 12-point *box* wrench at the other; nominal openings at both ends are the same. The open end is often angled at 15° from the handle, and the box end is often offset 15° from the plane of the handle to give hand clearance. Combination sets are made in various sizes of openings, lengths, offsets, and angles as discussed for the open-end and box wrenches. The combination wrench is often the choice of homeowners, mechanics, and technicians because it combines the open end for quick spin down of nuts or bolts and the box end for final tightening. Refer to Sections 17–5 and 17–11 for the use of the box and open-end wrenches, respectively.

17–8.   LOCKING PLIER WRENCH

A **locking plier wrench** provides a viselike grip around any nut, bolt, flat or round object placed between its serrated jaws. It is actually seven tools in one: clamp, gripping tool, pipe or locking wrench, pliers, adjustable wrench, portable vise, and a wire and bolt cutter. In essence, it's a pinch hitter where other tools fail. The upper jaw is fixed; the lower jaw is accurately adjusted to the desired jaw opening by turning the knurled adjustment screw. A locking handle locks the jaws onto an object with up to a ton of pressure by a toggle action of a lever being pushed past center. The lock release lever unlocks the jaws to allow removal of the wrench. Typical wrench jaws open up to 2 inches; the locking capacity is from $1\frac{1}{4}$ to $1\frac{3}{4}$ inches for wrench lengths of from $7\frac{1}{2}$ to 10 inches. The 5-inch locking plier wrench is also handy for small jobs.

The locking plier wrench can be locked onto an object of any shape. It can serve as a handle for files, chisels, screwdrivers, hot pans, or faucets and be used in any place where an extension or handle is required. It can be used to manipulate sheets of steel, plastic, or wood. It can be used to improvise tools, such as an awl, by simply clamping a heavy needle or nail in its jaws. A scraper can be made with a razor blade clamped between the jaws. It is an excellent clamp for use in gluing, soldering, riveting, welding, sawing, filing, or cutting any material. A saw may be fashioned by clamping a broken blade or a small blade into the jaws. It can be used as a plier to bend, form, twist, hold, and crimp metal and wire. It's also a small portable vise and can be locked into a larger vise when a small vise is needed to hold small objects for polishing, filing, grinding, or soldering. It will pull out headless nails, remove broken studs, and is an adjustable open-end and pipe wrench. In summary, the locking plier wrench is a necessity for numerous applications (Fig. 17–4). It should be in every toolbox or shop; it's also a fantastic multipurpose tool to carry in your automobile for emergency repairs.

Several other tools valuable to the homeowner, technician, machinist, and welder that are similar in design and operation to the locking plier wrench are illustrated in Fig. 17–5. The curved-jaw

Awkward fabricating jobs.

Quick powerful clamp for gluing and joining.

Pulling headless nail, even if nail is broken off flush with wood.

Holding pipe.

Emergency handle in camp or kitchen for a cool, lock-on handle for hot pans, pots, skillets.

Only VISE-GRIP® will hold without slipping on a job like this.

For holding small pieces while grinding. Positively will not slip. Lessens danger of being injured.

Perfect handle for holding and twisting star drill. No skinned knuckles.

Speed wrench—just lock to nut and give it a whirl.

Perfect pipe wrench for plumbers, pipe fitters.

Riveting

Removing oil filter easily.

Holding for machine work.

Pulls cotter pins without straightening prongs.

Work in close quarters.

Lock on handle for machine shop jobs.

Quickie handle for saw blades, awls, files, etc.

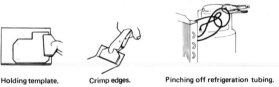

Holding template.

Crimp edges.

Pinching off refrigeration tubing.

Figure 17–4 The locking plier wrench and other similarly designed tools are used for numerous applications in the homeowner's shop as well as for professional applications.

locking plier wrench is the same as the straight jaw (Fig. 17–1) except that the curved jaw is superior for use as a pipe wrench or on other *round* objects. The curved jaw contacts hex nuts and bolts at four points, for extra gripping power. The wire cutter (below the jaws) can cut a quarter-inch bolt in two when successive bites are taken.

The C clamp is used to clamp angle iron; clamp I-beams; hold work on a drill-press table; hold workpieces for gluing, welding, and soldering; and to perform numerous other clamping applications. Unlike a screw C clamp, this C clamp is adjusted to the correct opening before use. It is then clamped by a squeeze of the hand for a positive locking grip. In factory tool work, it holds templates and parts for die work.

The sheet-metal tool is designed primarily for use in sheet-metal work, for clamping, bending, and fabrication. Furniture repairmen and upholsterers find this tool very versatile and valuable.

The chain clamp uses the same locking and leverage principles as the other tools, but its jaws are a chain and a body hook. This tool will hold any shaped part or parts that its chain will wrap around. It is an emergency tool that can accomplish seemingly impossible holding jobs.

The welding clamp permits alignment of the edges of pieces to be welded. Then it locks the pieces together. When clamped, both hands are free for welding. The U-shaped jaws allow visibility and working space for the welding operation. The pinch-off tool is a special tool for the refrigeration industry; it pinches off copper tubing instantly.

To grip an object with any of the locking plier wrenches or similar tools, grasp the tool with the locking lever slightly open. With the other hand, rotate the adjustment screw until the jaws just slip over the workpiece. Squeeze the handles together until locked. After the job is completed, hold the wrench with one hand and hook the fingers of the other hand around the screw end of the wrench. Push the lock release with the thumb. To use as pliers without locking, adjust the end screw so that the jaws don't quite snap shut on the workpiece. Practice using the locking plier wrench on workpieces of various sizes until you are fully acquainted with the procedures for locking and unlocking the wrench. The surface of some objects may be marred by the jaws and clamping pressure of these tools.

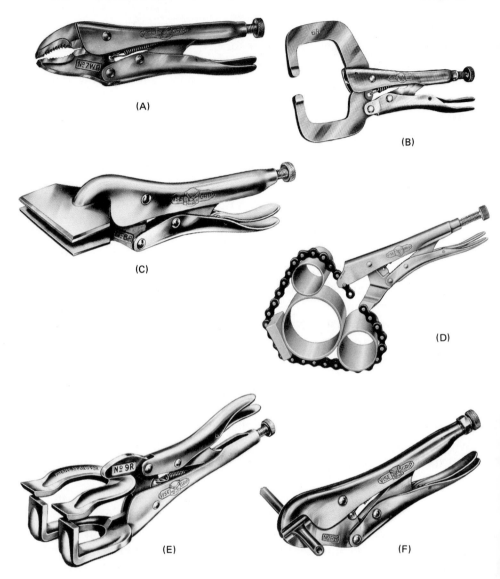

Figure 17–5 Several other types of tools similar to the locking plier wrench are: (A) curved jaw locking
plier wrench; (B) C clamp; (C) sheet metal
tool; (D) chain clamp; (E) welding clamp; (F)
pinch-off pliers.

Protect the workpiece surfaces with scraps of wood, soft metal, or other material.

Damaged serrated jaws or the adjustment screw can be renewed by filing. Place the jaw or screw into a vise and carefully file with a three square file. If the spring that is housed in the fixed handle becomes stretched or broken, it is easily replaced by following the manufacturer's recommendations. Occasionally place a drop of oil on all points of wear.

17–9.   NUT-DRIVER WRENCH

The **nut-driver wrench** is similar to the design of a screwdriver except that the tip is a six-point socket for hexagonal-shaped nuts and bolts. The nut driver speeds up the turning of nuts. Portions of the shanks are often hollow to accept the end of a bolt as the nut is turned down onto the bolt. There are nut drivers to fit sizes from $\frac{3}{16}$ to $\frac{5}{8}$ inch. The handles are shockproof butyrate plastic or wood and are fluted for a more positive grip; the handles are often color coded according to size. Nut drivers are available in midget pocket-clip styles, stubby, regular, and extra long.

The nut driver is used a great deal by the electronic technician to rapidly spin nuts and hex-headed sheet-metal screws. It is used like a screwdriver (Fig. 17–6). When the nut is tightened, care must

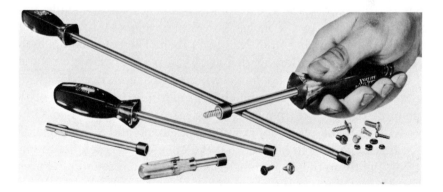

Figure 17–6 The nut driver wrench is used like a screwdriver.

be taken that the nut driver does not round the corners of the nut and that the corners of the nut driver do not become stripped.

Variable size nut drivers hold ¼- to ⁷⁄₁₆-inch hex nuts and bolts for easy starting and removal when you are working in tight spaces. The positive locking device holds the fastener. The harder you turn, the tighter it grips. This tool should be bought rather than a set of fixed nut drivers if you have only occasional need for this type of tool.

17–10.   OIL-FILTER WRENCH

Oil-filter wrenches are used by the home automobile repairman and the garage mechanic to remove standard *spin-on* oil filters. Force applied to the wrench hex nut is distributed over the surface of the oil filter to prevent the splitting or crushing of the filters. The continued force of the wrench grips the filter securely to loosen and remove it. This wrench is not used to replace the filter.

Place the oil-filter wrench over the oil filter; attach a hex socket, open-end, or box wrench to the hex nut and apply turning power to remove the filter.

17–11.   OPEN-END WRENCH

The **open-end wrench** is usually a double-ended wrench with openings of different sizes at each end. Wrenches are available with openings from ¼ to 1¾ inches and 6 to 28 mm. Midget wrenches have openings ranging from ¹³⁄₆₄ to ⅜ inch. The common open-end wrench has ends that are angled at 15° to permit complete rotation of 30° hex nuts. Other open-end wrenches have ends at 45, 60, 75, or 90°. The length of the wrench is proportioned to the size of the opening; the greater the length, the greater the leverage. Other types of open-end wrenches are single-open-end and S-shape-handle.

It is important to be sure that the open-end wrench fits the nut or bolt tightly so that the wrench does not slip and round off corners (Fig. 17–7). Offset open-end wrenches make it possible to turn a bolt or nut that is recessed or is in a limited space, where there is little room to turn the wrench. The wrench may be turned over, often after each partial turn, to aid in turning the nut or bolt in limited

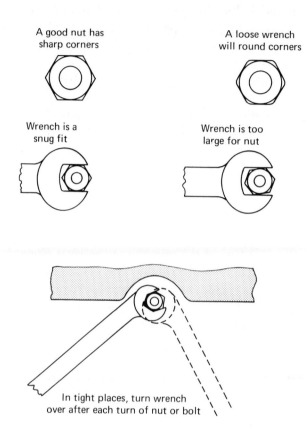

Figure 17–7 Fitting and using the open-end wrench.

areas. If possible, always pull the wrench toward you to move the nut or bolt in the desired direction. If you must push on the wrench, push with your palm (knuckles out of the way) so that if the wrench slips, your knuckles won't be skinned. To avoid slipping on the final tightening of the nut or bolt, make the final turns with a box wrench.

17–12.   PIPE WRENCH

A **pipe wrench** (often called a *Stillson wrench*) is used to rotate a round workpiece such as a pipe or the head of a worn nut or bolt that has had its corners rounded; the pipe wrench is not to be used on good nuts and bolts. The pipe wrench has two hardened jaws (with milled teeth) that are not parallel. The outer jaw, which is adjustable by means of a knurled nut, is called the *hook jaw*. This jaw is made with a small amount of play, which provides an automatic tight grip on a pipe when the wrench is turned in the direction of the movable jaw. The jaws always leave marks on the woodpieces; this can often be alleviated by placing a rag against the jaws. The *healjaw*, which is the fixed jaw, is replaceable. It is also spring-loaded to give it full floating action to increase the wrench grip. Pipe wrenches used by home repairmen, plumbers, and mechanical technicians are available in straight and offset patterns in lengths from 6 to 14 inches, with capacities of from $\frac{1}{4}$ to 6 inches. The 10- to 14-inch sizes are best for most applications around the home.

The pipe wrench will work in only one direction; the wrench is turned in the direction of the opening of the jaws. Force is applied to the back of the handle. Since the top jaw has slight angular movement, the grip on the workpiece is increased by the pressure on the handle. Correct direction of rotation for the pipe wrench is the same as for the adjustable open-end wrench shown in Fig. 17–2. In plumbing work, pipe wrenches are used in pairs, one to hold the threaded pipe and one to turn the fitting.

To replace the healjaw, cut the rivet with a cold chisel. Replace the healjaw and rerivet it into place.

17–13.   SETSCREW WRENCH

Setscrew wrenches, also called *Allen wrenches* and *hex keys*, are L-shaped, made of tool steel, and have a hexagonal section. The setscrew wrench is used to tighten or loosen socket setscrews, socket-head capscrews, button-head capscrews, socket-head shoulder screws, flathead capscrews, and true-round pressure plugs that have hexagonal sockets. These types of fasteners are used to hold handles, secure knobs and controls, and to lock pulleys to shafts. Dimensions across the flats are available from approximately 0.028 to 2 inches in English and metric units. A typical set includes setscrew wrenches of 0.028, 0.035, 0.050, $\frac{1}{16}$, $\frac{5}{64}$, $\frac{3}{32}$, $\frac{7}{64}$, $\frac{1}{8}$, $\frac{9}{64}$, $\frac{5}{32}$, $\frac{3}{16}$, $\frac{7}{32}$, $\frac{1}{4}$, and $\frac{5}{16}$ inch. In addition to the L shape, setscrew wrenches are available with loop handles, as a flexible driver, and in a holder similar to a pocket knife.

When using the setscrew wrench, be sure that a wrench of the proper size is selected and is inserted as far as possible into the fastener to be tightened or loosened. The long end is used to rapidly turn a fastener. The short end of the wrench is used to give a final tightening or to break loose a tight fastener.

17–14.   SOCKET WRENCH (WITH ALL DRIVES)

A **socket wrench** consists of a drive handle and one of a various number of English or metric-sized sockets. The socket wrench is used to tighten or loosen nuts, bolts, and headed screws. The socket wrench is made from parts within a socket wrench set: sets may contain as few as six pieces to over 220 pieces, consisting of drives, sockets, universal joints, adapters, and other related tools.

When a person needs a ¾-inch socket wrench, he is normally requesting a ¾-inch detachable socket plus a drive handle, which is usually either a ratchet-drive handle or a flex-drive handle. Prior to his request, he has determined the size of and number of nuts or bolts to be tightened or loosened. He has also determined his working space.

A basic socket wrench set usually consists of various-sized 12-point sockets, a ratchet drive, a flex handle, a slide bar handle, and an extension. The socket wrench drives are available in ¼-, ⅜-, ½-, ¾-, and 1-inch sizes and should be selected according to their required use. A ¼-inch drive is for light-duty work; ⅜- and ½-inch for automotive, industrial, and aircraft work; and ¾- and 1-inch drives are for heavy-duty use, including machinery and heavy-equipment installations.

There are four basic types of socket wrench drives: ratchet, flex handle, speeder, and slide bar handle. These drives attach to a variety of sizes of sockets, 4- or 8-point sockets for square-head nuts and bolts, and 6- or 12-point sockets for hexagonal-head nuts and bolts. Accessories such as socket adapters, universal joints, and extensions extend the capability of the socket wrenches.

The ratchet drive [Fig. 17–8(A)] is used with various-sized Eng-

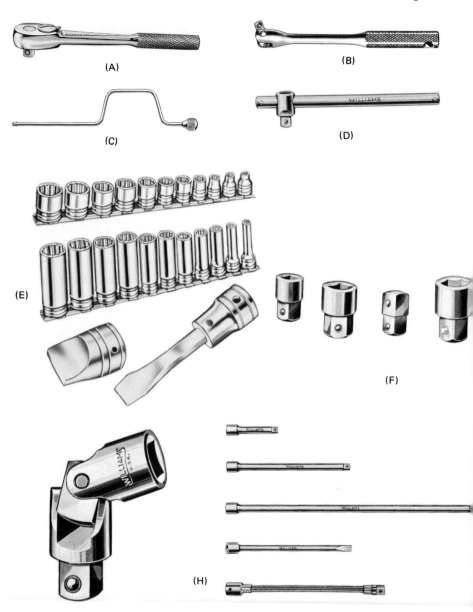

Figure 17–8 Socket wrench set: (A) ratchet drive; (B) flex handle drive; (C) speeder drive; (D) slide bar handle; (E) sockets; (F) socket adapters; (G) universal joint; (H) extensions.

lish and metric sockets to tighten or loosen nuts and bolts. The ratchet drive saves time in performing its functions because the socket does not have to be removed from the nut or bolt. It is particularly useful in close quarters; a fine-toothed-action ratchet drive permits handle movement in increments of 4 degrees.

Ratchet drives contain two and sometimes three *controls*. The quick-release push button releases spring pressure on the spring-tensioned ball in the square drive, allowing the socket to slide easily off the drive; a different socket readily slips on and locks over the spring-tensioned ball. The reversing lever allows the ratchet to slip (ratchet) in one direction for tightening and the opposite direction for loosening. A knurled speeder (on the ratchet) allows nuts to be quickly spun onto a bolt. The speeder accessory may be added to a ratchet drive if it is not on the original model (a speeder is not shown in Fig. 17–8).

The flex handle drive [Fig. 17–8(B)] is used with various sizes of English and metric sockets to tighten or loosen nuts and bolts. With the flex handle drive in a straight (perpendicular to the work) configuration, nuts or bolts are spun snugly. The flex handle is then turned 90° (parallel to the work). This provides additional leverage for final tightening of the fastener. In confined areas where the flex handle cannot be turned 90°, a sliding bar may be placed through a cross hole in the handle; this provides additional leverage for final tightening of the fastener.

The speeder drive [Fig. 17–8(C)] is used with various sizes of English and metric sockets as a rapid means of spinning (running) a number of nuts and bolts on or off. Final tightening or breaking of tight fasteners must be done with the ratchet or flex handle drives, which provide additional leverage.

The slide bar handle, often called a T or L handle drive [Fig. 17–8(D)], is used with various-sized English and metric sockets to tighten or loosen nuts and bolts. For additional leverage and for working in confined areas, the drive may be positioned anywhere along the handle; thus a T or an L shape is formed.

Sockets [Fig. 17–8(E)] have two openings: a square hole that fits the socket wrench drive and a circular hole with notched sides to fit the nut or bolt head to be turned. The square hole is ¼, ⅜, ½, ¾, or 1 inch across to mate with the respective socket wrench drive. The circular hole may be notched with 4 or 8 notches for square-shaped nuts and bolt heads or with 6 or 12 notches for hexagon-shaped nuts and bolt heads. The 8- and 12-notched sockets are recommended because they will last longer, turn in smaller angular increments, and are about the same price. Socket sizes usually range from $\frac{1}{8}$ to $\frac{9}{16}$ inch for $\frac{1}{4}$-inch drives; from $\frac{3}{8}$ to $\frac{3}{4}$ inch for $\frac{3}{8}$-inch drives; from $\frac{3}{8}$ to $1\frac{1}{4}$ inches for $\frac{1}{2}$-inch drives; from $\frac{3}{4}$ to $2\frac{1}{4}$ inches for $\frac{3}{4}$-inch drives; and from $1\frac{1}{16}$ to $3\frac{1}{8}$ inches for 1-inch drives. Metric sizes are available also.

Regular-sized and deep sockets, useful for spinning nuts onto long bolts because they allow a length of the bolt into the socket, are available. Sockets with conventional, Phillips head, hex, open-end, and box drivers are also available. Socket adapters [Fig. 17–8(F)] are attached to a socket wrench drive when it is desired to change from one square drive size to another square drive size. Socket adapters are available to change socket wrench drives of $\frac{3}{8}$ to $\frac{1}{4}$, $\frac{1}{4}$ to $\frac{3}{8}$, $\frac{3}{8}$ to $\frac{1}{2}$, $\frac{1}{2}$ to $\frac{3}{8}$, $\frac{1}{2}$ to $\frac{3}{4}$, $\frac{3}{4}$ to $\frac{1}{2}$, 1 to $\frac{3}{4}$, and $\frac{3}{4}$ to 1 inch.

A universal joint [Fig. 17–8(G)] makes it possible to turn nuts or bolts where a straight wrench could not be used because of lack of clearance. One end of the joint is attached to a socket wrench drive; the other end attaches to the square-hole end of a socket. The joint swings up to 90°. Spring tension holds the joint at any desired angle. Universal joints are also available that have a $\frac{1}{2}$-inch-square drive with 12-point sockets of $\frac{1}{2}$, $\frac{9}{16}$, $\frac{5}{8}$, $\frac{11}{16}$, and $\frac{3}{4}$ inch. These fixed-size universal joint sockets are useful for applications where the same size of universal joint is required for extended work.

Extensions [Fig. 17–8(H)] extend the length of socket wrench drives. The extension is connected between the drive and the socket.

To use a socket wrench, first select the shape (for square or hex nut or bolt) and the size of the socket that is required. Hand-try the socket for proper fit. Next, inspect the clearance area to determine which type of drive is the most satisfactory for the job. If the ratchet drive is selected, snap the socket onto the square drive. Flip the reversing lever to the applicable position for ratcheting in either the clockwise or counterclockwise direction. Use the ratchet wrench speeder to quickly spin the nut or bolt finger-tight. Finally, apply force to the handle and torque the nut taut (Fig. 17–9). It may be necessary to swing the handle back and forth, but the socket does not have to be removed from the nut. In loosening, reverse the process.

Figure 17–9 This socket wrench consists of a deep socket
and a reversible ratchet drive.

If the flex handle is selected, snap the proper-sized socket onto
the square drive. With the drive in a straight line with the handle,
spin the handle with the fingers until the nut or bolt is snug. Turn
the handle 90° (parallel to the workpiece) and apply pressure to the
handle to tighten the fastener.

The T or L handle drive is used because of its sliding, variable
handle length. The speeder is used in the same manner as a brace.
One hand holds the rear handle and applies a force toward the drive;
the other hand rotates the speeder, causing the nut or bolt to be
tightened or loosened.

17–15.   STRAP WRENCH

The **strap wrench** is used to rotate a round object such as a chrome
pipe without damaging the surface. The wrench handle (approximately 12 inches) is made of cast iron. The strap, generally made of

canvas, has a capacity of ⅛ to 2 inches and can be replaced when worn.

Place the workpiece within the strap loop [Fig. 17–1(L)]. Pull the strap tight and apply force to the handle. In Fig. 17–1(L), force is correctly applied to the handle in a downward direction.

17–16.   TORQUE WRENCH

A **torque wrench** is used to tighten nuts, bolts, cap screws, and so on, to *specified* pressures. The torque wrench is used on machines, automobile engines, and airplane engines in applications where one or more bolts or nuts are to be tightened to the same specified force to assure alignment, equal pressure for sealing, and so on. For example, the automobile mechanic would use a torque wrench when installing cylinder heads and main- and connecting-rod bearing caps.

Two available types of torque wrenches are the torque-limiting type and the deflecting beam-converging scale type. Each may incorporate one or more of the following features: square drives of ¼, ⅜, ½, ¾, or 1 inch; quick-release push button for release of the various English and metric sockets available (refer to the description of *sockets*, Section 17–14); ratchet and nonratchet drives; reversing levers to change the ratchet direction for tightening or loosening; torque measurement in one or both directions; and a scale that is calibrated to a National Bureau of Standards standard. These torque wrenches are available in calibrated units of inch-pounds and foot-pounds. Handle lengths vary from 13 to 40 inches.

The torque-limiting type of torque wrench is set to the predetermined specified torque by rotating the micrometer-style handle to the value specified on the scale. A snap lock holds the setting. The nut or bolt to be tightened is then turned. When the set torque pressure is reached, you feel and hear an audible click in the handle. It is not necessary to read the scale; this makes this wrench ideal for use in the dark, in blind spots, and even under water or oil. The wrench automatically resets to the value for the next operation.

On deflecting beam-converging scale torque wrenches, the torque-pressure value is read out on the scale as the nut or bolt is torqued. If the simple sound device is set for a predetermined specified torque value, there is also an audible sound when the predetermined value is reached.

Torque wrenches are operated the same as the socket wrench, composed of a ratchet drive and socket. First, if a torque wrench requiring a setting is used, the specified torque value is set into the wrench. Second, the proper-sized socket is selected and snapped onto the torque wrench drive. The ratchet reversing lever, if available, is placed in the proper position for tightening. The socket is then placed fully over the head of the nut or bolt to be tightened. The wrench is used to tighten the fastener until the proper torque pressure is indicated by either an audible click or by a visual indication on a gauge.

appendixes

appendixes

A

CHAPTER REVIEW QUESTIONS

This appendix contains chapter review questions that the reader can use to ensure his understanding of the material in each chapter. If you cannot answer a question, you should return to the chapter and reread the applicable material.

A course instructor can use these review questions to check his students' progress and understanding of the material (instructors should refer to Appendix B).

CHAPTER 1. YOU AND TOOLS

1. Make a list of the tools that are *required* for your particular application. Place an asterisk next to those tools that you now own.
2. Why is it necessary to store tools properly?
3. Name some ways to store tools.
4. Where is the most convenient location for your work area? Using ¼-inch grid line paper, construct a scaled drawing of the area and of the proposed location of your workbench and storage areas.
5. Name as many general tool-care procedures and practices as you can.

CHAPTER 2. BORING TOOLS

1. Describe how you would accurately drill a ½-inch-diameter hole through a 2-inch board with hand tools.

2. What is the difference between a push drill and a hand drill?
3. What does it mean to countersink? To counterbore?
4. What are the principal parts of a brace? What does each part do?
5. What is the difference between an expansive bit and a power-wood-boring bit? What tool(s) are used to drive each bit?
6. List methods of caring for boring tools.

CHAPTER 3.   CHISELS AND GOUGES

1. List the types of wood chisels.
2. How does a wood chisel differ from a wood gouge?
3. Describe how you would cut a bar of ¼-inch copper with a chisel.
4. Describe how to sharpen a cold chisel.
5. Describe how to sharpen and hone a wood chisel.
6. List some of the safety precautions to be used when cutting with wood chisels. With metal chisels.
7. Under what conditions is a mallet used to drive a wood chisel?
8. Describe how to use a wood chisel to cut a mortise.
9. Why must you be careful not to overheat a chisel during grinding operations?

CHAPTER 4.   CLAMPS AND VISES

1. What kind of clamps are used for light-duty clamping? Heavy-duty? Wood only? Metal only?
2. Which clamps are useful in clamping large workpieces that are being glued together?
3. Design (on paper) three improvised clamping jigs.
4. Describe the difference among fixed, swivel, clamp-on, and vacuum-vise bases. How do you mount each type?
5. Describe how to clamp two pieces of wood together using a hand screw.
6. List ways of protecting workpieces from being marred when using: bar clamp, C clamp, machinist's vise.

CHAPTER 5.   FASTENERS

1. Describe briefly the various types of anchoring devices available.
2. When are corrugated fasteners used?

3. What are the differences between common nails and finishing nails?
4. What types of heads are available on screws? On bolts?
5. Describe the different types of washers and the uses of each.

CHAPTER 6.   FILES

1. Describe the types of file cuts and coarsenesses.
2. What are the most common shapes of files? Which shapes might be best for your use and why?
3. Explain how to clean a file.
4. How is a file handle installed and removed?
5. Explain how to properly hold and stroke a file to cut a flat surface on a workpiece.
6. Explain draw filing.
7. Which files are useful for curved surfaces?
8. Which file is primarily used to sharpen saw blades?
9. How does a Swiss pattern file differ from other pattern files?

CHAPTER 7.   GLUES, ADHESIVES, AND CEMENTS

1. Describe proper glue-surface preparation.
2. What sources of flame and sparks must be removed from your work area when you are planning to use flammable glues?
3. What methods are used to spread glue?
4. How much glue should be placed on a surface?
5. Which glues are used to laminate countertops?
6. For what applications may epoxy glues be used?
7. Describe how to use a hot glue gun.
8. Which glues are good all-purpose indoor wood glues?

CHAPTER 8.   HAMMERS

1. Name the two kinds of claw hammers and explain their different appearances and uses.
2. How is a nail correctly driven?

3. How is a nail correctly pulled out of a board?
4. Explain how to toe and clinch nails.
5. Describe a soft-faced hammer. If a soft-faced hammer is not available, how can you improvise?
6. When are sledgehammers used? When are tack hammers used?

CHAPTER 9.   MEASURING AND MARKING TOOLS

1. Describe how to use a bevel. Describe its uses.
2. How is a caliper rule used?
3. Describe how you would ensure that the vertical edge of a picture frame is vertical on a wall.
4. How is a feeler gauge used?
5. What is parallax? How can you prevent parallax from affecting the accuracy of your measurements?
6. If you are reading an outside micrometer caliper and obtain 0.253 inch, what are the number of major, minor, and thimble divisions read on the micrometer?
7. What part of an inch does each of the following divisions on an English ten-thousandth micrometer represent?

   a. A major sleeve division.
   b. A minor sleeve division.
   c. A thimble sleeve division.
   d. A vernier division.

8. Describe the procedure of using an outside micrometer caliper to measure the thickness of a steel plate.
9. What are the values of the following divisions on the 50-division vernier caliper?

   a. An inch division.
   b. A major beam division.
   c. A minor beam division.
   d. A vernier division.

10. Describe how to make a measurement with a scale. With a steel tape.

CHAPTER 10.   MISCELLANEOUS HAND TOOLS

1. What are the different grades of sandpaper and when is each used?
2. Describe uses of the awl.
3. Describe the procedure for using a glass cutter.
4. Name the basic types of gouges/knives used by modelers.
5. How is a nail set used?
6. Describe the operation of a nibbler. How would you cut a square hole?
7. Describe the proper use and care of an oilstone.
8. How is a paint scraper used and how can you prevent it from gouging the workpiece?
9. Describe the uses of a propane torch. How do you use it to solder? To aid in paint removal?
10. Describe the operation of the hand riveter. What hole size do you drill for a rivet?
11. What are the uses for the terminal crimper? How do you know which groove in the jaws is used for a particular size of terminal?
12. Describe the various types of tin shears.

CHAPTER 11.   PLANES

1. What are the differences between block planes and jack planes?
2. Describe how a plane is used to smooth the edge of a workpiece.
3. How is a spoke shave used?
4. How should planes be stored?
5. How is the surface of a workpiece planed? How can you check that the surface is flat (square)?

CHAPTER 12.   PLIERS

1. Which of the pliers discussed in this chapter could be used for electronic assembly work?

2. Describe how to bend a small metal workpiece using duck-bill pliers.
3. Explain how end-cutting pliers differ from diagonal pliers. How do you use the pliers to cut wires?
4. How can you insulate plier handles?
5. Describe how to strip insulation from a wire with the cutting edges or notches of pliers.

CHAPTER 13.   POWERED HAND TOOLS

1. Describe safety precautions to be followed when using power tools.
2. Describe the proper procedures for using an electric drill to drill a ¼-inch hole through a block of aluminum.
3. List the accessories available for use with the electric drill.
4. List applications of the saber saw.
5. Describe the type of saber-saw blade used for thin metals. For wood.
6. Describe the procedure for making a compound cut with a circular saw (the compound cut is to be at a 45° bevel and a 30° angle across the workpiece).
7. List some safety procedures to be followed when using the circular saw.
8. Describe the use of grinders and grinding wheels.
9. Describe the procedures for using the power planes.
10. Describe the various types of bits available for use in the router.
11. What are the different kinds of electric sanders? What is the primary function of each?
12. Describe how to tin a soldering iron.
13. What kind of manufactured and improvised guides can be used to aid you in cutting straight lines with power saws?

CHAPTER 14.   PUNCHES

1. Describe the differences between a center punch and a prick punch. When is each used?
2. Describe the difference between a solid punch and a pin punch. When is each used?
3. Describe how you would recenter a center-punch indentation if the original punch was not exactly on the mark.

4. Explain how you would regrind a center-punch point and a pin-punch point.
5. What steps can be taken to ensure safe use of the punch?
6. Describe a mushroomed anvil. How can you repair this condition?

CHAPTER 15.   SAWS

1. When is a backsaw used? When is a compass saw used?
2. Explain the different uses of the cross-cut saw and the ripsaw. How can you distinguish the ripsaw from the cross-cut saw?
3. When is a miter box used? Which saw is used with the miter box?
4. Describe the general procedures for sawing.
5. How does a dovetail saw differ from a backsaw?
6. Describe how you change the angle of the blade in a coping saw.
7. How do you change the angle of the blade in a hacksaw?
8. When are fine-teeth hacksaw blades used? How do you start a cut with a hacksaw?

CHAPTER 16.   SCREWDRIVERS

1. Describe the difference between a Reed and Prince screwdriver (screw) and a Phillips head screwdriver (screw). How can you determine if you're using the proper screwdriver for a given screwhead?
2. Describe a proper-sized fit of a conventional screwdriver in a slotted bolt head.
3. What are the advantages of using an offset screwdriver over a straight-bladed screwdriver? Of using an offset ratchet screwdriver?
4. Describe how to use jewelers' screwdrivers. Spiral ratcheting screwdrivers.
5. In what applications could you use a spark-detecting screwdriver?
6. Make a list of the types and sizes of screwdrivers that you have in your tool box. Which additional screwdrivers do you need?

CHAPTER 17.   WRENCHES

1. What are the differences among box, open-end, and combination wrenches?

2. Describe some of the applications of a locking plier wrench.
3. Name the various parts and accessories of a socket wrench set.
4. Describe the proper use of an adjustable open-end wrench.
5. Which wrenches may be used to remove an automobile oil filter?
6. Describe how to use a torque wrench.
7. Which of the types of wrenches described are now in your tool box? Which wrenches would be your next three additions?

B

HOW ELSE CAN YOU USE THIS BOOK?

B–1. INTRODUCTION

This handbook is a valuable aid to you, the instructor, in teaching your students the fundamentals of basic hand tools and power tools and their applications in wood and metal shops. The handbook describes each tool, describes how to use the tool, and describes how to care for tools, including sharpening and parts replacement. In addition, the handbook describes the features of tools that students should consider in purchasing tools for their toolboxes and shops.

B–2. THE HANDBOOK AS A COURSE TEXT

The handbook is divided into 17 chapters, which correspond to a school's one-half-year program of 18 weeks. Thus, one chapter of material can be covered each week of the program. A suggested shop course outline that includes chapter coverage, terminal behaviors, lecture and demonstration outlines, workshop practical work suggestions, reading assignments, and written assignments is presented in Table B-1. You can alter the program to suit your particular needs.

B–3.   SUPPLEMENTARY TRAINING AIDS

You can supplement your course with visual aids, including:

    a. Films
    b. Filmstrips
    c. Filmloops
    d. Transparencies
    e. Merit awards and trophy plaques
    f. Instruction wallcharts
    g. Safety charts

You can make many of these visual aids yourself, can rent them from local libraries, or can purchase them inexpensively from tool manufacturers, including Stanley Tools, New Britain, Connecticut 06050, and The L. S. Starrett Company, Athol, Massachusetts 01331.

SHOP COURSE
PROCEDURE

TABLE B-1. Shop Course Outline

WEEKS OF PROGRAM	CHAPTER COVERAGE	TERMINAL BEHAVIOR	FIRST PERIOD: LECTURE & DEMONSTRATION
1	Ch. 1. YOU AND TOOLS	Student is aware of the tools he will use. He understands the course objectives and how the objectives will be accomplished.	Course introduction. What will be covered. What is expected of students. Description of quizzes and tests. Cover Ch. 1
2	Ch. 9. MEASURING AND MARKING TOOLS	Able to measure workpieces accurately. Can convert fractions to decimals and decimals to metric. Can use the measuring tools he needs.	Discuss measuring tools. Stress accuracy. Discuss conversion of fractions to decimal equivalents. Teach importance of metric-to-English and English-to-metric conversions.
3	Ch. 15. SAWS	Able to select proper saw for application. Able to start saw properly and make straight cut.	Discuss types of saws and applications. Stress methods of starting cuts to ensure that cuts are straight.
4	Ch. 5. FASTENERS and Ch. 7. GLUES, ADHESIVES, AND CEMENTS	Know the differences between, the application of, and the advantages of each type of fastener and glue.	Discuss the advantages and disadvantages of each type of fastener and glue.
5	Ch. 8. HAMMERS	Know how to use hammers properly.	Discuss types of hammers. Stress differences between straight claw and curved claw. Demonstrate methods of installing and removing nails. Also discuss nail set (Ch. 10).
6	Ch. 2. BORING TOOLS	Able to correctly use boring tools to bore straight holes.	Discuss and demonstrate types of boring tools. Define auger, countersink, counterbore. Show how to drill a perpendicular hole into a board by hand. Also discuss the awl (Ch. 10).
7	Ch. 16. SCREWDRIVERS	Able to recognize screwdriver heads and use the proper screwdriver to drive the screw.	Discuss screwdrivers and screwheads. Show differences among conventional, Phillips head, and Reed and Prince.

NOTE: Written assignments should be selected questions from Appendix A applicable to the reading assignment of the week.

WEEKS OF PROGRAM	SECOND PERIOD: WORKSHOP ON DAILY PRACTICAL PROBLEMS	THIRD PERIOD: WORKSHOP ON LONG-RANGE PROJECTS	READING AND WRITTEN* ASSIGNMENTS
1	Introduction to tools, work areas, tools available, storage, check-in and check-out procedures.	Suggest three long-range projects to students. Each student selects his own. Projects should be of about the same complexity.	Chs. 1 and 9
2	Select problems from Appendix C applicable to the reading material and to the first-period presentation.	Students continue work on their selected long-range project.	Ch. 15
3	Select problems from Appendix C applicable to the reading material and to the first-period presentation.	Students continue work on their selected long-range project.	Chs. 5 and 7
4	Select problems from Appendix C applicable to the reading material and to the first-period presentation.	Students continue work on their selected long-range project.	Ch. 8
5	Select problems from Appendix C applicable to the reading material and to the first-period presentation.	Students continue work on their selected long-range project.	Ch. 2
6	Select problems from Appendix C applicable to the reading material and to the first-period presentation.	Students continue work on their selected long-range project.	Ch. 16
7	Select problems from Appendix C applicable to the reading material and to the first-period presentation.	Students continue work on their selected long-range project.	Ch. 3

TABLE B-1. Shop Course Outline (continued)

WEEKS OF PROGRAM	CHAPTER COVERAGE	TERMINAL BEHAVIOR	FIRST PERIOD: LECTURE & DEMONSTRATION
8	Ch. 8 CHISELS AND GOUGES. COURSE REVIEW	Able to correctly use chisels and gouges. Know how to sharpen/hone.	Discuss types and uses of chisels and gouges. Demonstrate sharpening/honing. Cover modeler's knives and gouges, and oilstone (Ch. 10). Present course review of material and labs—Chs. 1, 2, 3, 5, 7, 8, 9, 15, and 16.
9	MID-TERM EXAMINATION	To indicate the comprehension of the students after 9 weeks. Students' strengths and weaknesses are pointed out.	Examination: use selected questions from Appendix A plus supplementary questions. Provide examination critique.
10	Ch. 11. PLANES	Able to correctly use planes. Knows procedures for sharpening planes.	Return and review examination. Discuss types and uses of planes. Demonstrate proper use and sharpening. Discuss abrasive papers (Ch. 10).
11	Ch. 6. FILES and Ch. 14. PUNCHES	Able to identify types of files. Able to select and correctly use files and file card. Able to select and use proper punch.	Discuss types of files and punches. Demonstrate proper use.
12	Ch. 4. CLAMPS AND VISES	Able to use clamps and vises. Can design and improvise various clamping devices.	Discuss clamps and vises. Discuss improvised clamps and have students design improvised clamps in the classroom.
13	Ch. 13 POWERED HAND TOOLS	Knows capabilities of the following tools and their accessories: drill, modeler's power tool, saber saw, circular saw, grinder, vacuum, plane, router, sander, soldering iron, and paint sprayer. Is safety conscious.	Discuss and demonstrate the following power tools: drill, modeler's power tool, saber saw, circular saw, grinder, and vacuum.
14	Ch. 13. POWERED HAND TOOLS		Discuss and demonstrate the following power tools: plane, router, sander, soldering iron, and paint sprayer.
15	Ch. 12. PLIERS	Know the use of and be able to correctly use pliers. Able to strip wire with pliers.	Discuss and demonstrate the use of pliers and tin snips (Ch. 10).

NOTE: **Written assignments should be selected questions from Appendix A applicable to the reading assignment of the week.**

WEEKS OF PROGRAM	SECOND PERIOD: WORKSHOP ON DAILY PRACTICAL PROBLEMS	THIRD PERIOD: WORKSHOP ON LONG-RANGE PROJECTS	READING AND WRITTEN* ASSIGNMENTS
8	Select problems from Appendix C applicable to the reading material and to the first-period presentation.	Students continue work on their selected long-range project.	Review of Chs. 1, 2, 3, 5, 7, 8, 9, 15, and 16
9	Select problems from Appendix C applicable to the reading material and to the first-period presentation.	Students continue work on their selected long-range project.	Ch. 11
10	Select problems from Appendix C applicable to the reading material and to the first-period presentation.	Students continue work on their selected long-range project.	Chs. 6 and 14
11	Select problems from Appendix C applicable to the reading material and to the first-period presentation.	Students continue work on their selected long-range project.	Ch. 4
12	Select problems from Appendix C applicable to the reading material and to the first-period presentation.	Students continue work on their selected long-range project.	Ch. 13
13	Select problems from Appendix C applicable to the reading material and to the first-period presentation.	Students continue work on their selected long-range project.	Ch. 13
14	Select problems from Appendix C applicable to the reading material and to the first-period presentation.	Students continue work on their selected long-range project.	Ch. 12
15	Select problems from Appendix C applicable to the reading material and to the first-period presentation.	Students continue work on their selected long-range project.	Ch. 17

TABLE B-1. Shop Course Outline (continued)

WEEKS OF PROGRAM	CHAPTER COVERAGE	TERMINAL BEHAVIOR	FIRST PERIOD: LECTURE & DEMONSTRATION
16	Ch. 17. WRENCHES	Able to use wrenches properly. Knows the proper wrench for different job applications.	Discuss and demonstrate the proper use of wrenches. Emphasize adjustable open-end, locking plier, socket, and nut-driver.
17	Ch. 10. MISCELLANEOUS HAND TOOLS. COURSE REVIEW.	Able to use miscellaneous tools discussed in Ch. 10.	Discuss and demonstrate miscellaneous tools. Present review of Chs. 4, 6, 10, 11, 12, 13, 14, and 17.
18	FINAL TERM EXAMINATION	To indicate the comprehension of the students' understanding of hand and power tools.	Examination: use selected questions from Appendix A plus supplementary questions. Provide examination critique.

NOTE: Written assignments should be selected questions from Appendix A applicable to the reading assignment of the week.

WEEKS OF PROGRAM	*SECOND PERIOD: WORKSHOP ON DAILY PRACTICAL PROBLEMS*	*THIRD PERIOD: WORKSHOP ON LONG-RANGE PROJECTS*	*READING AND WRITTEN* ASSIGNMENTS*
16	Select problems from Appendix C applicable to the reading material and to the first-period presentation.	Students continue work on their selected long-range project.	Ch. 10
17	Select problems from Appendix C applicable to the reading material and to the first-period presentation.	Students continue work on their selected long-range project.	Review of Chs. 4, 6, 10, 11, 12, 13, 14, and 17
18	Select problems from Appendix C applicable to the reading material and to the first-period presentation.	Students continue work on their selected long-range project.	

C

PRACTICAL BENCHWORK PROBLEMS

The instructor of a program in a high school, vocational school, technical institute, adult education program, and government or industry training program can utilize this appendix for the assignment of practical benchwork problems. These problems have been selected by the author as a means of suggesting supplementary instruction to help the instructor present an overall effective training program. The instructor should select problems in the areas where he feels practical benchwork is required. (Instructors should refer to Appendix B).

Readers that are not enrolled in a formal training program may use the practical benchwork problems presented in this appendix as a means of introduction to the practical applications of the tools covered in this handbook.

CHAPTER 1.   YOU AND TOOLS

1. Make a list of all the hand tools located within your shop tool storage area. In the list, place an ✕ next to those tools with which you are currently familiar: you know what the tool is for, how it is used, and any special care that it should receive.
2. Design and make a scaled drawing of a tote box.
3. Remove hand tools from your storage area, inspect the tools for apparent wear or damage, clean the tools, and apply a light coat of oil to the metallic parts of the tools. Any damage or wear that

is discovered should be noted (and brought to the attention of the instructor).

CHAPTER 2.   BORING TOOLS

1. Using the proper hand tools, bore a ⅜-inch hole into a piece of wood.
2. Drill a ¼-inch hole into a piece of wood at an angle of 45°.
3. Drill ¹⁄₁₆-inch pilot holes with a hand drill and a push drill.
4. Use a twist drill and an electric drill to drill a ¼-inch-diameter hole through a piece of aluminum. Clamp the workpiece with a piece of scrap wood under it to a workbench.
5. Use an expansive bit to bore a 2½-inch hole through a ¾-inch-thick piece of wood.
6. Join two pieces of wood together using No. 10 flatheaded wood screws. Use all hand tools and countersink the heads flush with the surface.
7. Drill a ¼-inch-diameter hole in a piece of ⅛-inch aluminum. Ream the hole to a ⅞-inch diameter.

CHAPTER 3.   CHISELS AND GOUGES

1. Using a cold chisel, cut 1 inch from a ¼-inch bar of soft metal.
2. Using a cold chisel, cut a piece of ⅛- by 4- by 6-inch soft metal into two pieces.
3. File or grind a mushroomed head on a cold chisel.
4. Using a wood chisel, cut a ½- by 1- by ¼-inch-deep mortise into a piece of soft wood.
5. Use a ripping chisel to separate some old joined lumber. Pull out old nails with the chisel.
6. Using a wood chisel, cut a 4-inch-radius convex curve around the end of a board.
7. Hone the edge of a wood chisel.

CHAPTER 4.   CLAMPS AND VISES

1. Make a set of aluminum vise-jaw caps for a machinist's vise.
2. Construct two types of improvised clamps, one for holding small workpieces and one for holding large workpieces.

3. Using two pieces of scrap wood, glue and clamp them together with C clamps.
4. Construct a pair of sawhorses (instead of using brackets, you could design your own leg supports).
5. Clamp a piece of metal tubing in a machinist's vise. Using a hacksaw, cut the tubing.
6. Using hand screws for clamping, glue two pieces of wood together.

CHAPTER 5.   FASTENERS

1. Attach two pieces of wood together with short nails, two others with long nails, two others by driving the nails at angles, and finally two others by clinch nailing. Now separate the nailed pieces of wood. Which nailing technique produced the strongest joint?
2. Screw two pieces of wood together. How does the strength of this joint compare with the nailed joints in problem 1?

CHAPTER 6.   FILES

1. Examine files with single, double, rasp, and curved-tooth cuts. Try each on a scrap workpiece. Examine various file shapes.
2. Using a piece of scrap metal, file one area with a bastard file followed by a second cut and smooth files on two other areas. How do the speed and surface finishes produced compare among the three types?
3. Using a piece of scrap metal $\frac{1}{4}$ inch thick, file $\frac{1}{16}$ inch off of one edge. File another edge so that its edges are rounded off.
4. Install and remove file handles.
5. Use a file card or brush to clean a file.
6. Using a scrap-metal workpiece about $\frac{1}{2}$ inch thick, remove $\frac{1}{8}$ inch. The surface should be finished by draw filing.
7. Using a wood-scrap workpiece, file a 2-inch-wide by $\frac{1}{8}$-inch-deep groove. Use a rasp. Finish the groove with a wood file.
8. Use a forming tool to shape a piece of scrap wood.

CHAPTER 7.   GLUES, ADHESIVES, AND CEMENTS

1. Using a hot glue gun, glue two pieces of scrap wood together.
2. Using contact cement, laminate two pieces of scrap wood.

3. Join two pieces of scrap wood with nails. Join two other similar pieces with white glue. Finally, join two other pieces with white glue and nails. After 24 hours drying time, determine which joint was the strongest.
4. Join two nails together crosswise with epoxy. After 24 hours, can you get them apart by hand?
5. Using rubber glue, *temporarily* glue a piece of paper to a piece of cardboard. After an hour, lift a corner of the paper with a knife and peel off the paper. Now, *permanently* glue a piece of paper to cardboard. After an hour, try to remove the paper.

CHAPTER 8.   HAMMERS

1. Attach two pieces of 1-inch-thick scrap wood together by driving two 5d common nails straight into the wood.
2. Attach two pieces of 1-inch-thick scrap wood together by toeing two 5d common nails into the wood.
3. Attach two pieces of 1-inch-thick scrap wood together by clinching two 12d common nails into the wood.
4. Using a ripping hammer or ripping chisel, disassemble the pieces of wood nailed together in problems 1, 2, and 3. Which nailing technique was the easiest to disassemble? Which was the hardest?
5. Using a soft-faced hammer or a rubber mallet, remove a dent from a piece of sheet metal.
6. Use a sledge hammer and a cold chisel to cut a piece of heavy wire or rod apart (review Section 3–5 if necessary).
7. Using upholster's tacks and hammer (or a tack hammer), attach a piece of woven material to a piece of scrap wood.

CHAPTER 9.   MEASURING AND MARKING TOOLS

1. Use a chalk line to mark a vertical line on a wall or a horizontal line on the floor.
2. Use a combination square or a try square to mark the ends of a workpiece for square cutting.
3. Construct a set of parallel lines 2 inches apart. Use dividers and a steel square.
4. Measure the inside measurements of a door frame with a folding rule (with extension) and/or a steel pocket tape.

5. Measure all dimensions of three different workpieces.
6. Using a feeler gauge, measure the gap in a spark plug or the opening in a pair of fingernail clippers.
7. Determine the levelness of a piece of wood placed upon the workbench. Shim the workpiece until it is level.
8. Check the walls and door frames of a room for plumb.
9. Using an outside micrometer caliper, measure the thickness of the following (either an English or a metric micrometer may be used): pencil lead, pencil diameter, steel square, human hair, thickness of this page, and thickness of the cover of this book.
10. Using a plumb bob from an overhead object, such as a light, locate a point on the floor directly below the object.
11. Using a steel square, measure the width, depth, and height of this book.
12. Using a steel tape, measure the width and depth of one of your rooms.
13. Using a vernier caliper, measure the following: diameter of a 25-cent coin; inside and outside diameter of a tin can; thickness of this book.
14. Use a wood-marking gauge to draw three parallel lines spaced ½ inch apart along the length of a scrap piece of wood.

CHAPTER 10.   MISCELLANEOUS HAND TOOLS

1. Using a piece of scrap wood, various grades of abrasive paper, and a sanding block, explore the use of the various grades of abrasive paper on the scrap wood. Sand against the grain and with the grain with a sanding block and without a block.
2. Using scrap hardwood, mark six hole centers. Using a ³⁄₁₆-inch drill, drill three holes. At the other three hole-center marks, use an awl to make a starting hole. Again drill three holes. Which holes were more accurately drilled in relation to the hole-center marks?
3. Using a piece of white pine scrap wood and modeler's gouges, chisels and knives, carve an object of your design.
4. Fasten two pieces of scrap wood together with finishing nails. Set the nails below the surface with a nail set.
5. Using a nibbler, cut a 1-inch-square hole into a piece of scrap aluminum.
6. Using an oilstone, sharpen a penknife blade.
7. Using a paint scraper, remove paint from a scrap area.

8. Use a propane torch to perform one or more of the following:

   a. Soften paint for paint removal.
   b. Solder two heavy copper wires together. (*Note*: Clean the copper ends with steel wool until bright.)

9. Using two pieces of scrap aluminum, select four rivets and drill the correct-sized holes through both pieces of aluminum. Using the riveter, fasten the two pieces together.
10. Strip insulation from two pieces of wire. Crimp proper-sized terminals to the wire ends.
11. Using scrap aluminum and tin snips, cut a 3-inch-diameter circle from the aluminum.

CHAPTER 11.   PLANES

1. Using a jack plane, plane the surface of a board.
2. Using a block plane, plane the edges of a board.
3. Using a plane, plane the edge of a board to a 30° angle.
4. Draw a concave pattern line near the edge of a board. Use a spoke shave to shave the pattern.
5. Plane the end grain of a board.

CHAPTER 12.   PLIERS

1. Using diagonal pliers, cut five 8-inch lengths of plastic-covered insulated wire. Use notched cutters to strip ½ inch of insulation from each end of each wire.
2. Using the wires in problem 1, bend the ends of the wire into loops. Use needle-nose, long-nose, or chain-nose pliers.
3. Drive five 1-inch brads ½ inch into a scrap piece of wood. Use end cutters to cut off two brads flush with the wood surface. Use the end cutters to pull the other three brads out of the wood.
4. Use lineman's pliers to cut No. 10 wire. Splice two pieces of No. 10 wire together.
5. Remove a spring-type hose clamp from your automobile with combination slip joint pliers. Remove a spring-type hose clamp with hose-clamp pliers.

CHAPTER 13.   POWERED HAND TOOLS

1. Using scrap wood, drill the following sizes of holes with an electric drill and drills: $\frac{1}{32}$-, $\frac{1}{8}$-, $\frac{1}{4}$-, $\frac{1}{2}$-, and 1-inch diameter.
2. Using soft scrap metal, drill the following sizes of holes with an electric drill and drills: $\frac{1}{32}$-, $\frac{1}{8}$-, and $\frac{1}{4}$-inch diameter. Ensure that all safety procedures are followed.
3. Draw a curved pattern on scrap wood. Cut out the pattern with a saber saw.
4. Use a circular saw to cut the ends squarely off a 2- by 4-inch length of wood.
5. Using scrap wood, cut a piece of wood across the grain.
6. Rip 1 inch off the edge of a piece of wood.
7. Using a grinder, sharpen a nail to a needle point. Use water to keep the nail cool. Observe all safety precautions. Hold the nail in a locking plier wrench.
8. Use a power plane to plane the end of a board.
9. Using a router and a straight bit, cut a groove in a board. Cut a groove with a V-groove bit. Observe all safety precautions.
10. Sand a board with a finishing sander. Use the sander first with an orbital action followed by a straight-line action.
11. Using a soldering iron, solder two wires together.

CHAPTER 14.   PUNCHES

1. On a piece of $\frac{1}{8}$-inch aluminum approximately 4 by 6 inches, lay out hole centers for four $\frac{1}{4}$-inch-diameter holes. One hole center is to be located in each corner at a distance of $\frac{3}{4}$ inch from each edge. Prick-punch the centers. Scribe diagonal lines from one hole center to the diagonally opposite hole center. Prick-punch a hole location at the line intersection and, using dividers, scribe a 1-inch-diameter circle from this intersection. Center punch the four corner prick punches.
2. Lay out a hole center on a piece of aluminum. Center-punch the hole slightly off from the mark. Repunch by moving the center punch to the proper location.
3. In a piece of $\frac{1}{4}$-inch scrap aluminum, mark two hole locations. Center-punch the second location. Clamp the material and drill

a ⅛-inch hole at the first location. Drill a hole at the second location. Which hole was more accurately drilled?

4. Drill an ⅛-inch hole into a bar of scrap metal. Insert a dowel pin. Use a starter punch and a pin punch to remove the pin.

CHAPTER 15.   SAWS

1. Using a cross-cut saw, cut a piece of scrap wood into three equal lengths.
2. Using a ripsaw, cut two 1-inch strips from a piece of scrap wood.
3. Using a backsaw and a miter box, cut pieces of molding at 45° angles so that right angles can be made.
4. In the center of a piece of ½-inch scrap wood, mark off a 4- by 6-inch square. Use a compass saw to remove the square.
5. Use a dovetail saw to cut a piece of 1-inch-square soft pine into 1-inch cubes.
6. Using a piece of ¼-inch scrap wood six inches square, design a wooden puzzle. Cut the pieces out with a coping saw.
7. Using a hacksaw, cut a piece of ¼-inch bar stock or tubing into several pieces.

CHAPTER 16.   SCREWDRIVERS

1. Given a set of slotted, Phillips, and Frearson screws, determine the correct type and size of screwdriver to use with each screw.
2. Join two pieces of ¾-inch scrap wood together using No. 10 1¼-inch wood screws. Use predrilled countersunk holes and a screw-starting screwdriver.
3. Join two pieces of metal together using binding-head sheet-metal screws. Predrill the holes.
4. Use Phillips head or Reed and Prince screws (and proper screwdriver) to fasten two pieces of metal together. Predrill the holes.
5. Tighten several screws with an offset screwdriver.
6. Using a spark-detecting screwdriver, check for the presence of high voltage in the ignition system of your car.
7. Regrind the tips of some of your old conventional screwdrivers.
8. Install several screws into a piece of scrap wood using a spiral ratchet screwdriver.

CHAPTER 17.   WRENCHES

1. Obtain two pieces of scrap metal that have ½-inch-diameter holes drilled in them and two ½-inch hex-head bolts and nuts. Obtain the proper-sized open-end, box, and combination wrenches and secure the two workpieces together.
2. Use an adjustable open-end wrench to remove the bolts installed in problem 1.
3. Using several different-sized bolts and nuts, install and tighten them using the locking plier wrench. Cut wire with the locking plier wrench.
4. Adjust and clamp the locking plier wrench onto several thicknesses of metal.
5. Use the nut driver to remove and reinstall hex-head nuts from a workpiece.
6. Using a pipe wrench, install nipples onto a piece of threaded pipe.
7. Use a socket wrench set to install or tighten bolts onto a workpiece.
8. Using a torque wrench, tighten nuts onto a workpiece to the torque value assigned by your instructor.
9. Use either an oil-filter wrench or a chain pipe wrench to remove an automobile oil filter.

D

ENGLISH-TO-METRIC AND METRIC-TO-ENGLISH CONVERSION FACTORS

This appendix provides conversion factors from English to metric and from metric to English. To convert from one measurement unit in one system to another unit in the other system, multiply the first unit measurement by the conversion factor. Thus

first system measurement and unit $\times$ conversion factor
$\qquad$ = second system measurement and unit $\qquad$ (D-1)

Example: Convert $3\frac{1}{4}$ inches to centimeters.

Since the metric system is based on 10 (the decimal system), it is first necessary to change the fraction of $\frac{1}{4}$ to a decimal. Thus

$$\frac{1}{4} = 1 \div 4 = 0.250$$

Now, convert 3.250 inches to centimeters. Use Table D to determine the conversion factor and equation (D-1) to find the answer:

$$3.250 \text{ inches} \times 2.540 = 8.255 \text{ centimeters}$$

Example: Convert 25 meters to feet. Use Table D and equation (D-1):

$$25 \text{ meters} \times 3.281 = 82.025 \text{ feet}$$

TABLE D Linear Measurement Conversions

To Convert	Into	Multiply by
	English to Metric	
inches	millimeters	25.40
inches	centimeters	2.540
inches	meters	0.0254
feet	millimeters	304.8
feet	centimeters	30.48
feet	meters	0.3048
cubic feet	cubic meters	0.02832
cubic inches	cubic meters	1.639×10^{-5}
square inches	square millimeters	645.2
	Metric to English	
millimeters	inches	0.03937
millimeters	feet	3.281×10^{-3}
centimeters	inches	0.3937
centimeters	feet	3.281×10^{-2}
meters	inches	39.37
meters	feet	3.281
cubic meters	cubic feet	35.31
cubic meters	cubic inches	61,023.0
square meters	square feet	10.76
square millimeters	square inches	1.550×10^{-3}

E

INCH-MILLIMETER EQUIVALENTS OF DECIMAL AND COMMON FRACTIONS

Inch	$\frac{1}{2}$'s	$\frac{1}{4}$'s	8ths	16ths	32nds	64ths	Millimeters	Decimals of an Inch[a]
						1	0.397	0.015 625
					1	2	0.794	0.031 25
						3	1.191	0.046 875
				1	2	4	1.588	0.062 5
						5	1.984	0.078 125
					3	6	2.381	0.093 75
						7	2.778	0.109 375
			1	2	4	8	3.175[a]	0.125 0
						9	3.572	0.140 625
					5	10	3.969	0.156 25
						11	4.366	0.171 875
				3	6	12	4.762	0.187 5
						13	5.159	0.203 125
					7	14	5.556	0.218 75
						15	5.953	0.234 375
		1	2	4	8	16	6.350[a]	0.250 0
						17	6.747	0.265 625
					9	18	7.144	0.281 25
						19	7.541	0.296 875
				5	10	20	7.938	0.312 5
						21	8.334	0.328 125
					11	22	8.731	0.343 75
						23	9.128	0.359 375
			3	6	12	24	9.525[a]	0.375 0
						25	9.922	0.390 625
					13	26	10.319	0.406 25
						27	10.716	0.421 875
				7	14	28	11.112	0.437 5

Inch	$\frac{1}{2}$'s	$\frac{1}{4}$'s	8ths	16ths	32nds	64ths	Millimeters	Decimals of an Inch[a]
						29	11.509	0.453 125
					15	30	11.906	0.468 75
						31	12.303	0.484 375
	1	2	4	8	16	32	12.700[a]	0.500 0
						33	13.097	0.515 625
					17	34	13.494	0.531 25
						35	13.891	0.546 875
				9	18	36	14.288	0.562 5
						37	14.684	0.578 125
					19	38	15.081	0.593 75
						39	15.478	0.609 375
			5	10	20	40	15.875[a]	0.625 0
						41	16.272	0.640 625
					21	42	16.669	0.656 25
						43	17.066	0.671 875
				11	22	44	17.462	0.687 5
						45	17.859	0.703 125
					23	46	18.256	0.718 75
						47	18.653	0.734 375
		3	6	12	24	48	19.050[a]	0.750 0
						49	19.447	0.765 625
					25	50	19.844	0.781 25
						51	20.241	0.796 875
				13	26	52	20.638	0.812 5
						53	21.034	0.828 125
					27	54	21.431	0.843 75
						55	21.828	0.859 375
			7	14	28	56	22.225[a]	0.875 0
						57	22.622	0.890 625
					29	58	23.019	0.906 25
						59	23.416	0.921 875
				15	30	60	23.812	0.937 5
						61	24.209	0.953 125
					31	62	24.606	0.968 75
						63	25.003	0.984 375
1	2	4	8	16	32	64	25.400[a]	1.000 0

[a] Exact.

F

DECIMAL EQUIVALENTS OF MILLIMETERS (0.01 TO 100mm)

mm.	Inches	mm.	Inches	mm.	Inches	mm.	Inches	mm.	Inches
0.01	0.00039	0.41	0.01614	0.81	0.03189	21	0.82677	61	2.40157
0.02	0.00079	0.42	0.01654	0.82	0.03228	22	0.86614	62	2.44094
0.03	0.00118	0.43	0.01693	0.83	0.03268	23	0.90551	63	2.48031
0.04	0.00157	0.44	0.01732	0.84	0.03307	24	0.94488	64	2.51968
0.05	0.00197	0.45	0.01772	0.85	0.03346	25	0.98425	65	2.55905
0.06	0.00236	0.46	0.01811	0.86	0.03386	26	1.02362	66	2.59842
0.07	0.00276	0.47	0.01850	0.87	0.03425	27	1.06299	67	2.63779
0.08	0.00315	0.48	0.01890	0.88	0.03465	28	1.10236	68	2.67716
0.09	0.00354	0.49	0.01929	0.89	0.03504	29	1.14173	69	2.71653
0.10	0.00394	0.50	0.01969	0.90	0.03543	30	1.18110	70	2.75590
0.11	0.00433	0.51	0.02008	0.91	0.03583	31	1.22047	71	2.79527
0.12	0.00472	0.52	0.02047	0.92	0.03622	32	1.25984	72	2.83464
0.13	0.00512	0.53	0.02087	0.93	0.03661	33	1.29921	73	2.87401
0.14	0.00551	0.54	0.02126	0.94	0.03701	34	1.33858	74	2.91338
0.15	0.00591	0.55	0.02165	0.95	0.03740	35	1.37795	75	2.95275
0.16	0.00630	0.56	0.02205	0.96	0.03780	36	1.41732	76	2.99212
0.17	0.00669	0.57	0.02244	0.97	0.03819	37	1.45669	77	3.03149
0.18	0.00709	0.58	0.02283	0.98	0.03858	38	1.49606	78	3.07086
0.19	0.00748	0.59	0.02323	0.99	0.03898	39	1.53543	79	3.11023
0.20	0.00787	0.60	0.02362	1.00	0.03937	40	1.57480	80	3.14960
0.21	0.00827	0.61	0.02402	1	0.03937	41	1.61417	81	3.18897
0.22	0.00866	0.62	0.02441	2	0.07874	42	1.65354	82	3.22834
0.23	0.00906	0.63	0.02480	3	0.11811	43	1.69291	83	3.26771
0.24	0.00945	0.64	0.02520	4	0.15748	44	1.73228	84	3.30708
0.25	0.00984	0.65	0.02559	5	0.19685	45	1.77165	85	3.34645
0.26	0.01024	0.66	0.02598	6	0.23622	46	1.81102	86	3.38582
0.27	0.01063	0.67	0.02638	7	0.27559	47	1.85039	87	3.42519
0.28	0.01102	0.68	0.02677	8	0.31496	48	1.88976	88	3.46456
0.29	0.01142	0.69	0.02717	9	0.35433	49	1.92913	89	3.50393
0.30	0.01181	0.70	0.02756	10	0.39370	50	1.96850	90	3.54330
0.31	0.01220	0.71	0.02795	11	0.43307	51	2.00787	91	3.58267
0.32	0.01260	0.72	0.02835	12	0.47244	52	2.04724	92	3.62204
0.33	0.01299	0.73	0.02874	13	0.51181	53	2.08661	93	3.66141
0.34	0.01339	0.74	0.02913	14	0.55118	54	2.12598	94	3.70078
0.35	0.01378	0.75	0.02953	15	0.59055	55	2.16535	95	3.74015
0.36	0.01417	0.76	0.02992	16	0.62992	56	2.20472	96	3.77952
0.37	0.01457	0.77	0.03032	17	0.66929	57	2.24409	97	3.81889
0.38	0.01496	0.78	0.03071	18	0.70866	58	2.28346	98	3.85826
0.39	0.01535	0.79	0.03110	19	0.74803	59	2.32283	99	3.89763
0.40	0.01575	0.80	0.03150	20	0.78740	60	2.36220	100	3.93700

G

ENGLISH SYSTEM OF WEIGHTS AND MEASURES

Linear Measure (Length)

1000 mils = 1 inch (in.)
12 inches = 1 foot (ft.)
3 feet = 1 yard (yd.)
5280 feet = 1 mile

Square Measure (Area)

144 square inches (sq.in.) = 1 square foot (sq.ft.)
9 square feet = 1 square yard (sq.yd.)

Cubic Measure (Volume)

1728 cubic inches (cu.in.) = 1 cubic foot (cu.ft.)
27 cubic feet = 1 cubic yard (cu.yd.)
231 cubic inches = 1 U.S. gallon (gal.)
277.27 cubic inches = 1 British imperial gallon (i.gal.)

Liquid Measure (Capacity)

4 fluid ounces (fl.oz.) = 1 gill (gi.)
2 pints = 1 quart (qt.)
4 quarts = 1 gallon

Dry Measure (Capacity)

2 pints = 1 quart
8 quarts = 1 peck (pk.)

Weight (Avoirdupois)

27.3438 grains = 1 dram (dr.)
16 drams = 1 ounce (oz.)
16 ounces = 1 pound (lb.)
100 pounds = 1 hundredweight (cwt.)
112 pounds = 1 long hundredweight (l.cwt.)
2000 pounds = 1 short ton (S.T.)
2240 pounds = 1 long ton (L.T.)

Weight (Troy)

24 grains = 1 pennyweight (dwt.)
20 pennyweights = 1 ounce (oz.t.)
12 ounces = 1 pound (lb.t.)

Angular or Circular Measure

60 seconds = 1 minute
60 minutes = 1 degree
57.2958 degrees = 1 radian
90 degrees = 1 quadrant or right angle
360 degrees = 1 circle or circumference

H

METRIC SYSTEM OF
WEIGHTS AND MEASURES

Linear Measure (Length)

1/10 meter = 1 decimeter (dm)
1/10 decimeter = 1 centimeter (cm)
1/10 centimeter = 1 millimeter (mm)
1/1000 millimeter = 1 micron (μ)
1/1000 micron = 1 millimicron $(m\mu)$
10 meters = 1 dekameter (dkm)
10 dekameters = 1 hectometer (hm)
10 hectometers = 1 kilometer (km)
10 kilometers = 1 myriameter

Square Measure (Area)

1 are = 1 square dekameter (dkm^2)
1 centare = 1 square meter (m^2)
1 hectare = 1 square hectometer (hm^2)

Cubic Measure (Volume)

1 stere = 1 cubic meter (m^3)
1 decistere = 1 cubic decimeter (dm^3)
1 centistere = 1 cubic centimeter (cm^3)
1 dekastere = 1 cubic dekameter (dkm^3)

Capacity

1/10 liter = 1 deciliter (dl)
1/10 deciliter = 1 centiliter (cl)
1/10 centiliter = 1 milliliter (ml)
10 liters = 1 dekaliter (dkl)
100 liters = 1 hectoliter (hl)
1000 liters = 1 kiloliter (kl)
1 kiloliter = 1 stere (s)

Weight

1/10 gram = 1 decigram (dg)
1/10 decigram = 1 centigram (cg)
1/10 centigram = 1 milligram (mg)
10 grams = 1 dekagram (dkg)
100 grams = 1 hectogram (hg)
1000 grams = 1 kilogram (kg)
10,000 grams = 1 myriagram
100,000 grams = 1 quintal (q)
1,000,000 grams = 1 metric ton (t)

I

CONVERSION BETWEEN ENGLISH AND METRIC UNITS

English to Metric   *Metric to English*

Units of Length

1 millimeter = 0.03937 inch or about 1/25 inch

1 inch = 2.540 centimeters	1 centimeter = 0.3937 inch
1 foot = 0.3048 meter	1 decimeter = 3.937 inches
1 yard = 0.9144 meter	1 meter = 39.37 inches
1 mile = 1.6093 kilometers	= 3.281 feet
	= 1.094 yards
	1 kilometer = 0.62137 mile

Units of Area

1 sq. inch = 6.4516 sq. centimeters	1 sq. centimeter = 0.1549997 sq. inch
1 sq. foot = 0.0929 sq. meter	1 sq. meter = 10.764 sq. feet
1 sq. mile = 2.590 sq. kilometers	1 sq. kilometer = 0.3861 sq. mile
1 acre = 0.4047 hectare	1 hectare = 2.471 acres

Units of Volume

1 cu. inch = 16.387 cu. centimeters	1 cu. centimeter = 0.061023 cu. inch
1 cu. foot = 0.028317 cu. meter	1 cu. meter = 35.31445 cu. feet

Capacity (Liquid)

1 gill = 0.11829 liter	1 liter = 8.4537 gills
1 pint = 0.4732 liter	1 liter = 2.1134 pints
1 quart = 0.9463 liter	1 liter = 1.0567 quarts

Capacity (Dry)

1 pint = 0.5506 liter	1 liter = 1.816 pints
1 quart = 1.1012 liters	1 liter = 0.908 quart
1 peck = 8.8096 liters	1 liter = 0.1135 peck
1 bushel = 3.52383 dekaliters	1 dekaliter = 0.28378 bushel

Units of Mass

1 grain = 0.0648 gram	1 gram = 15.432 grains
1 ounce (avdp.) = 28.3495 grams	1 kilogram = 35.274 oz. avdp.
1 pound (avdp.) = 0.45359 kilogram	1 kilogram = 2.2046 lbs. avdp.
1 short ton (2000 lb.) = 0.9072 metric ton	1 metric ton = 1.1023 short tons
1 long ton (2240 lb.) = 1.016 metric tons	1 metric ton = 0.9842 long ton

J

METRIC CONVERSION TABLE

Millimeters	× 0.03937	= Inches
Millimeters	= 25.400	× Inches
Meters	× 3.2809	= Feet
Meters	= 0.3048	× Feet
Kilometers	× 0.621377	= Miles
Kilometers	= 1.6093	× Miles
Square centimeters	× 0.15500	= Square inches
Square centimeters	= 6.4515	× Square inches
Square meters	× 10.76410	= Square feet
Square meters	= 0.09290	× Square feet
Cubic centimeters	× 0.061025	= Cubic inches
Cubic centimeters	= 16.3866	× Cubic inches
Cubic meters	× 35.3156	= Cubic feet
Cubic meters	= 0.02832	× Cubic feet
Cubic meters	× 1.308	= Cubic yards
Cubic meters	= 0.765	× Cubic yards
Liters	× 61.023	= Cubic inches
Liters	= 0.01639	× Cubic inches
Liters	× 0.26418	= U.S. gallons
Liters	= 3.7854	× U.S. gallons
Grams	× 15.4324	= Grains
Grams	= 0.0648	× Grains
Grams	× 0.03527	= Ounces, avoirdupois
Grams	= 28.3495	× Ounces, avoirdupois
Kilograms	× 2.2046	= Pounds
Kilograms	= 0.4536	× Pounds
Kilograms per square centimeter	× 14.2231	= Pounds per square inch
Kilograms per square centimeter	= 0.0703	× Pounds per square inch
Kilograms per cubic meter	× 0.06243	= Pounds per cubic foot
Kilograms per cubic meter	= 16.01890	× Pounds per cubic foot
Metric tons (1,000 kilograms)	× 1.1023	= Tons (2,000 pounds)
Metric tons	= 0.9072	× Tons (2,000 pounds)
Calories	× 3.9683	= B.T. units
Calories	= 0.2520	× B.T. units

K

LUMBER CONVERSION CHART

Lineal Feet to Board Feet
Example: 1 x 2 x 10 = 1–2/3 bd. ft.

				Length in (Feet)				
Size	10	12	14	16	18	20	22	24
1 x 2	1-2/3	2	2-1/3	2-2/3	3	3-1/3	3-2/3	4
1 x 3	2½	3	3½	4	4½	5	5½	6
1 x 4	3-1/3	4	4-2/3	5-1/3	6	6-2/3	7-1/3	8
1 x 5	4-1/6	5	5-5/6	6-2/3	7½	8-1/3	9-1/6	10
1 x 6	5	6	7	8	9	10	11	12
1 x 7	5-5/6	7	8-1/6	9-1/3	10½	11-2/3	12-5/6	14
1 x 8	6-2/3	8	9-1/3	10-2/3	12	13-1/3	14-2/3	16
1 x 9	7½	9	10½	12	13½	15	16½	18
1 x 10	8-1/3	10	11-2/3	13-1/3	15	16-2/3	18-1/3	20
1 x 12	10	12	14	16	18	20	22	24
1 x 14	11-2/3	14	16-1/3	18-2/3	21	23-1/3	25-2/3	28
1 x 16	13-1/3	16	18-2/3	21-1/3	24	26-2/3	29-1/3	32
1¼ x 4	4-1/6	5	5-5/6	6-2/3	7½	8-1/3	9-1/6	10
1¼ x 5	5-5/24	6¼	7-7/24	8-1/3	9-3/8	10-5/12	11-11/24	12½
1¼ x 6	6¼	7½	8¾	10	11¼	12½	13-3/4	15
1¼ x 8	8-1/3	10	11-2/3	13-1/3	15	16-2/3	18-1/3	20
1¼ x 9	9-3/8	11¼	13-1/8	15	16-7/8	18¾	20-5/8	22½
1¼ x 10	10-5/12	12½	14-7/12	16-2/3	18¾	20-5/6	22-11/12	25
1¼ x 12	12½	15	17½	20	22½	25	27½	30
2 x 2	3-1/3	4	4-2/3	5-1/3	6	6-2/3	7-1/3	8
2 x 3	5	6	7	8	9	10	11	12
2 x 4	6-2/3	8	9-1/3	10-2/3	12	13-1/3	14-2/3	16
2 x 6	10	12	14	16	18	20	22	24
2 x 8	13-1/3	16	18-2/3	21-1/3	24	26-2/3	29-1/3	32
2 x 9	15	18	21	24	27	30	33	36
2 x 10	16-2/3	20	23-1/3	26-2/3	30	33-1/3	36-2/3	40
2 x 12	20	24	28	32	36	40	44	48

L

NAILS

COMMON WIRE NAILS

Size	Length	Gauge	Approx. No. to lb.
2D	1 In.	No. 15	876
3D	1¼	14	568
4D	1½	12½	316
5D	1-3/4	12½	271
6D	2	11½	181
7D	2¼	11½	161
8D	2½	10¼	106
9D	2-3/4	10¼	96

Size	Length	Gauge	Approx. No. to lb.
10D	3 In.	No. 9	69
12D	3¼	9	63
16D	3½	8	49
20D	4	6	31
30D	4½	5	24
40D	5	4	18
50D	5½	3	14
60D	6	2	11

FLOORING BRADS

Size	Length	Gauge	Approx. No. to lb.
6D	2 In.	No. 11	157
7D	2¼	11	139
8D	2½	10	99
9D	2-3/4	10	90
10D	3	9	69
12D	3¼	8	54
16D	3½	7	43
20D	4	6	31

FINISHING NAILS

Size	Length	Gauge	Approx. No. to lb.
2D	1 In.	No. 16½	1351
3D	1¼	15½	807
4D	1½	15	584
5D	1-3/4	15	500
6D	2	13	309
7D	2¼	13	238
8D	2½	12½	189
9D	2-3/4	12½	172
10D	3	11½	121
12D	3¼	11½	113
16D	3½	11	90
20D	4	10	62

CASING NAILS

Size	Length	Gauge	Approx. No. to lb.
2D	1 In.	No. 15½	1010
3D	1¼	14½	635
4D	1½	14	473
5D	1-3/4	14	406
6D	2	12½	236
7D	2¼	12½	210
8D	2½	11½	145
9D	2-3/4	11½	132
10D	3	10½	94
12D	3¼	10½	87
16D	3½	10	71
20D	4	9	52
30D	4½	9	46

SMOOTH AND BARBED BOX NAILS

Size	Length	Gauge	Approx. No. to lb.
2D	1 In.	No. 15½	1010
3D	1¼	14½	635
4D	1½	14	473
5D	1-3/4	14	406
6D	2	12½	236
7D	2¼	12½	210
8D	2½	11½	145
9D	2-3/4	11½	132
10D	3	10½	94
12D	3¼	10½	88
16D	3½	10	71
20D	4	9	52
30D	4½	9	46
40D	5	8	35

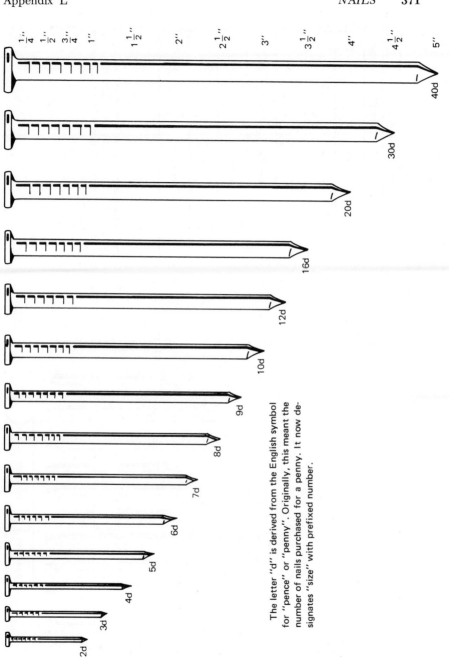

The letter "d" is derived from the English symbol for "pence" or "penny". Originally, this meant the number of nails purchased for a penny. It now designates "size" with prefixed number.

Wire nails and brads					
Length	Gauges		Length	Gauges	
$\frac{3}{16}''$	20 to 24		$1''$	7 to 20	
$\frac{1}{4}''$	19 to 26		$1\frac{1}{8}''$	7 to 19	
$\frac{3}{8}''$	18 to 26		$1\frac{1}{4}''$	6 to 17	
$\frac{1}{2}''$	14 to 24		$1\frac{3}{8}''$	6 to 17	
$\frac{5}{8}''$	12 to 24		$1\frac{1}{2}''$	4 to 17	
$\frac{3}{4}''$	10 to 21		$1\frac{5}{8}''$	4 to 17	
$\frac{7}{8}''$	8 to 20		$1\frac{3}{4}''$	4 to 17	

*The letter "d" is derived from the English symbol for "pence" or "penny". Originally, this meant the number of nails purchased for a penny. It now designates "size" with prefixed number.

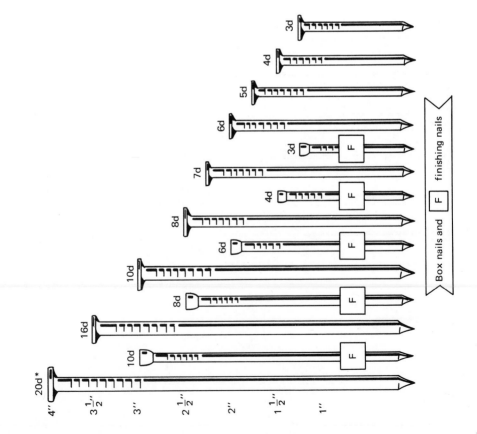

M

SCREW REFERENCE CHART

Listed below are screw lengths from $\frac{1}{4}''$ to $4''$. Shank dimensions are shown from 0 to 24. These sizes are most frequently used and are more generally available.

Length	\multicolumn{18}{c}{Shank numbers}
	0	1	2	3	4	5	6	7	8	9	10	11	12	14	16	18	20	24
$\frac{1}{4}$ inch	0	1	2	3														
$\frac{3}{8}$ inch			2	3	4	5	6	7										
$\frac{1}{2}$ inch			2	3	4	5	6	7	8									
$\frac{5}{8}$ inch				3	4	5	6	7	8	9	10							
$\frac{3}{4}$ inch					4	5	6	7	8	9	10	11						
$\frac{7}{8}$ inch							6	7	8	9	10	11	12					
1 inch							6	7	8	9	10	11	12	14				
$1\frac{1}{4}$ inch								7	8	9	10	11	12	14	16			
$1\frac{1}{2}$ inch							6	7	8	9	10	11	12	14	16	18		
$1\frac{3}{4}$ inch									8	9	10	11	12	14	16	18	20	
2 inch									8	9	10	11	12	14	16	18	20	
$2\frac{1}{4}$ inch										9	10	11	12	14	16	18	20	
$2\frac{1}{2}$ inch													12	14	16	18	20	
$2\frac{3}{4}$ inch														14	16	18	20	
3 inch															16	18	20	
$3\frac{1}{2}$ inch																18	20	24
4 inch																18	20	24
0 to 24 diameter dimensions in inches at body	0.060	0.073	0.086	0.099	0.112	0.125	0.138	0.151	0.164	0.177	0.190	0.203	0.216	0.242	0.268	0.294	0.320	0.372

Twist bit sizes for round, flat and oval head screws in drilling shank and pilot holes.

	0	1	2	3	4	5	6	7	8	9	10	11	12	14	16	18	20	24
Shank holes hard and softwood	1/16	5/64	3/32	7/64	7/64	1/8	9/64	5/32	11/64	3/16	3/16	13/64	7/32	1/4	17/64	19/64	21/64	3/8
Pilot hole softwood	1/64	1/32	1/32	3/64	3/64	1/16	1/16	1/16	5/64	5/64	3/32	3/32	7/64	9/64	9/64	9/64	11/64	3/16
Pilot hole hardwood	1/32	1/32	3/64	1/16	1/16	5/64	5/64	3/32	3/32	7/64	7/64	1/8	1/8	9/64	5/32	3/16	3/64	7/32
Auger bit sizes for countersunk heads			3	4	4	4	5	5	6	6	6	7	7	8	9	10	11	12

\multicolumn{2}{l}{Twist drill sizes for round, oval and flat head screws in drilling shank and pilot holes.}																			
Screw sizes—common, slotted head		0	1	2	3	4	5	6	7	8	9	10	11	12	14	16	18	20	24
Shank hole—hard and softwood	Fractional	1/16	5/64	3/32	7/64	7/64	1/8	9/64	5/32	11/64	3/16	3/16	13/64	7/32	1/4	17/64	19/64	21/64	3/8
	number-letter	52	47	42	37	32	30	27	22	18	14	10	4	2	D	I	N	P	V
Pilot hole—softwood	Fractional	1/64	1/32	1/32	3/64	3/64	1/16	1/16	1/16	5/64	5/64	3/32	3/32	7/64	9/64	9/64	9/64	11/64	3/16
	number	75	71	65	58	55	53	52	51	48	45	43	40	38	32	29	26	19	15
Pilot hole—hardwood	Fractional	1/32	1/32	3/64	1/16	1/16	5/64	5/64	3/32	3/32	7/64	7/64	1/8	1/8	9/64	5/32	3/16	13/64	7/32
	number	70	66	56	54	52	49	47	44	40	37	33	31	30	25	18	13	4	1

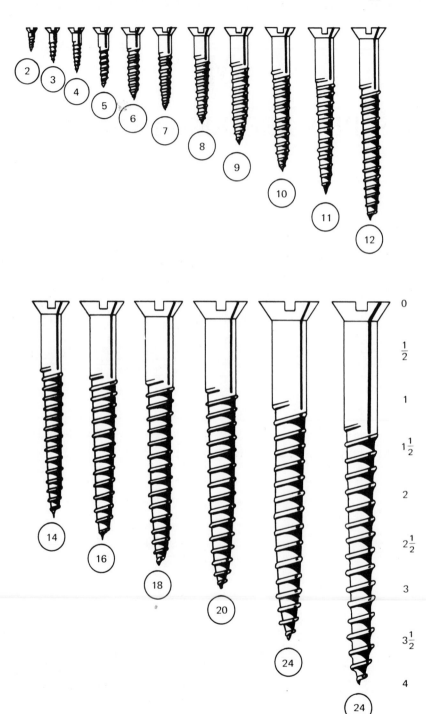

N

DECIMAL EQUIVALENTS OF NUMBER AND LETTER DRILL SIZES

NUMBER SIZE DRILLS

No.	Size of Drill In Inches	No.	Size of Drill In Inches	No.	Size of Drill In Inches	No.	Size of Drill In Inches
1	.2280	21	.1590	41	.0960	61	.0390
2	.2210	22	.1570	42	.0935	62	.0380
3	.2130	23	.1540	43	.0890	63	.0370
4	.2090	24	.1520	44	.0860	64	.0360
5	.2055	25	.1495	45	.0820	65	.0350
6	.2040	26	.1470	46	.0810	66	.0330
7	.2010	27	.1440	47	.0785	67	.0320
8	.1990	28	.1405	48	.0760	68	.0310
9	.1960	29	.1360	49	.0730	69	.0292
10	.1935	30	.1285	50	.0700	70	.0280
11	.1910	31	.1200	51	.0670	71	.0260
12	.1890	32	.1160	52	.0635	72	.0250
13	.1850	33	.1130	53	.0595	73	.0240
14	.1820	34	.1110	54	.0550	74	.0225
15	.1800	35	.1100	55	.0520	75	.0210
16	.1770	36	.1065	56	.0465	76	.0200
17	.1730	37	.1040	57	.0430	77	.0180
18	.1695	38	.1015	58	.0420	78	.0160
19	.1660	39	.0995	59	.0410	79	.0145
20	.1610	40	.0980	60	.0400	80	.0135

LETTER SIZE DRILLS

A	0.234	J	0.277	S	0.348
B	0.238	K	0.281	T	0.358
C	0.242	L	0.290	U	0.368
D	0.246	M	0.295	V	0.377
E	0.250	N	0.302	W	0.386
F	0.257	O	0.316	X	0.397
G	0.261	P	0.323	Y	0.404
H	0.266	Q	0.332	Z	0.413
I	0.272	R	0.339		

O

HARDENING AND TEMPERING PROCEDURES

To harden and temper a chisel, punch, or other tool, first heat the tool to a cherry red color in a furnace or with a hand torch. Hold the tool in the center with a pair of tongs and dip the cutting end into cold water or oil to a depth of slightly over 1 inch. Dip the other end of the tool to the same depth. Using heat-resistant protective gloves, polish the hardened ends with an aluminum oxide abrasive cloth. Watch for the color to return to the ends from the hot center. Each time the cutting end turns purple, dip it. Everytime the head turns blue, redip it. When the red color disappears from the tool, dip the complete tool in water until it is cool. This checks further drawing of the temper. This procedure produces a hard cutting edge and head and a softer, tougher center section that withstands shock.

Glossary

This glossary lists shop and tool terms which are used in this handbook and with which you may be unfamiliar. Specific tool definitions and descriptions are contained throughout the handbook; use the index to locate them.

Acute — an angle or formation of an angle of less than 90°.

Anvil — the flat end of a tool, such as a punch or chisel, that is struck with a hammer to cause the tool to function; the flat part of a machinist's vise; a heavy steel-faced iron block on which metal is shaped.

Arbor — a shaft on which a revolving cutting tool is mounted.

Bead — a projecting rim, band, or molding.

Bevel Cut — a cut made on one surface at an angle (except a right angle) to another surface; oblique; also a tool for making angles (refer to Section 9–5).

Burr — a rough protuberance, ridge, or area left on metal after cutting or drilling; to form a rough point or edge.

Casein — a phosphoprotein of milk, precipitated from milk by heating with an acid, or by the action of lactic acid in souring, and used in making paints and adhesives.

Catalysis — a modification in the rate of a chemical reaction induced by material unchanged chemically at the end of the reaction.

Catalyst — a substance that initiates a chemical reaction and enables it to proceed under milder conditions than would otherwise be possible.

Catalytic — causing, involving, or relating to catalysis.

Chamfer — an oblique surface, usually 45°, cut on the edge or corner of a board.

Chuck — an attachment for holding a workpiece or tool in a machine (as in an electric drill).

Collet — a metal band, collar, ferrule, or flange; used to hold small-diameter bits.

Concave — hollowed or rounded inward like the inside of a bowl.

Convex — curved like a circle or sphere when viewed from without; bulging and curved.

Counterbore — to enlarge the upper part of a hole to receive and allow the head of a screw or bolt to be recessed below the surface.

Countersink — to enlarge the upper part of a hole by chamfering to receive the cone-shaped head of a screw or bolt.

Dado — to cut a rectangular groove into a workpiece; the blade used to cut the rectangular groove; a rectangular groove cut into a workpiece.

Dog — the retractable bar on a wood vise used with a bench stop or other device to clamp a workpiece.

Dovetail — a joint or fastening formed by one or more tenons and mortises spread in the shape of a dove's tail.

End Grain — the grain at the end of a board, in the direction across the grain of the wood. See **Grain**.

Ferrous Metal — a metal that contains iron.

Flats (drill shank flats, chuck flats) — the flat areas on the end of some drill shanks (power-wood-boring bits) that are placed against the flats in the drill chuck. These flats align the bit into the chuck and also prevent the shank from slipping in the chuck.

Flux — a substance used to promote fusion, especially of metals.

Grain (of wood) — the stratification of the wood fibers in a piece of wood. Cutting *with the grain* is the process of cutting in the direction of the stratification.

Hasp — a clasp for a door, lid, and so on, especially one passing over a staple and fastened by a pin or a padlock.

Helical — having the form of a helix.

Helix — something spiral in form; a curve traced on a cylinder by the rotation of a point crossing its right sections at a constant oblique angle.

Hone — a fine-grit stone for sharpening a cutting implement; to sharpen, enlarge, or smooth with a hone.

Kerf — the cut or incision made by a saw or other instrument.

Keyway — a groove or channel for a key or spline.

Kiln — a furnace or oven used to dry something such as wood, brick, or ceramic.

Laminate — to make by uniting superimposed layers of one or more materials, such as countertopping on wood counters, fabric on wood, and so on.

Lateral — of or relating to the side; situated on, directed toward, or coming from the side.

Layout — the marking off of points, lines, circles, arcs, and angles on metal or wood as a guide for cutting, matching parts, drilling, and so on.

Malleable — capable of being extended or shaped by beating with a hammer or by the pressure of rollers.

Meter — the fundamental unit of length in the metric system equal to 39.37 inches or 3.281 feet. The meter is measured in cadmium-red light waves and is equal to 1,553,164.13 of the waves.

Miter — the abutting surface or bevel on either of the pieces joined in a miter joint. A *mitered joint* is a joint formed when two pieces of identical cross section are joined at the ends, and where the joined ends are beveled at equal angles.

Mortise — a rectangular cut of considerable depth in a piece of wood for receiving a corresponding projection (tenon) on another piece of wood to form a joint.

Mushrooming — the spreading out of the metal of a tool when it is hammered; as the head of a chisel spreading out from repeated hammering during chisel cutting operations.

Ogee — a molding with an S-shaped profile.

Pantograph — an instrument for copying on a predetermined scale, consisting of four light rigid bars joined in parallelogram form.

Parallax — the apparent displacement of the reading mark or graduation on a scale due to a change of direction in the position of the observer.

Parallel — lying in the same plane but never meeting, no matter how far extended.

Pawl — a pivoted tongue or sliding bolt on one part of a machine that is adapted to fall into notches on another part (as a ratchet wheel) so as to permit motion in only one direction.

Perpendicular — vertical; upright; meeting a given line or surface at right angles.

Pilot Hole — a small-diameter hole drilled into material to lead the point of a larger drill.

Porous (material) — a material that is permeable to liquids; for example, wood fibers allow glue to soak into them.

Quench — to cool rapidly with water.

Rabbet — a cut, groove, or recess made on the edge or surface of a board to receive the end or edge of another board or the like which is similarly shaped.

Ratchet — a mechanism that consists of a wheel having inclined teeth into which a pawl drops so that motion can be imparted to the wheel, governed, or prevented, and that is used in a hand tool to allow effective motion in one direction only.

Right Angle — the angle formed by two perpendicular lines intercepting a quarter of a circle drawn about its vertex. A right angle is an angle of 90°.

Scrollwork — ornamental work cut out with a coping saw or power jig or scroll saw.

Shaper — a power tool having cutters used to shape wood workpiece edges, moldings, and so on.

Shim — a thin strip of metal or wood for filling in to bring one workpiece in line with another.

Solder — a metal or metallic alloy used when melted to join metallic surfaces; especially an alloy of lead and tin used to solder electrical/electronic component connections.

Spline — a thin wood or metal strip used in building construction; a key that is fixed to one of two connected mechanical parts and fits into a keyway in the other.

Strop — a strip of leather or other flexible material used to sharpen razors or tool edges.

Stylus — an instrument for writing, marking, or incising.

Tang — a long, slender projecting strip, tongue, or prong that forms part of an object, as a file or bit, and serves as a means of attachment for another part, as a handle or brace.

Tangent — touching, as a straight line in relation to a curve or surface.

Temper — to soften by reheating at a lower temperature; to harden (steel) by reheating and cooling in oil.

Template — a gauge, pattern, or mold (as a thin plate or board) used as a guide to the form of a piece being made.

Tenon — a projection fashioned on an end of a piece of wood for insertion into a corresponding cavity (mortise) in another piece of wood to form a joint.

Tensile Strength — the greatest longitudinal stress a substance can bear without tearing apart.

Vial — a small glass or acrylic tube with a liquid. The vial in a level is not completely filled; therefore, an air bubble remains that indicates a level condition when centered between marks on the vial.

Viscosity — a property of a fluid which resists change in the shape or arrangement of its elements during flow.

Viscous — sticky, adhesive; of a thick nature; having the property of viscosity.

Vitrify — to convert into glass or a glassy substance by heat and fusion; to become vitrified.

Whet — to sharpen by rubbing on or with a stone; to make keen.

Whetstone — a tool for whetting the edges of tools.

INDEX